SHOPS AND THE MALLS

SHOPS AND THE MALLS
A Sociological Exploration of Indian Retail Business

Rachana Sharma

KALPAZ

ISBN: 978-93-5128-140-5

Price: ₹ 650

First Published, 2015

Published by

Kalpaz Publications
C-30, Satyawati Nagar,
Delhi-110052
Ph. : 9212142040
E-mail: kalpaz@hotmail.com

Cataloging in Publication Data—DK
Courtesy: D.K. Agencies (P) Ltd. <docinfo@dkagencies.com>

Sharma, Rachana, author.
Shops and the malls : a sociological exploration of Indian retail business / Rachana Sharma.
pages cm
Includes bibliographical references (pages).
ISBN 9789351281405

1. Retail trade—Social aspects—India—Amritsar. 2. Shopping centers—Social aspects—India—Amritsar. 3. Shopping malls—Social aspects—India—Amritsar. I. Title.

DDC 306.30954552 23

Contents

Preface

Globalisation is an inevitable reality and has become an expression of common usage. In contemporary times, process of global integration has speeded up as a result of which societies are transforming drastically, like goes with markets. In more than one way, discourse on Globalisation has become contentious primarily due to the pace at which global integration is taking place and secondly, the way it is convincing people to adjust themselves in the changing settings. The phase of 1990s was eventful in Indian economic history which brought a gradual shift in development strategy from state centric to market centric. With the adoption of New Economic Policy (NEP), Indian economy has seen a magnificent growth. After the success of manufacturing sector, Indian government showed a keen interest in further extending liberalisation, privatisation and Globalisation policy to the service sector. Opening up of Indian retail sector to foreign investors has attracted much of attention in scholarly publications, of recent. Within a short span of time, there has been a creeping internationalization in the Indian retail sector which has generated lot of unrest in socio-political environment in India. The share of traditional retail is quite high as Indian consumers have long relied upon it for their requirements but of recent, the rapid growth of modern retail formats have raised concerns over the retail policy adopted by Indian government on several accounts.

Retailing is not a mere economic activity in India rather; it is embedded in the social-cultural framework. In India, retail sector is the second largest employer after agriculture and now is highly fragmented (traditional and modern retail). With major industrial houses and Multinational Corporations firming up their businesses in

Indian market and setting up retail chains in collaboration with Indian companies, concerns are being raised that adverse impact may be felt on the local retail market. The entire discussion on Indian retail policy broadly revolves around two issues, firstly, it is feared that international retailers and corporate retail houses will bring traditional retail on the verge of extinction as traditional retailers may not be able to compete with international retailers having deep pockets. Secondly, it is assumed that modern retail will yield efficiency in supply chain, enable better access to products and services in the market, would lower prices to customer products and generate employment at the large. Thus, it becomes important to substantively address the contrasting theses concerning implications of retail Globalisation policy. Based on these insights, the present work would help in constructing some possible trajectories that this sector might take in near future and would also discuss potential challenges to be faced.

In a disciplinary sense this is a crossover book as, elements of the analysis are drawn from development economics, economic geography, international political economy, sociology, and management studies. However, the purpose of writing this book has been to provide a sociological insight to the issue which has been largely dealt with and is considered to be purely economics. By focussing upon implications of new retail policy in India, the book will provide its readers with a broad outlook on Indian retail businesses and its transformation into economic powerhouse. By documenting, analyzing and interpreting transformations in work, spatial expression, consumption, and market this volume tries to pinpoint the consequences (adoption, adaptation and challanges) of retail Globalisation policy on Indian market. It is expected that the book will provide a good reading material and research material to researchers, teachers and students in social sciences as well in management studies.

The list of people who have provided friendship and support over the last years is long and includes family, friends and colleagues. Of all, a few must be signalled out for special mention. In particular, I am extremely grateful to Dr. Gurpreet Bal (Professor in Department of Sociology, GNDU) for her guidance. I wish to put on record my appreciation for the encouragement I have received from her for undertaking this study. Also, I would like to thank Dr. Paramjit Singh Judge (Professor in Department of Sociology, GNDU) for his thoughtful and encouraging comments and for always inspiring me. From him, I learned that books are fun, that they follow a system of organization that works, and that libraries are sacred places. I learned that the written word can spark creative endeavour in others. Dr Bal and Dr Judge have always been an excellent teacher and have inspired me to continue learning with an open and positive mind.

It would really not have been easy to bring this work to light without the kind help of my family and their unwavering support in all the ways. Special thanks to my Mother who has taught me so much throughout my life. She has always been a great role model for me because she is a strong independent women who always inspired me. She is the person that made me think that what I do now is what I will be doing in my future. I thank my all family (especially, My Mama Ji, Naani, Brothers and Sisters) for their confidence and enthusiasm throughout. I would also like to thank publishers, respondents and anonymous reviewers for their suggestions. I do not take the full credit for the ideas presented in this book for myself as I have depended upon many writers and scholars who have written on this issue and on whose works I have built up my arguments. I thank them all. The list of acknowledgement goes long therefore, I confine my words of gratitude to all those who have directly and indirectly helped in bringing this work to light. Lastly, I would also like to thank the publishers for publishing my work.

Rachana Sharma

2015

1

Globalisation and Beyond: An Introduction

Since the mid-1980s, sociologists have become interested in market, as it has emerged as a dominant institution. Its role and functions have undergone change over a period of time because it is not only an economic institution but also a social institution consisting of social relationships, thereby affecting social life in significant ways. Integration of markets as world systems is not a new phenomenon. The history of commerce and industry of various societies across time shows evidence of free mingling of markets, but the process of integration as followed today is somehow different in comparison to the past as countries now opt for integration in world system either out of compulsion or by choice. What is of much interest is that, irrespective of consequences brought in by such integration of markets, no nation in the present times and in the fast changing settings can afford to stay in isolation.

In this context, the decades of 1970s and 1980s were eventful ones, largely due to much flow of commercial debts from the west to the developing countries. Under the guidance of World Bank and IMF, funds were provided to countries on stringent conditions, requiring borrowers to stabilise their economies through fiscal and monetary policies which included de-regulation, de-nationalisation and trade liberalisation. Liberalisation policy was hence adopted by shattered economies to strengthen the economic growth of their respective countries. Such a move provided new challenges as well as opportunities for development as a result of which countries witnessed profound changes in their economies. Nayyar (2006) sees the decade of 1990's as more significant as it witnessed more policy changes, nationally as well as internationally. Both developing as well as developed countries were differently motivated to partner in new economic regime. On one hand, this shift was driven by debt on the economies, on the other hand, the developed and developing countries opened their economies for need of more FDIs (Kambhampati, 2004). Developing countries shifted from strongly inward looking policies of 1960s and early 70s towards greater outward orientation in 1980s and 1990s as a result, commercial debts were replaced by flow of FDIs.

As a result of adoption of policy of liberalisation, changes have taken place at three different levels: global, national and sectoral. Under the auspices of General Agreement on Trade and Tariff (GATT), which had provided the rules for system since 1948 to make trade regime transparent around the world, a series of agreements took place to remove restrictions on free trade and reduce the cost of trade. Of all the GATT rounds, the last and largest Uruguay Round (November 1982) lasted from 1986 to 1994 and was the most significant one. It led to creation of World Trade Organization (WTO) on 1 January, 1995 to mediate trade disputes and set up a uniform platform for trading and it brought about biggest reform to the world's trading system. The major thrust of this round was to establish a legal framework of rules and disciplines to cover services in trade and to commit governments at a minimum to the extent of market access provided by current regulations. GATT mainly dealt with trade in goods, whereas WTO covered wider issues such as, trade in services and in traded inventions, creations and designs (intellectual property) and dealt with the rules of trade between nations at a global or near-global level. As an organization for liberalizing trade, WTO has been working as a forum for governments to negotiate trade agreements and operate a system of trade rules (Nayyar, 2006).

Chanda (2003) puts forward that another major contribution of Uruguay Round was that it broadened the scope of multilateral trade negotiations to include 'Services' for the first time in the history of trade negotiations. While, multilateral liberalisation of trade in goods took place in the last half century, liberalisation of trade in services began only in 1994 with the end of Uruguay Round. The outcome of these negotiations was General Agreement on Trade and Services (GATS) which entered into force in January 1995 with a set of binding rules and disciplines to promote orderly and transparent trade and investment liberalisation in services. GATS contained a built-in agenda mandating members to initiate progressive liberalisation negotiation on services from January 2000. As a comprehensive legal framework of rules and disciplines covering 161 sector activities across and twelve classified sectors including wide range of activities like: trade, financial, business, communication, personal services, transportation, insurance, public utilities, health care, education, distribution services (wholesale and retail). It was argued that GATS would be of great significance for both developing as well as developed counties and will result in increasing competition, greater transparency and predictability in trade and investment flows.

Although liberalisation of trade in services among developed countries was already there, liberalisation of trade in services among developing countries is a new phenomenon. Overall, it can be said that liberalisation under GATS has progressed at a relatively slow pace. In the Uruguay Round, a total of ninety six countries made commitment in services, but a close analysis of commitment schedule shows that most of the countries have undertaken a very limited liberalisation. It was seen that low and middle income countries scheduled only 12 per cent of the service sector, whereas high income countries scheduled 45 per cent of their services sector (Wattal, 1997). In case of high income countires, between 1985 and 2005, the service sector accounted for 90 per cent of GDP growth. Services also accounted for all employment growth, as in 2008 the service sector employed 72 per cent of the labor force (http://carnegieendowment.org). Economies of several advanced countries like USA, UK, Germany, Japan, Canada and Australia rapidly adopted liberalisation policy and changed from goods-dominated to services dominated. In case of developing countries, service sector is of paramount importance both in terms of its contribution to growth and export expansion. It is so, they initially showed reluctance in adopting liberalisation in services as quickly as developed countries.

Over the past quarter of a century, in order to respond to demands of Globalisation and international pressures they often bring, governments of developing countires have become more open and participating than before. Few economies of the world have been more profoundly affected by the current wave of Globalisation than all. In case of Asian countries, momentous change has occurred over the past few years due to increasing interdependence of Asian countries with each other and with the rest of the world. The economic and social indicators assessed in the following part of the chapter suggest that amongst Asian countires, India has made an impressive progress post liberalisation period.

Backdrop to the Launch of New Economic Policy in India

If one looks at economic history of India, it cannot be stated exactly whence the process of Globalisation started in India, yet it can be said that it became a business phenomena in 17th century with the establishment of East India Company (EIC). Robins (2006), puts forward that EIC laid the foundations of modern Multinational culture, i.e., the modern business administration in India. The basic strategy it adopted to ensure high profits and market domination to establish its base in India was to buy cheap and sell dear. Therefore, the idea of exchange of goods/ Foreign Direct Investments/ Multinational Corporations and the current patterns of Globalisation were prevalent much before independence in India. It was in the post independence period India took a selfsufficient course of development when second five year plan was introduced in mid-1950s (Timberg, 2004). The growth rates during the earlier period didnot help the economy much as Indian economy was much inward looking. If one looks at the growth patterns, it indicates that India grew about 3.5 per cent per annum against the target of 5 per cent during 1960-80, which was quite disappointing (Nagraj, 2003).

Rajiv Gandhi's government in early 1980s introduced a series of reform that spurred growth though not rapid structural reform. India remained comprehensively and stringently controlled economy both internally as well as externally. Reforms that were initiated hesitatingly around 1985, experimented with internal liberalisation such as selective price, decontrol and deregulation of industries, increased exchange rate adjustments and monetary policy reforms (Bhati 2006 and Siddharth 2005). However, foreign investments were permitted in designated industries, subjected to various conditions on setting up joint ventures with foreign partners. At that time, even international development and donor agencies showed a concern with the fate of newly independent country like India and propagated westernized development model for growth. This included four indices: urban industrialization, open economies, modernization and urbanization. Though, Indian economy was opening up itself to the larger market, yet the growth rate did not improve much. By the late 1980s, the economy was sagging under the weight of excessive government control, stifling in the same stew of inefficiency and bureaucratic mismanagement that was bringing down the Soviet empire. Refusing to deal with World Bank, India turned to USSR and East Europe for help in developing its public sector which was a close partner of India at that time.

But, the restructuring of Indian economy coincided with the collapse of Soviet Union. In the summer of 1991, leaders of the Soviet formally decided to dissolve their nation (www.nytimes.com). The breakup of the Soviet Union had a great impact on Indian economy. India confronted a severe balance of payments crisis. The economic crises composing of a steep fall in foreign exchange reserve, galloping inflation, huge public, current account deficits and left with foreign currency reserves worth just weeks of imports forced the adoption of economic reforms. In many ways, it paved the way for a reinvention of the country: from a socialist economy to a more dynamic, capitalist one. The historic step of changing tracks of Indian economy came from international financial institutions (particularly, the World Bank) which imposed the condition of liberalisation of economy on the loan payment so as to respond to the balance of payment crises by borrowing money. The attitude of World Bank and developed countries towards India's public sector was hostile and they wanted India to either abandon search for industrialization or rely on west based multinational companies for industrial investments. Seeing the current form of liberalisation of economies, increasing flow of FDIs towards other emerging markets, the Indian government, under the stewardship of Manmohan Singh as the then finance minister adopted the policy of liberalisation in 1991 to attract greater share of foreign direct flows (Kumar, 2000). Thus, NewEconomic policy (NEP) came to India as a crises driven response as Indian government had no option but to comply with conditions imposed on it by world powers to come out of crises (Ahlawat, 2008).

The financial crises of the 1990s, dramatically affected the Indian economy as a consequence of which India has experienced a large increase in globalisation. There has been a large rise in integration with respect to product and capital markets. Post 1990s, there has been a sharp reduction in the barriers to international trade, a large increase in portfolio capital and foreign direct investments as compared to the earlier decades.

In order to assess the effects of liberalisation or pro- business orientation on Indian economy it is at first necessary to have a look at changes in economic growth rate. Growth rates reveal that from 1980's there is a climb up to a rate of 5 per cent per annum, while in earlier decades it went up around 3 to 3.5 per cent per annum only. Nevertheless, since then, for the two decades spanning 1981-2001, the growth rate was 5.6 per cent per annum barring a few years of fluctuation. It got picked up to 6.7 per cent in 2002-2005 (Ray, 2003 and Ahluwalia: E-Book).

The total accumulated debt burden was $92 billion in early 1997 thereby making India the fourth largest borrower after Brazil, Mexico and China (Dasgupta, 2005: Dholakia, 2001 and Derne, 2008). The balance of payment from 1990s showed consistent deficits, i.e., imports grew at 10.1 per cent higher than exports (Dasgupta, 2005). India's foreign exchange reserve rose from a pathetic figure of $1 billion prior to 90s to $21 billion in 1994-95. The most striking argument raised against the Indian economic reforms is that higher growth rate has made no dent in bringing down poverty, unemployment and growing disparities in incomes of people.

Interestingly enough, the rapid economic growth after liberalisation of 90s turned the economy from what Nayyar (2006) calls as lumbering elephant into running tiger. It can be said that economic liberalisation in India gathered momentum against background of a worldwide push towards free movements in goods and services between countries as India was undergoing the phase of economic challenges (Ray, 2003). NEP in India which was purely an economic move primarily involved three components: Liberalisation, Privatisation and Globalisation that covered wide spectrum of policy including fiscal, industry, trade etc and in totality, so as to make Indian market globally competitive.

(a) Privatisation process was the first significant attempt at reducing the interventionist role of the state by ending licensing and other forms of controls pursued since independence. The government undertook two steps towards privatisation (a) De-nationalisation that involved shifting of ownership of public sector assets to private sector, and (b) De-regulation that involved opening up of sectors which were earlier reserved exclusively for public sector (Judge and Bal, 1996). It meant increasing the share of participation of private players in Indian market. In response to IMFs demands, the government ended licensing for all but 18 industries and reduced the number of procedures required for Multinational firms in Indian enterprises. The principle objective behind privatisation as Mehta (1997) notices was (a) to stabilize balance of payments, (b) to encourage industrialization (c) to fulfil the objective of self sufficiency (d) to help in reallocation of resources (f) to provide budget revenue. As a result, foreign in 1995 declined to $ 17 billion (but reached $35 billion by 2001 and debt burden became $98 billion by 2000, an issue apart). Under this move, India has been overtaken by several countries such as Russia, Turkey, Korea, Argentina, Brazil, Mexico, China and Indonesia which have relegated India to ninth position (Dasgupta, 2005).

(b) Marketization was the second component of liberalisation policy. It meant making Indian economy market oriented in which there is free competition, efficacy and integration with the global economy (Judge and Bal, 1996). A broader conception of market implies that all markets in the economy are connected and that change in one of them would lead to change in other. Earlier, businesses in India were dominated by traditional way of life, traditional rate of profit, traditional manner of regulating their relationship with labour and traditional circle of customers and manner of attracting new ones. Therefore, Indian market was fairly restrictive not free, more internal and essentially local that supplied people with items from their immediate surroundings. Also to say, embedded relation were important in governing economic relations due to which Indian market evolved at a slower pace. However, as a result of adoption of liberalisation policy, there has been natural progression from small and simple markets to large and complex ones. The markets now operating in global settings are more networked and ally with different nations. Through this strategic move, it was expected that Indian market would also undergo dramatic changes as opening of markets and entry of foreign firms will increase competition, improve the variety of competition and will help in diminishing inequalities among the market and market players (Nijman, 2000).

The objective is not far fetched if we look into the kind of transformation that has taked place in the Indian market. An October 2007 study (c.f. Kaushik and Dutta 2012) found that for the past one and a half decade, Indian multinationals began to aggressively use overseas acquisition as a preferred expansion strategy into the world market. Likewise, new age business owners have completely altered the Indian business landscape in a short span of time and have helped raise the general standard of conduct of traditional business as well. The forbes 2008 list of richest people around the globe included four Indians in top ten position. In 2010, India stil had 52 billionaires in USD terms despite global slow down and its effect on the stock indices. All of them were owners and controllers of business empires.

(c) Globalisation was the third attempt at bringing more Foreign Direct Investments (FDIs) into industrial sector. Globalisation is thus, yet another way of putting the fact that capitalist regime gets extended beyond political boundaries of nation states. Systems of formal governance are relegated to the status of subordinate partners while, business dominated by MNCs and their managerial class controls the decision making process and occupies a pre-eminent position in global economy (Dhanagare, 2012). Kumar (2002:308) states, "With the breakdown of national boundaries as a result of globalisation, there has been creation of new markets (service, financial and consumer), new actors (MNCs, WTOs and regional groups) and new, faster and cheaper means of communication channels. It implies free movement of factor inputs (both capital and labour) as well as output between countries (Stiglitz, 2002). Thus, the process of Globalisation with its domination of market logic is minimizing the sphere of activities of the state and making individuals as the units of market.

Globalisation : Contents and Discontents

During past decades and a half, no other concept has stirred a major discourse in social sciences as the term Globalisation did. To be sure, Globalisation is not a new phenomenon. The roots of Globalisation or the modern world-system lie in European world-economy that was created in late fifteenth and early-sixteenth century but got consolidated in its current form by the mid of seventeenth century. In academia, the debate over the first part (historicity) is almost over which was blurred since long, due to multidimensionality of the concept itself (C.f. Dasgupta, 2006). But, it is now well established that Globalisation does not constitute a new phenomenon as world-system has maintained some of its main features over several centuries. Literary scholars reduce the complexity over historicity of globalisation, by broadly classifying phases of the process into two stages (a) 1870-1913 as the period of Globalisation I and (b) contemporary period as Globalisation II or second stage (Nayyar, 2006). The works of Adam Smith, David Ricardo and Herbert Spencer describe neo-liberalism, whereas Franks (1971) dependency theory, Wallersteins (1974) world system theory (C.f. Wallerstein: E-Book), Giddens (1991) theory of reflexivity and space distanciation, Smart (1993) and Appadurais (1990) concept of postmodernization and Globalisation linkage and Castells (1996) global network (C.f. Castells: E-Book), all describe the Globalisation from different perspectives.

The second debate on Globalisation revolves around the very concept of globalisation. The term Globalisation came to business as well as academic field more speedily in 1960s. As the process of Globalisation is not mere relevant from the economic context but also social for this, the term has been defined in two broad contexts, i.e., economic and non-economic. As a theory of economic development, Globalisation can be defined as a policy that involves two elements (a) Approval of proposal for Foreign Direct Investments (FDI) (b) Removal of business barriers to commercial activity (Balakrishnan, 2003). On the other hand, social aspects of Globalisation are in fact more complex as it includes all aspects of human life. The Globalisation debate in general is focussed largely on more recent development, whose impact is not confined to economic sphere but also spread over a wide range of non economic spheres of life all over the world. It is therefore necessary to explicate the sociological notion of Globalisation first. The idea of global vllage as introduced by Mc Luhan implied a sort of compression of the world and intensification of consciousnesses of wold as a single entitiy. The idea of shrinking world was then attributed to the growing impact of media revolution. The later sociologist approached the problematic via considerations of modernity and define the term Globalisation as a fundamental change in the spatial and temporal contours of social existence so that time and space is annihilated (Kambhampti, 2004: 100).

Giddens (1990) looks at it as the intensification of worldwide social relations which link distant localities in such a way that local happenings are shaped by the events many miles away and vice-versa. Robertson (1992) puts forward another connotation of the term Globalisation "the concept refers both to the compression of the world and intensification of consciousness of the world as a whole". While, Waters (1995) defines Globalisation as, "A social process in which the constraints of geography on the social and cultural arrangements recede and in which people become interestingly aware that they are receding". Appadurai (C.f. Judge, et.al., 2003), puts forward the notion of 'global cultural economy' and 'political economy' as better perspectives to understand Globalisation as a process of historic progression of the world towards acquiring world in a global social-cultural configuration cutting across national boundaries. While, the political economy perspective looks at it as a transformative project of unifying the world in accordance with the logic of global capitalism. He notes that contemporary global order is marked by disjunctive between and within five dimensions or 'Scapes' of global cultural flows. These scapes (Ethnoscapes, Technoscapes, Financescapes, Mediascapes and Ideoscapes) form the basis of fluidity of today's world and multiple perspectives that image the meanings informing the worldview of social actors (individuals, communities, corporations, nation-states). In simple terms, Globalisation involves change that is too simple and yet paradoxically too complicated to gapple with.

As a reaction to the inadequacy of development theory, Globalisation theories have emerged as of recent a new-fangled perspective to understand the real world concerns in modern world system which forms the third part of the discussion on Globalisation issue. The current Globalisation theories differ from the earlier development theories but somehow share linkages as it bases its theoretical foundations on the structural and functionalist sociological movement. It tends more toward a gradual transition rather than a violent or revolutionary transformation in which different social groups adapt themselves to changing global exchange relations. It also looks at global capitalism as not mere process of economic hegemony or relationship of unequal bargaining and multilayered exploitation, but as a process that has powerful economic, political, cultural and social dimensions.

Across each of these foci, theories are categorized on different grounds such as, whether Globalisation results in homogenization or heterogenization of different social systems. Some cultural theorists see Globalisation as producing homogeneity as a consequence of cultural imperialism while; others see it as producing distinctive local forms. Among economic theorists, some assert that globalism produces homogeneity as a result of the spread of the market economy with the aid of international organizations. For still others, it is about heterogeneity of local markets and the existence of flexible specialization (glocalization). Some theories focus on the growth of a single model of governance around the world while, others assert that Globalisation has resulted in intense nationalist retrenchment (http://socyberty.com). The characteristics of Globalisation as it is now unfolding are multifarious and are influencing societies and their economies.

Held (C.f. Giddens, 2006) after intense research on Globalisation brings out four major schools of thought in this regard: Sceptics (Regional Block Theory), Hyperglobalizers (World Economy Theory) and Transformationalists (Third Way Theory) and Homogenists (World Culture Theory). As per the Regional Block Theory or Sceptics, Globalisation is not a new phenomenon but differs from the past only in intensity of interaction between the nations. Though, it appears that there is an increasing contact between countries, yet current world economy is not sufficiently integrated as bulk of trade occurs within three regional groups: Europe, Asia-Pacific and North America.

They believe that there has been regionalisation within the world economy which points towards emergence of major trading blocks and world economy a less global in a way. In such settings the national governments continue to play key role in governing economic activity which shows that the world is not fully integrated. Whereas; Hyperglobalizers or World Economy Theorist stand in contrast to the Sceptics. According to hyperglobalizers, Globalisation has led to emergence of a new social order whose consequences are visible in all aspects. They oppose sceptics for undermining the role of global institutions as power groups who challenge the power of national governments in exercising control over the policies and economies of the nations.

Third Way Theorists take a mid way stand by stressing that the world is changing but many of the old patterns remain same. They see Globalisation as a dynamic, multidimensional and reflexive process characterised by links and cultural flows that work in multidirectional way and see countries as active and outward looking entities actively involved in restructuring economic and social organization. Whereas, World Culture Theorists stand a little off the earlier perspectives, as they tend to see Globalisation more broadly that is, in terms of increasing uniformity of cultures across the world, instead from mere economic perspective.

They are also different from the previous theorists who viewed growth of single world culture as a consequence of globalisation, which they view as a part of Globalisation (http://socyberty.com). They focus on the way in which participants in the process become conscious of and give meanings to living in the world as a single place. World culture denotes the multiple ways of defining the global situation, conceived as responses to this shared predicament, in which units (actors and practices) engaged in process of relativization assume a position relative to emerging global whole and lose their autonomy.

Castells (2004), network theory has also emerged as a promising one for analysing the current global networking. By networks, he means open structures that are able to expand without limits. For him, networks are appropriate instruments for a capitalist economy based on innovation, Globalisation and a source of dramatic reorganization of power relationship.

Since networks in global society are multiple, the inter-operating codes and switches (power holders, i.e., world economic institutions) between networks become a major source in shaping societies and social structures. As such, new economy is organized around global networks of capital, management and information. According to him, the current pattern of capitalism is different from predecessors as it is global and structured around network of financial flows.

Capital is invested globally in all the sectors of activity and businesses, some of which are more profitable than others as they go through ups and downs and profits earned thereby are reverted to the meta-network of financial flows where all the capital is equalized in commodified democracy of profit making (Giddens, 2006). From the various theories discussed above, it can be drawn that Globalisation in the sense of connectivity across the world has been growing for centuries but; the current situation is of fundamentally different order than the previous one.

There are divergent views upon the nature and dynamics of current pattern of globalisation. The speed of communication and exchange, the complexity, size of the networks involved and the sheer volume of trade, interaction and risk involved is much different in the bygone era (www.infed.org). The current phase is consciously evolved agreement based on formal and legal rationality with an objective to enhance world output, employment and economic welfare through liberalisation of trade. In the present phase, MNCs and financial institutions are playing a major role in enforcing asymmetrical rules and perpetuating unequal development among the nations. Scholars such as Prasad (1997), Omvedt (2005), Nayyar (2006), Mohammad (2006), Harshe (2006) define the process involving hegemonic relation as central to the debate from conflict perspective but at the same time they also view it as a development strategy for the low developing economies. Also, the current debate on Globalisation is centred more on implications of Globalisation than the development or underdevelopment of nations and societies.

In this context, the triumph of TNCs their finance capitalism over the microcosms of nation states has led to question the future of nation states. Two divergent opinions are advanced. On the brighter side, proponents see that Globalisation has strengthened the position of state by redefining its role in changed economic settings. On the other hand, pessimists see it as a process which will hasten the demise of nation states. In the history of markets, no economic theorist has ever claimed markets to be a pro-poor institution, as the general nature of market is that it tends to polarise societies not only in the relative but also in absolute terms. Likewise, from this, it can nevertheless be said that there is total absence of power blocks as the major political and economic institutions act as mediators between countries for addressing their grievances. Reddy (2008), views the current process of Globalisation as equivalent to 'Americanization', 'Westernization' or what Sharma (2003) calls as 'Amglobalisation' that involves popularization and internalization of predominant values, technology and way of life. The current pattern of Globalisation symbolizes global reach of certain forms of economic system in which all nation states are included as partners (Judge, 2008). It can be said that the influence of nation states may have shrunk as part of the process of Globalisation but it has not disappeared. Nation-states have become subject to both advancement as well as loss of status within the world system as important decisions are made globally. However, it is global finance capitalism compels nation states to adopt neo liberal policies to stay in the competitive world market.

Far more from the inherent contradictions that Globalisation involves, much pronounced have been consequences of Globalisation that covers wider spheres of social life. The social benefits and cost brought upon by Globalisation has also generated debate in academia. World Commission on the Social Dimensions of Globalisation (2004) states 'Our primary concerns are that Globalisation should benefit all the countries and should raise the welfare of all the people throughout world'. It implies that Globalisation should help and facilitate in raising the rate of economic growth in poor countries and reduce world poverty rather than increasing inequalities or undermining socio-economic security within the countries. Of the various facets that Globalisation has affected profoundly, socio-economic inequality has been crucial and considerable attention is now being paid to this question in the debate on globalisation.

New Economic Policy and its Implications

The final debate which has gained ground in academics is on implications of globalisation. As Dasgupta (2010) puts, Globalisation is neither in itself a positive or negative trend. Rather, its ultimate effects on the well being of people depend upon several unresolved factors which include who is involved in decisions that drive the process, which values are to dominate it, and whether the often vast inequalities that now exist between regions, nations, classes and the like will endure, increase or diminish (C.f., Jayaram, 2010). A significant change brought in by Globalisation has been, that the old international division of labour based on core- periphery relation has been replaced by new division of labour in which cost effective labour is procured from across the globe. Conditions of working class in developing world seems to be no better under globalizing economies on many accounts.

Increasing internationalization along with changing patterns and composition of trade has brought number of developing countries into global production network and has created new opportunities for economic growth. By bringing sectoral changes in economies, industry has outstripped agriculture as a source of economic growth in both developed as well as developing countries. Trade shares of newly developing countries in world trade has increased from 23 per cent in 1985 to 25 per cent in 1995 to 47 per cent in 2008 (http://www.wto.org). The share of developing countries in world service exports has also increased from 14% in 1990 to 21% in 2008 (http://www.voxeu.org). Likewise, intra-developing country trade has also increased from 31 per cent of total developing country trade in 1985 to 37 per cent in 1995 (ISSER, 2002). In developing economies, organised non industrial labour is a small fraction of total workforce and a great bulk is found in the background and are likely to become invisible because of tertiarization, feminization, casualization and precarization (Jayaram, 2012).

Service sector is paramount for economic development both in terms of its contribution to growth and export expansion therefore, developing countries are more cautiously considering opening up of service sector. Many developing countries adopted policy of liberalisation in service sector in haste without undertaking assessment of its effect and few others are still evolving regulatory frameworks and institutions to govern services sector in their domestic economies. Service sector in Sri Lanka contributes 57.1% to GDP whereas in India, Pakistan and Bangladesh it accounts for 58.1 per cent, 52.3 per cent and 49.1 per cent respectively. In recent years, service sector has experienced a phenomenal growth as compared to past (Chaudhari, 2003). The sector has grown at an average of 6 per cent since 2000 (Kelegama, 2009). There has been a steady decline in contribution of agriculture (22.1 % in 2002-2003) and industrial sector to GDP since 1960s, with shift towards service sector. Service sector in India accounted for 28% of GDP in 1960-61, 31% in 1970-71, 37% in 1980-81, 47% in 1999-2000 and 56.1% in 2002-2003 (Brahmanandan: E-Book). India's GDP at 2010-2011 was recorded 8.5 per cent which previously (2009-2010) was 8 per cent (www.rediff.com). It also accounts for more employment in comparison to other sectors in at present. Although the progress is slow, yet it is widely recognised that exposing service sector to international competition has potential to unleash significant economic gains. Increased market access will improve both access and efficiency of many services reducing their cost and increasing quality.

Liberalisation of trade in services under GATS framework has been criticized on equity, cost, distribution and priorities in servicing sector. There is a lot of pessimism among the critics on potential of Globalisation of trade. The most common criticism is that it would force countries to open up their services which would result in 'corporate takeover' of the service sector by the Multinational Corporations and force privatisation of services (Ray, 2004). Initially, there were considerable apprehensions that international firms with their superiority would wipe out the domestic firms in many of the industries (Shastri, 2004 and Biswas, 1996). It was also expected that the Globalisation led economic growth would bring about structural changes in the job market and render people jobless (Rao, 2008). This holds true in case of traditional sector, which has been dominant employer and is ten times larger than the service sector. Unemployment is increasing, reaching 185 million job seekers in 2003 in this sector.

Due to Globalisation and inclination towards formal economy the low skilled people will have to face problems of absorption in formal settings that would require highly skilful and educated people with placement in cities. In most of the cities in developing world, informal sector allows everyone to find employment to make both ends meet. With the implementation of new technologies, there has been increase in structural unemployment particularly in developing countries. The source of competitive advantages has changed as, now role of innovation in stimulating economic growth has increased (which the developing countries lack). There has been a shift in labour (as a result of fall in wages) from agriculture to other high value added manufacturing sector and service sector. That also means that the developing countries are facing acute crises of demand for skilled labourers with displacement of labour from agriculture to more specialized occupations like service sector. As a result, the growing number of unskilled and agricultural workers will migrate to urban centres and formal economy will have to struggle to absorb the huge influx into workforce.

There is no doubt that Globalisation has created a world full of job opportunities. 'Consumer Insight into Globalisation Report, August 2006' (http://pl.neilson.com) too highlights this point that over half of Latin Americans (57%) and consumers in Asia Pacific (53%), believe that more global business in their markets brought greater job opportunities and better working lives. Most in agreement were found to be Indians (78%), followed by Filipinos (73%) and Chinese (71%). It brings out that out of top ten countries, six (from the Asia Pacific region) are in agreement that Globalisation brings about increased job and career opportunities.

Economic survey (2001-2002) data indicates the fact that employment levels were in 1990s stagnant in India. During 1991-2001, 1.6 million jobs were added in service sector, 1 million were added in private sector during 1991-2001. It is indicative of the fact that private sector has become major source for incremental employment in modern sector of the economy over the last one and half decade (Dholakia, 2003).

The organization of economic corporation and development (OECD) estimates that a billion new jobs will be needed by 2025 to sustain estimated population growth in cities of developing countries and it is likely that these jobs would be created in formal sector (Giddens, 2006). For example in India alone, there would be a demand for net new employment (and of course, not in primary sector) of 70 per cent by 2030 in cities (The Tribune, 14/1/11). Employment in sectors like trade, construction, financial services, transport, storage and communication has also grown rapidly in post reform period as compared to pre reform period. Not surprisingly, indigenous industry, particularly small scale units have been affected by MNCs (Judge, et.al. 2003). Free trade has encouraged competition leading to efficiency in production which involves merging and acquisition on one hand and on the other has accelerated the process of labour proletarianization (Kannan, 2004).

Mein (1999) makes it explicit that the industrial and trade structure of a country is determined by both exogenous and endogenous factors. Endogenous factors comprise industrial and trade policies that are implemented and factor endowment of a country. While, exogenous factors encompass external influences which are beyond the control of most countries including impacts from FDI and MNC. In this context, the increasing role of FDIs and MNCs in developing countries has become widely debated. Development theories understood FDI as an indicator of market disequilibrium and distortion. They were of the opinion that MNCs make global inequality worse by creating jobs by blocking development local industries and pushing them to export thereby making them poorer. Studies carried by dependency school on Latin America and Africa equally identified high concentration of TNC flows as negatively affecting their domestic economies (Kambhampti, 2004). The school of though was of the opinion that development of less developed economies takes place at the mercy of high developing economies who invest their capital in these economies. On the other hand, Globalisation theorists argue that FDI inflows or MNC's activity is essential for development and see FDIs as indicator of market failures and market imperfections that need to be corrected through foreign aid.

Anyhow, it is equally argued by development and Globalisation theorists that presence of MNCs/ FDIs in developing countries would help in eliminating poverty as a result of rise in income of people (ISSER, 2002). They also admit that Multinational Corporations would raise standard of people living in poorer nations by creating more jobs and suggest integration of market as a key to progress and affluence for all (Macionis, 2005). Therefore, there has been intense 'global race' among countries for foreign investments as they are regarded as GDP boosters (Rajan, 2004). It can be said, where earlier development theories understood FDIs as an indicator of market disequilibrium and distortions. The current Globalisation theories see FDIs as an indicator of market failures and market imperfections that need to be corrected through foreign aid and countries are striving for getting maximum through direct investments.

Equally significant are the changes that have taken place in technological patterns of developing countries. With the incoming of MNCs, host countries have been benefited in many ways. MNCs create an inflow of funds in the form of foreign exchange, increase employment, bring in new technology, managerial and marketing skills and improve competition in the markets. With market liberalisation and reforms in economy changes in perception about role of public sector has taken place as areas that were previously reserved exclusively for public sector were thrown open to private sector. Parallel with the reforms in real economy, reforms in other sectors like financial, banking, non bank financial intermediaries, capital market were also made to provide greater role for private sector and market forces and promote financial stability. As a result, the rate of annual growth in FDI in developing countries has risen dramatically as compared to post reform period (ISSER, 2002). However, it has not benefitted all the countries equally as FDIs are strategically and geographically located. Developing countries in general, get a very small share and most countries get hardly any FDI at all. During 1992-1997, ten leading emerging market economies accounted for more than three quarters of total FDI inflows to developing countries. China, Brazil and Mexico accounted for half of the total inflows (ISSER, 2002). It can be said that benefits from the increase in flow of FDI to developing countries have been accrued to only a few developing countries. One of the major factors behind widening gap in FDI flows among region and countries included the policy of trade openness which was hurriedly followed by countries in East- Asia and China.

On the role of FDIs Ramasamy (2003), puts forward the argument that the countries with liberal FDI are not necessarily the examples of successful industrialization. Kannan (2004) supports his argument by saying that since 1980s, more than hundred countries adopted significant liberalisation measures to attract foreign investments, but ninety per cent of them remained disappointed. He gives example of string of dramatic crises in the emerging markets like Mexico, Indonesia, Korea, Thailand, Brazil, Russia, Argentina and Turkey leading understandably to the speculation that the unfettered movement of capital does not sets well with emerging markets. He opinionated, these countries overlooked the fact that all flows of FDI/ MNCs do not benefit their host countries. Kambhapati (2004), states that MNC largely borrow within the host countries and by investing in developing countries they take advantage of domestic markets than to export. They exercise monopolistic power practices especially in the countries with the weak domestic market by creating unskilled, low value employment and not employing local management staff and so are criticized for slowing down development of local managerial talent. Despite this, states have often been engaged in intense competition to attract them as they expand market relations, push back state and interstate interference, bring in capital, expand employment opportunities and create global free markets (Nayyar, 2003).

Therefore, the general feeling shared in the developing world is that Globalisation defies all principles of equity, social justice, autonomy and sovereignity and there is erosion of local culture and national sensitivities. Irrespective of the fact that such reforms were regarded as 'anti-poor' and despite the protests from various sections of the society, Indian government continued with NEP (Ahlawat, 2008). Keeping into consideration the pros and cons of introducing liberalisation reforms in Indian economy Siddharthan (2004) views, there seem to have been no alternative to make Indian market more efficient and globally competitive but to globalize if it was to survive as a nation. To further motivate the discussion of links with globalisation, let us now look at the business transmutation in India. Contrary to conventional wisdom, Globalisation entails more than economic transactions across national borders by global corporation. Equally important is the cross border diffusion of business norms and practices that fundamentally shape the ways in which businesses are organised and managed in a global economy (Rondinelli, 2008).

Indian Business Entrepreneurship: Nature and Dynamics

There are different approaches and theories to understand characteristics, formation and role of market. Weberian approach conceptualized market from system's perspective and looks at it as a social action that begins with competition and ends with exchange followed by conflict in the market (market struggle). This approach asserts that market requires regulation and highest degree of market freedom or rationality is reached in capitalist society.

On the other hand, network theorist see markets as network that have emerged out of social relations. Baker (C.f. Swedberg, 2004) too makes it explicit that though markets are heterogeneous, social structure of a market and the relationship that exists in market plays an important role in the way the market operates. For him, a mix of market ties (economic) and embedded ties (social) is important for business to survive.

If one tries to explain it in simple terms, markets everywhere have grown out and are a replica of social structure of the cities and nations. Sharma (1986), underpins that developing nations largely have traditional market structure, individual orientation, unorganised sector, resistance to technological changes and modernization which has resulted in their underdevelopment. Modern sector on the contrary, is commercially sophisticated, risk taking and change seeking has evolved at a slower pace in India.

This assumption holds true in case of businesses in India which have since long evolved from traditional to modern in this fashion. It is unique in itself as religion, sex, caste, kinship and family system had played an influential role in shaping economic activities. Indian entrepreneurship historically evolved on the principle of hereditary occupations. Caste system has so keenly been observed in the country that it played an important role in industrial development of India.

A caste was identified with hereditary occupation. According to 'Varna' scheme, Vaishaya caste specialized in trade. Caste and occupation in India were so closely linked that many a times the name of caste corresponded with the occupation. Gadgil (1959) in his work outlines castes that were mainly responsible for trading activities in various regions of India in 18th century. Mishra (1961) also cites example of some Indian merchant communities that are proficiently dominating the Indian market for example, Baniyas and

Khatris of North India were the most distinguished of the traders. Bruno (2003), notes that 128 merchant castes/ Jatis in Rajasthan (known as Marwari for a long time) have been actively practicing banking, trade, money lending. The history of Indian business entrepreneurship indicates that these entrepreneurial communities such as Marwari, Sindhi, Parsis and Gujrati have been actively involved in trade activities ever since (Tripathi, 1971).

Entrepreneur ship in India had another unique characteristic that broadly entrepreneurship in India has been confined to few regions which lead to enrichment of few areas more than others. Some kind of business entrepreneurship has been evident even long ago among the artisans in various cities like Banaras, Ahmedabad, Surat, Gaya, and Lucknow.

The network of traditional trade activities was magnificent in India and Indian traders had trade relations with outside world. Other than this, caste system, kinship system and joint family system also remained as a strong backbone behind the success of business communities in India (Chacko: 1991 and Hazlehurst: 1966). Many of the business communities like Marwaris, Gujratis long relied upon joint family system and kinship network for generating investments as well as labour.

Businesses were run jointly by the male members of the family. Likewise, kinship played an important role in networking among business communities. As in India, rules of endogamy are followed therefore; traders also use to marry off their children within their own caste which eased expansion of not only their social but also economic network (Timberg, 1978).

Ancient cities in India had a very different market structure from the one that exists today. There were separate bazaars that were operated by indigenous bankers and trader. These bazaars were well integrated complex of Shroffs, Arthiyas and wholesale merchants who hailed from traditional business caste groups and were engaged in number of activities. These bazaars served as a link between towns and villages and between urbanites and villagers (Chacko, 1991). Weekly markets and itinerant traders formed a link between villages and towns. The word 'Bazaar' though, sounds primitive and less magnificent than industry yet, it nevertheless was the same. Neither, the traditional business communities were primitive nor laid back in their vocation in any way. The bazaars were so much in profitable activities that business caste groups stayed away from industrial ventures till 1914. Likewise, credit which forms a major part of transaction today was widespread in bazaars. Businesses were run and established on credit taken from Arthiyas, who were money lenders (mostly from Baniya caste) (Ray, 1992 and Tripathi, 2007). The whole bazaar system was well integrated and businesses as well as credit used to be given even by word-of-mouth.

As compared to the earlier bazaars, the later bazaars contained not only merchants and their customers, but also shop assistants and body of casual worker. These modern bazaars were the places in the packed areas of cities where bulk transactions were made; the roads were crowded with hawkers, buyers, bullock carts and hand carts that a pedestrian has to negotiate his way with great difficulty. The shops were well structured but small in size, tilled, quite old, low roofed and in vicinity of residential areas. It took long for Indian business entrepreneurship to develop properly due to several internal as well as external factors. Infrastructural problems including lack of capital, lack of political unity, network of custom barriers, and low prestige accorded to business person were a few challanges faced by Indian businesses in India. Nonetheless, it was company rule in India that brought about a major change in Indian business entrepreneurship and linked traditional businessmen to modern sector.

By giving a push to manufacturing sector, Britishers in a way gave stimulous to Indian businessmen by inflicting various changes in economy and influencing trading communities particularly, Parsis, Marwais and Gujaratis to move in various trades and commercial occupations (Trivedi, 1991). Whilst, it was only after independence that a major change in Indian market structure was visible. Traditional Indian market has changed and become more rational. Also, attitude of people towards business has changed, and is no more looked down upon. The earlier myths associated with entrepreneurship that it is an exclusive domain of the socially conservative, traditional trading communities were broken. In 1960, study of small business entrepreneurs in the then state of Madras, James Bean observed that entrepreneurs could emerge from a wide range of social and economical backgrounds. The late sixties and early seventies also witnessed a few sporadic attempts to create entrepreneurs from non traditional communities with a view to breaking the monopoly of the dominant groups and diversifying the entrepreneurial base in the country. The state of Gujarat was on the forefront of this movement. Due to rapid industrialization and urbanisation, many of non- industrial or non- business communities like Ramgharia, Ramdasis, Nadar, Kanojia, Sindhi, Chettior, Jat, Scheduled Castes and many others have shown presence. They have entered into business and industry and scattered to emerging entrepreneurial hubs in different parts of the country. With the flow of immigrants and integration of markets, the local traders lost good deal of their business to the immigrant trading communities who were large minded, stronger and hard working than the local traders.

Apart from a few organised industrial houses, there is a magnificent share of businesses in the unorganised sector. The complicated tissue of cultural economy of the cities is today complicated by multinational corporations and private corporate houses. However, small enterprises had a definite role to play not only in contributing towards employment and income generation but also in attending to the specific needs of a diverse consumers. Modern as well as traditional businesses have altogether maintained their own set of work practices and have adjusted themselves by changing the way in which people communicate and conduct business. In order to cater to the needs of the busier lifestyle of consumers, local businessmen turned investments to modern ventures and are diversifying their practices and work ethics.

The traditional image of Indian businessman is no longer valid in the changing market settings. With the change in entrepreneurial environment, young entrepreneurs have entered the market. This generation of new age entrepreneurs is much aggressive, methodical, goal oriented, educated, have wider perception, are more enterprising and risk taking as compared to the earlier generation of businessmen.

They have assimilated themselves to the new ways of doing business. Post liberalisation, as opposed to the earlier phases has brought drastic transformation in the Indian market. Liberalisation as a whole, has enlarged growth opportunities for all.

Twith the changes in macro environment, the pressure of increasing competition in domestic and international market has forced domestic firms to improve the efficiency of their operations through organizational restructuring, better capacity utilization has benefited business in general (Baijal, 2002). The large scale entry of modern organizations has resulted in increased competition, leading to greater choice and quality improvement; a desirable outcome for consumers and employment for the unemployed. The policy of liberalisation has in a way provided way for addressing market imperfection by inducing behavioural changes among entrepreneurs but at the same time,also aggrevated vulnerabilities of businesses.

Similarly, Globalisation has made women economically independent by providing them opportunities in business which earlier was though of to be male domain. Though, many women have proved their mettle by becoming successful businesswomen yet how much Globalisation has in real contributed in imporoving their conditions remain debateable. As regards the effects of Globalisation on female labour in india, studies have come up with diverse, at times even conflicting findings.

Amidst celebrations of globalisation, rise of Indian middle class has also gained a drawing attention. India today boasts a middle class of 60-80 million people whose craze for goods turns out to be in sharp contrast to the Gandhian vision of India dedicated to traditional crafts (Thakur, 2012). The intensifying appetitie for various kinds of goods among the middle and aspiring middle has further helped in extension of liberalisation policy which has brought transformation in Indian market. It is seen in the ever increasing exports and imports of goods and services on one hand and acquisition and merger of business units on the other. An impression is thus sought to be created that businesses/ market is fast shrinking off national anchorages and a global community has arrived not only in economic but also in social and political terms which would entail a near complete homogenisation. Of course, under the bulldozing effects of globalisation, there are good as well as bad turns which need to be scrutinised with great care and caution. More fundamentally, reaping the benefits of Globalisation depends upon domestic structure that supports the creation and destruction of activities that are central to long term growth. Thus, for a country like India, rapidly integrating into global market, fast growing and undergoing major internal and exonomic and social transformation does make a sense.

2

Retail Globalisation: Prospects and Challanges

Structural change has taken place in the economies of both developed as well as developing countries as contemporary market is characterized by predominance of service sector. In the age of Globalisation and societal transformation, the composition of GDP has witnessed shifting trends. As per UN Conference on Trade and Development (UNCTAD) since 1995 to 2005, there has been an increase in GDP from 62 per cent to 72 per cent in developed countries whereas, in case of developing countries, it has increased from 45 per cent to 52 per cent. The larger credit goes to the steep rise of service sector which on an average accounts for 70 per cent of employment in developed countries and 35 per cent of total employment in developing countries (Kelegama, 2009). Though all three sectors (primary, secondary and tertiary) of Indian economy have seen tremendous growth and contributed to the GDP during the last sixty four years, the growing importance of service sector particularly in the aftermath of reform is a sign of India's being projected as a superpower for future. From 1991 onwards, structural changes were made in Indian economy which included; opening of various sectors of economy, allowing FDI to attract capital and talent, disinvestment of PSUs, financial sector reforms including banking, insurance, stock market etc and telecom sector reforms which not only fuelled the growth but also envisaged service oriented economy driven by technology and IT. Since eighth plan (1992-97) the share of service sector (42.99%) has inceased in GDP as compared to agriculture (30.03%) and manufacturing (26.97%) (Tiwari, 2011). Also, phenomenal shift in the service growth which has crossed more than half contribution at present in terms of percentage share in GDP has led to significant shoot in some of the sub-service categories like trade, hotel, transportation and communication which stood at 44.29 per cent in 2008-2009 (Tiwari, 2011). It would be difficult to analyse and summarise each reform and its repercussion on Indian economy, it is quite necessary to give an account of transformation in business sector which is current major growth driver.

Over the last few years, retail has emerged as fastest growing sectors in economies all over and there is hectic activity in terms of expansion, entry of international brands and retailers. In developed economies, modern retail constitutes 75-80 per cent of total retail but the share of modern retail in developing countries is comparatively low. India is now one of the fastest growing economies in the world. It is second most attractive developing market, ahead of China and fifth among the thirty emerging markets for new retailers. With over 600 million effective consumers by 2010, India has emerged as one of the largest consumer markets in the world attracting market players from all over the world (Rao, 1998). The Indian government is also not inconsiderate about potentiality this sector offers for economic growth for, which it has been over and again reviewing its policy of retail globalisation. Retail liberalisation policy has gained a considerable attention in India and elsewhere because of consequence it would bring to the diverse sections of society. It is not only in India that retail Globalisation has raised concern, rather similar things have happened in other South Asian countries that opened their retail sector to foreign investors. In case of India, issue of organized retailing or modern retailing has become more litigious because proportion of traditional retail is much higher (96%) in india than any other country and primarily conjecture revolves around marginalisation of the majority (traditional retailers). The issue of modern and traditional retail sector is pertinent not only because it involves question of exclusion of the traditional retailers but also because it carries social, economic and cultural consequences.

In the subsequent chapters, readers will come across some of the terms which have been used 'operationly' such as 'traditional formats/retail' has been used to refer to shops that are owned and run by local traditional businessmen. By 'modern formats/ retail' it is meant the emerging formats of retailing (that include malls, stores and marts) having newer work practices that largely represent global work culture, organization as well as structures. At large, the terms mall/ store and marts have been used synonymously as modern retail is in nascent stage in India, therefore there is no clear cut visible categorisation of these modern formats in practice. However, at some point these terms have been purposefully used differently so as to distinguish them. No distinction has been made between foreign and national modern retailers to access its implications on other segments.

Evolution of Retail in India

The trajectory of retail sector begins by setting the context within which it grew and flourished. Wholesale and retail are the two magnificent trade sectors in India. Any organization of business, selling goods to final consumers whether, a manufacturer, wholesaler or retailer means doing retailing. With a contribution of 14 per cent to the national GDP and employing 7 per cent of the total workforce in the country, retail industry is definitely one of the pillars of Indian economy (Guruswamy, 2005). Retail in India started at its earliest with the weekly markets *(Mandi's)* and village fair that were larger in size. Wide variety of goods were bought and sold in these bazaars and catered to the daily needs of the villagers. The village markets usually called *'Hatt'* (shops) were held weekly or more frequently in the open spaces. In these hatt's, various articles of common household consumption were available. Though, the main business was done through regular hatt's in the mandi's or market, yet the petty shopkeepers had small hatti's (shops) through which they carried on with their retail business.

The later era saw emergence of neighbourhood 'kiryana shop' to cater to convenience of consumers. These shops (largely of small sizes) were situated in proximity to residential areas and so were easily accessible market places and more convenient to womenfolks for whom it was easier to shop from locations near to their residence than going to far-off places for shopping. The shops were usually maintained by Hindu Baniya who were an important part of economic structure. Later era of government support, saw an indigenous franchise model of store chains run by Khadi and Village Industries Commission. This period also witnessed the popularisation of shopping centres and shopping complexes with parking facilities and mixture of shops at one location. Such formats of retailing were largely visible in metros and cosmopolitan cities of India.

Until 1990s, there were just three international style shopping formats (malls) in India- Ansal in Delhi, Spencer in Chennai and Crossroad in Mumbai (Purohit, 2009). There is a great difference in modern retail formats as they are existing in India as compared to those in western countries. Indian malls are not exactly replicas of western malls as they are customized for specific cultures and localities. Also, they are smaller and located in high density urban areas in contrast to peripheral locations (www.palgravejournals.com). It is only in a span of a few years that much more evolved form of exclusive retail formats of various sizes with a complete range of products available under single roof are now visible in many of cities in India. It can be said that retail as it has evolved over a period of time has grown out of the specific requirements or demands of the people. Modern retail has grown out of changes that have taken place in social and economic lives of people. As discussed in the introductory chapter that post 1990s, there has been a significant improvement in the lives of people in all societies, changes in lifestyles of people are also visible as they are now much exposed to goods, services and places of consumption.

With the change in market structure, Indian retail industry has got highly fragmented and now comprises of modern and traditional retail sector. Modern retailing refers to trade activities undertaken by licensed retailers which includes the corporate- backed hypermarkets and retail chains and privately owned large retail businesses. Traditional retailing on the other hand, includes traditional formats of low cost retailing such as; local kiryana shops, convenience stores, pavement vendors, chemists, footwear shops, apparel shops, hand-cart hawkers etc. Traditionally, small shop (kiryana) or neighbourhood retailing has been one of the easiest ways to generate self-employment as it requires limited investment in land, capital and labour (Sharma, 2005).

Despite its immense contribution to the economy, traditional retailing has been one of the least evolved industries till now. There are number of factors responsible for slow growth of retail sector in India, the foremost being the structure. The traditional retail thrives on informal relationship between buyer and seller and credit was a common mode of transaction between them. As shops were located in residential areas, it was natural that both knew each other personally and so they largely had an informal relationship of transactions and dealings, it was a common practice among retailers to sell on credit and maintain transaction record of goods in their accounts ledger known as 'bahi-khaata'. Far more, as shops were easily approachable and convenient for shoppers and the sellers also information about the buyer. Shops in India were locally run by people hailing from business families, they lacked technical standardization as they acquired business acumen through informal socialization as formal education was looked down upon by business communities. It was one of the major reason behind slow growth of retail in India. Businesses were jointly run by household labour that still continues to be a major portion of workforce in traditional retail. More than 80% of the 12 million outlets in India are even today run as small family business with the help of housegold labour (www.indiaretailing.com). Development of retail was also obstructed by distribution chain, involving number of intermediaries between transactions who would minus profit in hands of retailers which affected their interest in business and hindered growth.

Lastly, traditional retailers enjoyed monopoly practices in market over consumers as it was the only option available for consumers. They were not much interested in adopting innovative methods or modernising their ventures as they knew there was lesser scope for consumers as market was quite homogenous because of several advantages traditional retail has maintained itself and it continues to be on rise. According to Economic census of 2005, the number of establishments in India, under retail trade were around 15 million. While 52% of these were in rural areas, the rest 48% were in urban areas. During the earlier economic census of 1998, the total number of establishments engaged in retail trade was 10.6 million (with 49% in rural and 51% in urban areas). The period has seen an average growth of about 6% per year in the number of retail establishments (www.nabard.org). Traditional retail employs 39.5 million. With about 12 million retail outlets spread across, India earns the epithet of a 'nation of shopkeepers' (The India Retail report, 2007).

The massive employment in traditional retailing speaks volume about how vital this business is to the socioeconomic equilibrium in India. As agriculture sector is over-crowded and manufacturing sector stagnant hence millions of young Indians are virtually forced into the service sector. Aided by the second stage economic reforms, modern retailing has emerged from the shadows of traditional retailing and is contributing significantly to the growth of Indian retail sector.Modern retail formats roughly employs 0.5 million people. Expansion of modern retail along with entry of the foreign retailers has become a major concern as well as challenge for traditional retailers. It is assumed that modern retailers with deep pockets and strategies will intensify competition in the market and eliminate traditional retail players from the market. Why are such contentions or arguments raised is mainly because both forms of retail sharply contrast each other in many aspects and represents challanges and demands of their times.

Modern retailing is increasingly an expression of consumer consciousness in society. These formats have made a noticeable entry in almost all the cities of India. The transformation of Indian markets started with an overnight transformation of the Gurgaon by housing the headquarters of many MNCs and banks and witnessing a spread of malls all over the country creating a tough time for the traditional retailers. Therefore, retailing is one of the businesses that have most rapid, most visible and deepest impact on economic development and growth. Largely owned and managed by Indians, but some foreign retailers have also made an entry through franchises and export-oriented wholesale activity. Raheja and Singh (2010) have identified the following pull factors that have brought changes in the Indian retail market. The demographic and occupational changes in India such as, increasing active and independent (youth) population and expansion of middle and upper middle class with increased personal income in hand has been one of the predominant factor of retail expansion. As compared to several advanced countries having more of ageing population, India has more young and middle aged population. More than 70% of its population is below 40 years and more than 47% is of 20 years age group. Population of working woman in India has also increased from 22% in 1991 to 26% in 2001 (Census, 2001). Participation of woman in workforce has redefined the rules of economic behaviour, as the purchasing habit of working woman is different from non working woman.

Apart from economic changes, expansion of media has made significant change in the way consumers live and spend. There is an easier acceptance of luxury and increased willingness to experiment with the mainstream fashion. With proliferation of new ideas through advertisement radical change in mindset of consumer regarding credit and easy availability of finance has led to easier acceptance of luxury and conspicuous consumption. Consumers are rapidly accepting modern formats overwhelmingly. These places have some kind of resemblance with the global formats and gives an international experience of shopping. Emergence of tier two and three cities in India are also seen as significant markets for investment by retailers and developers. Therefore, condition which are also required for modern formats are conducive for its growth which has led to increase in investment activities.

Due to change in form of retailing, several changes have taken place in the form as well as the relations of market, i.e., 'market power' has now shifted away from manufacturers to distributors. The earlier integrated manufacturing model which left the entire market risk with the manufacturer is now being replaced by 'share risk' practices that distribute risk at several points in the manufacturing chain despite, retailers de-risk their business (Jhaweri, 2003). As a result of competition between traditional and modern retailers, and with the introduction of branded stores the traditional market got redesigned. The trade practices of local retailers have improved and many have adopted innovative approaches in retailing and are offering better facilities to the consumers while, some are continuing with old ways of selling goods. It is argued that dynamism and re-structuration of Indian economy had not been possible without adopting policy of liberalisation as an outcome of which it is fast emerging as a market ahead of china. However, overall attitude of Indian government as well as people has not been much in favour as it is hypothesized that modern retail will push the traditional retail to the periphery of market with its strategic moves. The following discussion reviews the experiences of South Asian countries on retail FDI.

Experience in South-East Asia: Dissent against Modern Retailing and FDIs

Since long, Government of India has been considering opening up of retail sector to FDI but, due to opposition from the left and various trade associations, retail sector had to wait for sometime. The Indian policy makers have spent ample time assessing the retail Globalisation experiences of China, Thailand and Malaysia and other developing economies to analyze impact of how supermarket chains would hit the gross traditional retail sector (Guruswamy, 2005). India has a big advantage of learning from success and failure of mature retail markets such as: US, Canada, UK as well as emerging markets such as China and UAE as these markets are quite similar to Indian retail market.

Supermarkets started in US in 1920s, 1930s and became dominant in late 1950s. In developing countries, it has been around for half a century and was confined to metros cities, upper class and were largely domestic capital chains. For example, the first departmental store was opened in Thailand in 1956 and first shopping centre in 1967. In Greece, first store was opened in 1991 and till 1972 there was no foreign influence on stores in Brazil (Mulky, 2003). In contrast, supermarket revolution took place in early to mid 1990s or early 2000s in developing countries (Joseph, 2009). The arrival of modern retail in developing countries occurred in three successive waves (ICRIER,

2008). The first wave took place in the early to mid-1990s in South America (e.g., Argentina, Brazil, and Chile), East Asia outside China (South Korea, Malaysia, Philippines, Thailand, and Taiwan), North-Central Europe.(e.g., Poland, Hungary, and Czech Republic) and South Africa. The second wave happened during the mid to late 1990s in Mexico, Central America (e.g., Ecuador, Colombia, and Guatemala), Southeast Asian countries (e.g., Indonesia), Southern-Central Europe (e.g., Bulgaria). The third wave has begun in late 1990s and early 2000s in parts of Africa (e.g., Kenya), some countries in Central and South America (e.g., Nicaragua, Peru, and Bolivia), Southeast Asia (e.g., Vietnam), China, India, and Russia (ICRIER Report, 2008). The following figures show composition of traditional as well as modern retail formats in different countries.

South Asian countries in the initial stage adopted liberalisation policy fully by allowing large number of FDI to their countries for the development. Later, there was dissent against modern retailing and FDIs as it badly affected their local market. In Indonesia, 90 per cent of fresh food and 70 per cent of all food is controlled by traditional retailers. It is also seen that, in absolute terms, both modern and traditional retail are growing. In 1998, Indonesia faced riots which were directed at giant foreign retailers that had squeezed out the traditional retail industry. Likewise, impact on the traditional retail trade in Malaysia was also so sudden and adverse that the Government had to step in with immediate restrictions (non-tariff barriers). Thailand has been cited as another country in which expansion of modern formats of retailing caused dislocation to traditional supply chains during 1997-98 Asian financial crises (Sarma: 2005).

Modern Retailing in South Asian Countries 2006

Countries	Modern Retailing	Traditional Retailing
Malaysia	50%	50%
Thailand	40%	60%
Philippines	35%	65%
Indonesia	25%	75%
South Korea	15%	85%
China	20%	80%
India	4%	96%

**Source: Indiafdiwatch.org*

In China, supermarkets moved faster into the cities and started capturing an increasing share of the total retail in food and grocery.As a result, these countries started following more regulatory restrictions on the growth in modern retail. Since late 1990s and early 2000s, governments all over became aware of the demands and future of the traditional retailers and imposed restrictions involving the use of a combination of competition laws, FDI regulation, land use restrictions (zoning laws) and limits on operating hours.

Retail experience of China and Indonesia shows that traditional and modern retail can coexist and grow at different rates. It is established through experiences of other countries that structural changes in retail will affect large numbers of traditional retailers at some stage. These studies sugest that *Kiryana* traders operating at the periphery of the modern sector will be the first ones to bear the brunt of rapid expansion of modern formats and will loose their businesses relatively early. While, small and marginal traders farther away from supermarkets continue to survive and flourish.

While, several countries continue to hold and move ahead with retail liberalisation policy, seeing the benefits it would bring. The issue of opening of retail sector to FDIs has become a major concern in India as it is believed that modern retail would completely disrupt the livelihood of traditional retailers as India has the largest share of traditional retailer as compared to any other South-Asian countries. Where on one hand, proponents of FDI in retail trade talk of how ultimately consumers will be benefited by both price reduction and improved selection brought about by technology and knowhow of foreign players in the market. On the other hand, opponents of FDI in retail raise concerns over labour displacement and cut throat competition that would exist retailers. They also assume that it would promote cartels, create monopoly, increase real estate prices, result in absence of regulatory guidelines and unfair trade practices and will disrupt the current balance of the economy.

Indian Retail Policy: An Overview

India has been identified as 'second' most attractive destinations globally among thirty emergent markets and fourth largest economy in people's purchasing power (PPP) after china, USA and Japan. India is likely to reach ahead in the next 10 years or so, provided the growth rates in modern retailing remain as they are today or even accelerate under a more benign policy environment. After manufacturing sector, retail finance is contributing fifty per cent to the growth of Indian economy. There is huge pressure on government from foreign multinationals to allow FDI in other sectors as in manufacturing. FDI in retail is fundamentally different from that in manufacturing as FDI in retail trade may create job losses and displacement of traditional supply chain or disrupt the livelihood of many. For this, Indian Government was in a fix over issue of allowing FDI in retail. There were no specific restrictions on the entry of foreign retailers into the Indian market earlier. Till 1990s, modern formats included company owned, single branded retail outlets. The second half of 1990s saw a transformation in the modern retail industry with arrival and spread of multi brand and multi product retailing. By 1996, a few foreign players were granted permission for retailing. However, in 1997 it was decided to prohibit FDI in retailing. It was only in January, 2006 that a partial liberalisation took place in retail policy. Conflicting reports emerged in year 2007-08 on the investment ceiling to be permitted for opening up the sector to foreign competitors.

FDI Policy- Milestone

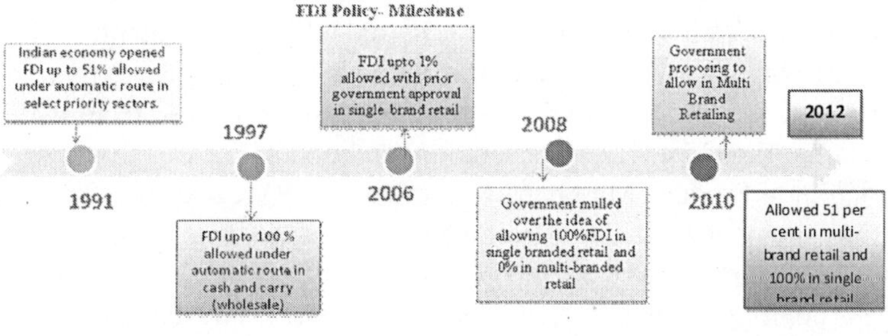

Source: www.deloitte.com

In the initial stage, it was decided that FDI up to 49 per cent should be allowed which would be raised to 100 per cent in 3 to 5 years (depending on the growth of the sector) (Mehta, 2003). The idea was that FDI should be restricted in any way with regard to branded products or retail formats. These reports strongly advocated that foreign direct investment be allowed in retailing, so as to speed up the growth of modern formats. After going through several reports and researches, the Indian government dropped its traditionally protectionist stance and opened up its retail market to greater overseas investments by allowing 51 per cent foreign stakes in single brand consumer stores, private labels approved by the Foreign Investment Promotion Board (FIPB) subjected to condition that the products to be sold should be of single brand only while, 100 per cent FDI is allowed in cash-and-carry wholesale formats (Mukherjee, 2005). Mukherjee (2005), and Indian Council for Research in International Economic Relation (ICRIER) report suggested opening up of FDI regime should be gradual to give the domestic industry enough time to adjust to the changes. Though nearly half of the retail sector has been opened for foreign investments, yet domestic investors constitute 60-65 per cent of total investments in retail chains in India (Athique, 2010) which indicates the possibility of more expansion of foreign retailer if policy is further liberalised.

In order to check sudden shock to the traditional market and untamed expansion of modern retail formats, the government framed a certain rules and regulations for domestic and international retailers. Regarding domestic regulation, the modern retailers will have to secure several licenses and clearances from various central, state, and local authorities before starting its operations. The number of licenses would vary from state to state and depend on the type of store format. First, a retailer has to obtain a trade license from the local authority (Municipal Corporation) and obtain licenses from the Agricultural Produce Marketing Committees (APMCs) of each state for procurement and sale of fruit, vegetables, and staples within the respective market areas *(mandis)* of each APMC. In addition, in case a new building or mall is to be constructed for use in retailing, the retailer would have to obtain 'No Objection Certificate' (NOC) from the different state authorities in charge of traffic, electricity, water, fire and pollution control. Zoning restrictions are also applicable to the modern retail outlets which can be set up only on land earmark for the local authority for commercial establishments (ICRIER, 2008). Despite strict rules, retail tycoons (foreign and Indian) are firming their feet through collaborations and backdoor entries. point of Inall, it can be said that though Indian government opted for retail liberalisation, yet in many ways it is still restricted and inward looking. Interesting to note here is that partial liberalisation has brought drastic change in lives of people, market composition and economic growth which needs to be investigated. .

India is on radar of global retailers and suppliers worldwide are willing to partner with local retailers in India (Basant, 2000). Of top six retailers of the world, Wal-Mart (USA), Carrefour (France), Ahold (Germany), Metro (Germany) and Tesco (UK) are making every effort to extend their retail network in India. FDI restrictions have not deterred prominent international players from setting up stores in India. Few foreign entrants have already marked their presence in different segments of retailing. The world's biggest retailer Wal-Mart has joined hands with Bharti enterprises (Indian retailer) and opened two stores in Punjab (Amritsar, Jallandhar). Shopper's Stop has signed a deal with UK's home retail group to develop Agros retail stores. Bombay Dyeing has tied up with France's Auchen. This indicates that in future there will be a flood of foreign retailers in the Indian market who would set up their business through joint venture (www.scribbed.com).

Keeping into consideration the investment trends, India's overall retail sector (both modern and traditional) is expected to rise to US$ 833 billion by 2013 and to US$ 1.3 trillion by 2018, at a Compound Annual Growth Rate (CAGR) of 10 per cent (Goel, 2010). This indicates, magnificent shift to what Sharma (www.cpasind.com/reports.html) noted in the year 2004 when the size of Indian modern retail sector was mere ₹ 28,000 Crore, which was only 3% of the total retailing market. The traditional retail sector has grown at approximately 10 per cent per annum with sales rising from US$ 309 billion in 2006-07 to US$ 496 billion in India. Organised retail segment is expanding at 20 per cent a year in india (http://www.ibef.org). In short, the trend show a possibility that both traditional and modern retail will coexist and achieve rapid and sustained growth in the years to come (www.slideshare.net).

Based on the projections of India Retail Report: 2007 (www.indiaretailing.com), the top five modern retail categories by 2015 would be food, grocery and general merchandise, apparel, durables, food service and home decoration. At present, food retail is a very large segment of the total economic activity in India, accounting for 63 per cent of the total retail sales. The largest share of retail is in food and grocery on which consumers spend about 76 per cent. Of 12 million retail outlets, nearly 5 millions sell food and related products and only 1 per cent of this market is covered by modern formats till date. The remaining ninety nine per cent of this market is dominated by neighbourhood kiryana stores. Such large consumer base along with export potential has attracted a large number of corporate houses into agricultural retail segment.

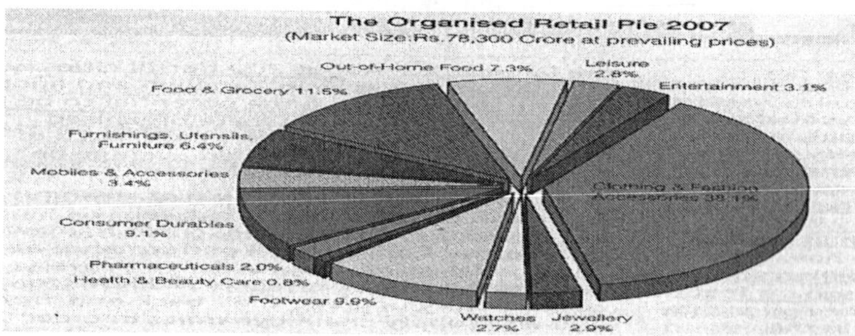

Source: Indian Retail Report, 2008

KSA Technopak Consumer Outlook Report (www.retail-report.com) shows that the average Indian spends 40% of his monthly salary on food and grocery. This is the reason that new players such as, Bharti- Wal-Mart, AV Birla Group, Future Group, Trent Ltd, RPG Enterprise, Vishal Retail Ltd, Wadias, Godrej Agrovert Ltd, and DCM - Hariyali Kisaan Bazaar, Pepsi Co, Field Fresh, Subhiksha are entering the food and grocery industry. MNCs have also shown interest towards developing supermarkets and hypermarket formats along with wholesale, cash & carry outlets. India's largest retailer Pantaloon has a continuous store rollout schedule for its Big Bazaar hypermarkets and Food Bazaar supermarkets in various cities (http://www.indiaRetailing.com/). The most bullish is Reliance with investment of ₹ 25,000 crore in its food segments in almost all the major cities of the country (Sridhar, 2007).

Similarly, India's luxury market is estimated to be 12th largest in the world and has been growing at the rate of 25 per cent per annum. Consequently, a number of foreign brands including French Connection, Sanrio of Hello Kitty fame, Jimmy Choo, La Pearla and Calvin Klein among others have already lined up for permission to infuse foreign direct investment through the single-brand retail window. Indian corporate groups like Tata, Reliance, Raheja, ITC, Bombay Dyeing, Murugappa & Piramal Groups and foreign investors are firming up their plans to identify investment opportunities in the Indian luxury sector. Many companies such as Bang & Olufsen, Escada, Brioni, Chanel, Louis Vuitton, Versace, Fendi, Valentino, Shoppers Stop and Swarovski among others have already opened stores in tier two and three cities (India Luxury Trends, 2006).

Retailers are experimenting with a variety of formats, ranging from discount stores to supermarts to hyper-marts to specialty chains thereby, transforming the traditional structure of the Indian market. Small-sized, single-category-specialty stores dominated the modern formats of retailing in 2001 with almost two thirds of total space. Departmental stores (large retail formats ranging from 20,000-50,000 sq ft that carry a broad variety and deep assortment, offer customer services and are modern into separate departments for displaying merchandise) came next with nearly a quarter of total space (www.nsdcindia.org). Supermarkets (self service food stores with grocery and located in or near residential high streets. They can be classified into mini-mart typically 1000 sq ft to 2000 sq ft and large marts ranging from 3500 to 5000 sq ft) account for the balance of about 12 per cent of modern retail space. There were no hypermarkets (large formats ranging between 80,000 to 2,00,000 sq ft. Its product assortment goes beyond routinely purchased goods and includes almost everything) in India till 2001 (www.fibre2fashion.com,). The impact of modern retailing is also visible in the change in retail formats. During the late 1990s, Indian retailers underwent an experimentation phase when new formats were introduced (Technopak, 2007). Modern retailing has entered in the form of sprawling malls, huge complexes offering shopping, entertainment, and leisure to consumers.

Specialty stores are still the most common modern retail formats covering over a half of total modern retail space in 2006. Such stores concentrate on a limited number of complementary merchandise categories and provide a high level of service in area under 8000 sq ft with less diverse product range (www.nsdcindia.org). Supermarkets and departmental stores occupied nearly an equal space of 15-16 per cent each in 2006. In 2006, India had about 75 large-sized hypermarkets carrying a tenth of the total modern retail space in the country. Hypermarket or supermarket route are the most preferred formats of international retailers. Upto 2006, there were fifty hyper-marts operated by 4-5 large retailers spread over 67 cities catering to a population of half a million or more (IT Retailing,2006). Modernization of retail has also led to changing preferences in demand for lifestyle goods as mindset of people is shifting towards experiencing modern formats.

Source: IT Retailing: Are You In The Loop?

With the spread of modern formats, it was anticipated that local markets would go through metamorphoses of a change and local stores would soon become thing of past or restricted to last minute unplanned buying. However, the issue of traditional v/s modern formats in India has become litigious and number of studies (regional as well as national) has emerged with different findings. Some studies focus on the co- existence of traditional formats with the modern formats of retailing and accept shopping malls as area of new activity which does no harm to traditional retail shops. They also anticipate that with increasing competition direct selling by small order or door to door will see tremendous growth.

On the other hand, some antagonists claim that within a few years, an estimated two crore traders have been rendered jobless due to opening up of big shopping malls in the country (www.retailrise.com). According to ICIER, traditional sector witnessed a closure rate of 4.2 per cent of which 1.7 per cent closures were because of modern retail. Athique (2010) in his study found that impact of modern retail has been modest as Indian malls have emerged as primary site for entertainment than shopping. There may indeed be a kernel of truth in the hyped-up slogan of "retail revolution", which is an attempt to overturn the traditional ways of selling goods. In the name of eliminating the much abused 'middleman' they have already established niche in urban as well as rural India. Malls and multiplexes are making headway into class II and III cities after saturating the metros. It is evident from the huge expansion of Shriram Group and Godrej who have entered the rural and semi-urban areas with their retail projects. Shriram group has already set up 27 rural malls and 172 in various states and targeting thousand more retails in rural areas (The Tribune, 21/4/2008). Therefore, it is not too simplicit to label the economic move as negative or positive.

The Methodology

The research was designed to discuss the important issues related to expansion of modern retail formats in Amritsar city. It was found that only a very few studies have been conducted on the social impact of retail surge in India. The present study attempts to explore impact of modern retail incursion on various sections of society. Therefore, to some extent the research design was exploratory in nature. In order to understand the nature of development taking place in the city and impact of emerging modern retail formats on different sections of society the following objectives were formulated:

1. To examine the socio- economic changes taking place in the city due to emergence and growth of mall culture.

2. To know the popular attitude toward retail Globalisation and its effect on the livelihood of traditional business entrepreneurs.
3. To assess the impact of modern retailing on consumers.
4. To explore the work life of employees working at the modern retail formats.
5. To understand change in the social lives of people as a result of changing market structure.

Amritsar city which is one of the major commercial centres of Punjab state of India was selected as universe of the study. The case of Amritsar city has been distinctive one in several accounts. Though, the city emerged as a prime site for religion yet, religion and politics accounted for only a part of life of Amritsar city as it has always been an important centre of manufacturing and trade (Gauba, 1980). The most important dimension to the issue of modern retail incursion is that trade and tourism are the major source of income of people of Amritsar. For the purpose of study, the sample was drawn from three different areas of the city namely Lawrence Road, Putligarh and surrounding areas of Hall Bazaar representing the diversity of economic activities of the city and symbolizing modern, medium and traditional markets of the city. A sample of 300 respondents was selected for the purpose. Sampling units included traditional retailers, employees working at modern retail formats and consumers. Out of these units, a total of 200 respondents, i.e., 100 from set of both sets of respondents (traditional retailers and consumers) were interviewed. For this, a sub-sample of 33 respondents from both the categories were chosen from three areas (different lanes and sub-streets, so as include diverse population) of the city. For selecting the traditional retail shop and household, a list of all shops and houses was prepared from the areas under consideration and then the required sample was selected. In case of traditional retail shop, every alternate shop was considered for interviewing. The traditional retailers interviewed from these three areas in the survey included the kiryana shopkeepers, owners of general stores, textile and readymade garment shop owners, home decor shops, shoe shop, jewellery shops, toy shop, fruit and vegetable selling shopkeepers.

Likewise for household interviewing, sample was drawn from every third household (from list) from the selected areas so as to include people of different socio- economic background, areas near and far from new market places so as to understand the impact on different segments of people. For the third category, i.e., employees of modern formats were interviewed randomly as stores/marts and malls are located at different locations of the city so an effort was made to include the employees working at different stores/ malls/ marts and at different designations (Appendix IV).

Till 2008, there were approximately 7 food and grocery chains with their stores located in different parts of the city and there were 4 marts/ superstores in the city. A list of all these retail chains was prepared and from each marts and superstore chains 6 to 7 respondents were selected from each for interviewing. While, from each grocery store 3 to 4 respondents were selected for interviewing. Snowball technique was also adopted for data collection as it was not easy for the researcher to approach and interview the employees working at the modern formats due to the restrictions imposed by the mall managers who wanted to maintain privacy of their management practices. The respondents were interviewed off-the working hours outside their respective retail chains depending upon the availability.

The data for the present study was collected both through primary as well as secondary sources. The primary sources consisted of interview schedule designed for determining information on different aspects of the research problem. The secondary sources consist of information derived from office of Municipal Corporation of Amritsar, Municipal Town Planning Amritsar, gazetteers (district and state), Census reports, study reports, relevant publications of the Government and other agencies, books, journals, dissertations, internet and other archival sources. The quantitative method was used for primary data collection and data analysis.

Data was collected through interview method with the help of an interview schedule. Snow Ball technique was also adopted to collect data from store employees. In addition, Observation was also made on the various aspects of their life including their place of work, working conditions, their interpersonal skills. It was interesting to note that most of the employees working at malls and stores preferred to reply in either Hindi or English. Whereas, the traditional traders largely gave responses in Punjabi (the local dialect) or a very few in Hindi. The researcher was not able to include big formats like Bharti-Wall Mart, Omaxe, and Alfa Mall as they were under construction during the time of data collection however, researcher has discussed them in text for the additional information. After data collection, information was compressed into significant and manageable categories and then the categories were assigned codes and further subjected to simple tabulation and cross tabulation. The graphical presentation (bar diagrams, pie charts) were used for simple pictorial analysis. Largely, the percentage method was used. Some simple statistical tests were also used wherever necessary. For all these purposes, MS Office program was applied. The analyzed data was subjected for interpretation with the help of secondary data.

3

City and the Business: A Case of Amritsar

Initially, cities were regarded as unpleasant and unnatural places and city life was regarded as superficial and impersonal. However, cities have always played a privileged role as centres of economic and cultural activity.

In present times, cities are increasingly been seen as economic assets than urban liabilities as there has been very real signs of renewed investments, cultural development and appetite for urban lifestyle (Boddy, 2004). This wholesale rethinking of cities is being recognised due to changing landscapes in which cities of present times operate. The cities of today are increasingly involved in intense competition in an increasingly globalised economy, are seeing rapid shifts in technological capacity and innovation and have increasing predominance of market in production and reproduction of goods and services. In strict economic terms, it may be quite correct to argue that in current economic environment, which is global in scope, it is not cities or regions that are competing with each other but businesses which have some real implications on the city formation as well as people.

Competitiveness has become a powerful mantra in economic and spatial policy durig the last decade. Although, there is a considerable body of theory concerned with increasing our understanding of forces underpinning long run differences in urban growth and competitiveness, there is a relative dearth of research that focuses upon the urban system as a whole. As academics, we need to study city cultures, economy, design and sociology as well as try to tell coherent historical narratives of how cities became what they are now. The purpose of presenting this chapter is to provide readers with an overview of economic, socio-spatial practices and processes relating to cities that have much to tell us about contemporary urban change. The development of uneven space by taking the case of Amritsar city was examined in the socio-historcial context. Capitalist development leads to geographical concentration of wealth in few spaces which develop and enrich themselves in the due process in comparison to the other spaces. It is so because capitalism requires it that way for process of accumulation to continue by re-production of space. The activity of changing the existing space suitable to the needs of imperialist capital involves change in the built environment, people and their life style, the new social-economic infrastructure for accumulation of wealth. The chapter firstly, presents diverse account of patterns of social and economic change and shift in the spatial structure of the city of Amritsar, including the edge expansion. It looks at the role of business activity, which is seen as key drivers of competitive strength both nationally as well as internationally, before finally discussing role of retail policy in shaping city -region and the broader implications that can be drawn from it. Each part of chapter would analyse key themes as spatial structure, change, competitiveness and business milieu.

Since 1960s and early 1990s, the focus of city texts has been on urban problems and challanges posed by the inner cities. The phase of 1990s saw a sea change in how towns and cities were viewed (Boddy, 2004). Throughout history, we can see that capitalism builds and rebuilds the geographies of regions, cities, countires in its own image giving rise to distinct socio-economic landscape with production of space in order to facilitate capital accumulation (Sebastain, 2007). The creation of aggolomeration is result of this constant search to gain relative surplus value through surplus location and by reducing the exchange time, i.e., new physical infrastructure has to be created in new areas/ locations. Globalisation process of present times, if we see is nothing more but a post modern expression of historical process of capitalism (Sebastian, 2007). Therefore, one needs to look at the emerging spatial configurations of cities under Globalisation in light of the above dynamics of global space under capitalism (Buck, 2005).

Cities of today exhibit global pattern of development. Analysis of differences and changing roles of cities as reflected in their changing industrial structures over the past few years and in their response to differetial patterns of growth and decline, signals that the urban system is adjusting to market forces. Cities are competing with each other intensily for attaining more investments, unlike never before. Some cities have in this process gained much at the cost of others. Large cities in modern capitalist environment are typically the ones leading in economic activites in form of substantial agglomeration of investments, business activities because of several competitive advantages and are becoming a model for the cities left behind. This could be substantiated with the notion of modernization theories that foreign investment correlates with urban growth, i.e., more the city grows, more foreign investments it attracts and more it develops and disperse from core to outer city. Also, power relations informing the notion of city have legitimised the design and construction of potential symbols of supremacy in form of monuments, streetscapes, buildings and locations. The modern infrastructural development has become symbols of determining and attaining power and contributes to positioning of cities. Hence, market has always been an important driving force for development of cities.

If one looks at micro level, i.e., at socio-economic organization of Indian cities. One can say that cities are not growing in an even manner. In India, highly developed cities arc the major economic, political, social as well as cultural centres and are at relatively advantageous position with respect to investment, development and policy formation as compared to other cities. Cities in India are quite distinct in character that the western ones as most of the cities in India have evolved from villages through a long development process while; others have historical character and distinctive culture and identity. Indian cities at first were primitive and gradually grew into modern urban centres and so continue to exhibit traditional sociography. They have a unique pattern of spatial dynamics, i..e, many of the oldest ciies in India have evolved out in quite a similar manner somehow maintaining their own specificites with regard to social-econommic and cultural pattern, in contrast cities have grown in more strategic manner and have matured over a period of time. Of the several internal as well as external forces that impact upon competitiveness and cohesion of cities, the national and international economic relationship and business connections and the role of central government play a major role in protecting cities from inequalities and cumulative process of decline that might arise from economic shifts (Turok, 2004). In this context, the discussion of Amritsar city and its market cannot be carried without understanding the entrepreneurial environment of the state of Punjab (India). The case of Punjab presents a specific example of competitive success. In the following part of the chapter, an effort has been made to analyse how liberalisation policy (particularly, post retail liberalisation policy) has aided development in an agrarian state (which was long neglected by the state) as a consequence of which dramatic change has taken place in entrepreneurial environment of Punjab and transformation of cities in Punjab.

Changing Entrepreneurship in Punjab

On the economic front, Punjab economy has performed well both in regional as well as national context. Punjab has its own unique socio-economic-cultural and historical specifications. It has been one of the important states of the northern zone of the country and had been neglected for long by state as well as investors which led to its marginalisation. Development activity was by and large confined to certain pockets of the region. Punjab is popularly known as an agricultural state but for a fairly long time the economy of the state was dependent much on trade and commerce, than the poplular notion of agriculture. The state has been one of the major commercial centres in the past. In urban as well as rural areas, trade was a major economic activity. *Shahukars* (in villages), merchants and traders (in cities and towns) contributed to the economic activities of the state.

The business and industry before and after British period in Punjab was characterised by small units that composed of artisans who possessed specialized skills, hailed from certain caste groups and followed traditional economic and ethical norms.

Multani and Baniya were the most important trading communities in Punjab during sixteenth century whereas Khatri became a prosperous community in seventeenth century primarily among Khannas, Kapoors and Mehtas (Singh, 2004). Their importance grew throughout British period. From 1849 to 1947, Khatri, Arora, Baniya and Khoja were the prominent business communities in Punjab. Aroras ranked next to Khatris and above the Baniyas in trade who largely worked as money lenders and shopkeepers. Total number of persons in shop keeping from business castes in Punjab in 1891 was 5,00,000. (Kaur, 1985). Khoja were engaged in peddling and hawking and were more mobile, i.e., they moved from hawking to trade to money lending to improve their social and economic status. Rajputs were involved in business of wholesale trade. Parchas (Muslim traders converted among Khatri) dealt in cloth, silk, indigo and tea. Business communities were numerous in towns and cities of Punjab and were the highly evaluated communities as they had better economic resources. Amongst them, Khatris were the owners of big business houses and Aroras were largely the book sellers, sweetmeat makers and medicine sellers. Business communities were not only confined to trade but also actively controlled industries. The number of persons belonging to the business communities who were engaged in industries was 39605, i.e., 1 per cent of the total 4195297 in 1911. Though, they formed the minority, yet they were controllers of the capital (Kaur, 1985). Out of all, Khatri's were the most enterprising business communities who readily entered the industrial sector as compared to the Baniya community that continued to stick strictly to their hereditary occupations of money lending and shop keeping. Only Aggarwal Baniyas who were educated took advantage of opportunities provided by the British.

During British rule, industrial development in Punjab as compared to other parts of India was extremely limited. The main aim of commercial development of Punjab agriculture was to make and retain it as a supplier of raw material and a market for British industrial commodity. The partition of country in 1947 completely shattered the production structure of Punjab economy as most of the areas of agriculture production and industrial establishment were left with Pakistan. After independence too, there was no basic change in strategy of Indian state towards Punjab economy. The fear and panic of partition, a long border with Pakistan, Indo-Pak conflict in 1965, 1971 and mainly the communal character of Punjab politics caused serious setback to the industrial growth of the state (Bawa, 2007).

Other than this, certain inherent reasons were rooted in the socio-economic structure of Punjabi society which had been responsible for a shift from industry to agriculture. Of the main manifestations of sociology of predominant peasant culture of Punjab, of industrial entrepreneurs and managerial talent. Historically, peasantry was always found to be lacking in industrial entrepreneurial tradition and therefore, in spite of prosperity rich peasants did not move into industry. Also, by reducing Punjab to the status of satellite state, the centre did not allow development of long term perspectives of industrial development, economic growth and social change (Singh: 1987, 1988). With the reorganization of state in 1966, developing industrial complex around Delhi fell into the state of Haryana and whatever mineral and forest resources that were available went over to Himachal Pradesh. This was another severe attack to the growth of industrial growth in the state. Till today, whatever industrial development has taken place in Punjab is very limited in scope, unbalanced in its structure and small scale in size. Though, in the period of 1969-1970 to 1979-1980 some increase in the number of large sized registered units and workers employed in them was noticed, yet the state was and remained an area of small scale industrial segment (Singh, 1987).

The structure of small industrial units was not very broad based and mainly composed of eight types of industries: woollen textile and hosiery, steel re-rolling, cotton and textile spinning, cycle and cycle parts, cotton grinning and processing, agricultural implements and machine tools, sewing machines and parts and sports goods. Further, development of these industries is uneven in different areas of the state with large concentration in three districts namely- Ludhiana, Jallandhar and Amritsar. Medium and large scale industries were largely concentrated at a few places namely Ludhiana, Amritsar, Patiala and Ropar (Bal, 1995). Till 2008, Punjab had a predominance of 0.2 million small scale industries and 600 large and medium scale industries functioning and involved fixed capital investment of ₹ 54,000 Million and 20,400 Million respectively (http//:www. punjabgovt. nic.in). About 1.18 Million people were employed in industrial sector in the state. Agriculture continues to be the dominant sector of employment and has been contributing to increasing affluence of the state and its people. The share of service sector in Punjab was recorded 43.91 per cent in 2008-2009, with decline in share of primary sector (29.87 %) and slow growth of secondary sector (26.22%) (www.businessstandard.com). The rise of service sector in Punjab somehow has given a boost to Punjab economy. Both real estate and retail have emerged as a promising sector of investment in Punjab by national as well as international market players.

Punjab as it exists today is one of the densely populated (550) states as compared to the All-India average (382). The state constitutes 27704236 total population, i.e., 2.29 per cent of India's total population and covers 50362 sq kms, i.e., it accounts for 1.5 per cent of total area of the country and has registered 76.7 per cent total literacy rate (81.5 males and 71.3 females) (Provisional Census of India, Punjab 2011). It is also seen that there has been increase in the share of urban population from past few decades, i.e., from 23.73 per cent in 1971 it has increased by 27.68 per cent in 1981 and 29.55 per cent and 33.92 per cent in 1991 and 2001 (Punjab handbook 2005-06). Likewise, sex ratio has also improved to certain extent in 2011 that is 893 as compared to 874 in 2001. The share of total GDP of Punjab in 2010 was recorded as 3.20 per cent and per capita income (INR) was 62153 (www.unidow.com). Estimated percentage of population in Punjab below poverty line is 2 per cent as compared to 19.34 per cent for all India in 2005-2006 (www.ibef.org).

Punjab has always been referred to as a prosperous state and this is evident from the fact that consumer spending in Punjab is quite high than the national average. Punjab has been consuming more than most other states and is significantly higher than the all-India average in almost every retailing category (food and beverages, footwear, clothing and communication) which are higher than the national average of ₹ 1149.52 per person (www.images.com). Unlike other states, unique feature about Punjab is that it has an equal support from urban as well as rural consumers as far as growth in consumption is concerned so this factor points to a tremendous potential for modern retail. The average monthly consumption expenditure for rural consumers in Punjab is ₹ 1,022.05 only marginally lower in comparison to the state's urban average, much higher than the national average of ₹ 635.72 per person per month (Statistical Abstracts 2001). Also the census 1991 indicates that the state has a significant young population (15-34), i.e., 35.12 per cent forming a major share of consumers (Punjab handbook 2005-06). For this, the state is fast becoming a favoured destination for retail developers that are keen to tap the huge consumption potential. With more disposable money to invest, the people of leading fuelling the retail boom.

Realising the potential of the state in real estate and retail, the New Industrial Policy (2003) adopted by the Punjab government aimed to create conducive investment climate through infrastructure creation, reduced regulation and general facilitation so as to rejuvenate and make existing industry competitive through improved technology, product quality and marketing. Other than the restructuring of the economic policy by the state, the contributions of Punjabi Non Resident Indians (NRIs) in economic development of Punjab cannot be missed out. There is huge reservoir of resources and talent in Punjabi diaspora which has been aptly tapped by the state government through policy intervention. The diaspora communities always feel connected to their homeland and wish to visit places of religious worship in Punjab which are associated with the history of Sikhs and Sikh Gurus. Their hard work helps building the host countries while their remittances sustain their families and local community in Punjab. Some also start, strengthen or diversify business ventures run by their close or distant relatives. Young NRIs having wealth and knowledge bring financial resources and entrepreneurial acumen to

Punjab to explore the possibility of foreign collaboration and ventures with the corporate houses (www.itftindia.com). As a result of outward looking policy adopted by Punjab government there has been an increasing inclination towards service sector and the agriculture sector in Punjab as well as in India is on decline. The unemployment rate in Punjab has been falling since 2005, with increasing opportunites for employment in allied sectors (Judge, 2008).

The retail projection for the year 2005 was ₹ 35,000 Crore (http://www.emgreen.in). In the beginning of 2005, there were just two operational malls with a total area of 2.70 lakh sq.ft. With nine new projects slated up by the end of 2006 taking the total mall space to 31.80 lakh sq.ft and about ₹ 600 billion has been made in the real estate sector in Punjab till 2009. As many as 60 more malls were expected to come up (www.indianexpress.com). Construction activity is in full swing in a number of projects visible in cities like Amritsar, Ludhiana, Gurdaspur, Sangrur, Jalandhar, Patiala, Firozpur, Hoshiarpur, Bathinda, Roopnagar, Moga, Muktsar, Kapurthala, Mansa, Nawashehr, Faridkot and Fatehgarh Sahib (Bal, 1995). Punjab is on the threshold of a major retail boom as leading corporate houses like Reliance, Spencer, Birla, Subhiksha, Piramals, Tatas, Rahejas, ITC, Godrej, S Kumar, RPG Enterprises, Future Group (formerly PRIL) and fast-food retailer McDonald have already started with their major plans to enliven up the retail sector in Punjab. Reliance with its aggressive plans in food and grocery segment has opened up their stores in different cities of the state like Jalandhar, Amritsar and Ludhiana (www.expressindia.com). Likewise Tatas have initiated their major retail project in Amritsar under name 'Trilliam'. German retail enterprise Metro Cash and Carry has also planned to invest ₹ 900 crore to start its retail chain of distribution and retail centres in Punjab with its prime operations in cities like Jallandhar, Ludhiana, and Amritsar, the company will provide over 18000 items both food and non-food (Dainik Bhaskar, 24/10/ 2007). Punjab is set to change with major retail penetration and the coming of several MNCs and big corporate houses in the business (www.tribuneindia.com). Modern retail expansion has given a facelift to cities of Punjab and its economy. Also, it has brought change in the market composition and structure.

Retail activity continues to be on rise because of positive response of the state government as well as aspiring classes who have shown interest in the modern retail space.

On the other head, despite the changes which are taking place in market, shop keeping continues to be a major employment option to many as it playes a key role in providing self employment to the masses. The table given herein shows, how vital this unorganised sector is which is facing severe threat because of the modern retail expansion.

Shops and Shop Employees in Punjab

Year	Shops	Shop Employees
1980	172831	42764
1990	247729	59912
2000	260529	67518
2002	217104	83990
2003	298336	85307
2004	210922	91278
2005	210243	98515
2006	211770	98377
2007	211817	101234
2008	213847	98569

Source- Statistical Abstracts of Punjab 2005-2009

Taking into consideration hue and cry raised all over India, over corporate invasion, the Chief Minister of Punjab made a clear stand to close the doors for entry of corporate retailers in Punjab. The India retail icon Reliance faced violence and shutter downs at several places in UP and Orissa for the fear of hacking the local retail market (The Tribune, Oct 11,2007) but situation was much peaceful in Punjab. The Punjab government opposed Reliance and other corporate houses over opening retail businesses in Punjab as it feared that modern retailers will steal away bread and butter from traditional shopkeepers and farmers in state and both will suffer heavy losses. However, penetration of world's biggest retailer, Wall Mart in the market with its first 'Best Price' Store in Amritsar and second in Jalandhar in alliance with Bharti Enterprises reflects that the state gave a welcoming response to modern retailers for its development.

With this, many of the cities of Punjab have seen a makeover. Amritsar, which has remained one of the important commercial centres of Punjab is also witnessing newer developments as a result of modern retail expansion. The case study of Amritsar city would provide an instance of how change in economic regime has affected city and its businesses. The other cities in India also by and large have similar traditional market structure and composition and so trajectory of Amritsari market might help us in asessing how retail transmutation (market shift) would affect Indian cityscape and traditional businesses.

The Walled City of Amritsar

From historical beginnings, cities have functioned in important ways as the sites of agglomerated and specialized production activities. Most of the ancient cities of the world shared certain common features with respect to the spatial organization. The cities during their initiation were quite different from the modern cities as they were usually surrounded by high walls that served as military defence and emphasised separation of urban community from countryside. The central area of the city was occupied by religious temple or a royal palace. This ceremonial, commercial and political centre (core) was sometimes enclosed within a second inner wall with a marker in center. People of different ethnic groups lived in their own ghettos, where members of their own community lived and worked. Streets were usually unplanned and unconstructed as only merchants and soldiers were regular travellers (Giddens, 2006). This may not be universal pattern for development and growth of all the cities, but to large extent most of the oldest cities all over the world have developed through this pattern.

Amritsar is a distinctive city in itself and has nothing in common with other cities of India because it was founded and brought up in different circumstances. The city has inherited rich historical, cultural, social and economic history and has passed through several stages of development and decay (Jolly, 2010). Amritsar is an important city in Punjab and a major commercial, cultural, and transportation centre and is also the centre of Sikhism (http://amritsar.nic.in). The origin of Amritsar dates back to the medieval period and was founded by the fourth Sikh Guru (Guru Ram Das) in 1577. Originally built in midst of tank excavated by Guru Ramdas, the city was chosen as a centre for pilgrimage. It was by 1601, when Darbar Sahib (sacred Sikh temple) was fully constructed there was surge in the concentration of trading communities in the city that largely settled their business in the vicinity of Darbar Sahib (Grewal, 2006).

Gauba (1988) and Singh (2004) in their works on Amritsar have given an elaborated scheme of dynamics of market in Amritsar during several periods. As a living organism, the city has followed its own development pattern. The *bazaars* (markets) and *galis* (lanes) of the city of present times have evolved since times of the Sikh gurus. The whole walled city development is a combination of katras, mohalla, bazaars and galis. To begin with in the Guru period, Guru Ka Mehal was the pivot around which whole development took place in the city (Map 1). All streets / roads terminated at Guru ka Mehal as the central place as people wanted to live close to Guru ka Mehal (residence of Guru). The fifth Sikh Guru was much interested in developing trade (especially horse trade) in Amritsar and through the system of '*Masand*' he gave a boost to trade in city. Caste groups of fifty two different trades and crafts (52 Kittey) from surrounding villages especially from Patti, Kasaur and Kalanaur were called upon by him to take up residence in Amritsar. These people from different caste groups took up professions as carpentry, masonry, brick making and horse trading (Kaur, 1977:63). Batti-Hattan (32 shops) were the first market places which was close to Guru ka Mehal. Guru Bazaar was another main commercial area and was located on the main streets.

However, during Misl period, there was a change in development pattern. Bungas, Forts and Katras were erected around Harmander sahib complex (several of them dated back to second half of eighteenth century) by various Sikh Chiefs and so traders and artisans were encouraged to settle down in the *Katras* (that were a mix of market and residential areas) (Singh, 1994). Each Bunga/ Katra had its own shopping square, its own market and specialized in particular trade carried on by traders of particular caste group. The katras were named after their chieftains such as Katra Dal Singh had its rice market (Chawal Mandi), Katra Mehtab Singh had Bazaar Paprian and Nihal Singh Attariwala had Bazaar Mishri as chief trading centre.. Shopping centres like Mai Sewan, Rama Nand, Katra Ahluwalia dates back to eighteen century. Jassa Singh Ahluwalia invited Nauhrias, a business community of Rajputana to settle down in Amritsar and gave them more than hundred shops to run trade (Jaggi, 1989).

During Maharaja Ranjit Singh's reign, a few of the forts/ Bungas were demolished that paved way for emergence of new localities and Katras in the city. The city life was confined within the twelve Darwazas/ Gates of the city, i.e., gate *Khazana, Hakima, Ranjan Nangalia (Bhagtawala), Gilwali, Ramgharia(Chatiwind), Doburji (Ghee Mandi), Ahluwalia (Sultanwind), Deori Kalan (Mahan Singh Gate), Rambagh, Deori Shehzada (Hathi gate) and Lohgarh* got constructed during Maharaja Ranjit Singh reign in 1825. Through these gates, the city was connected with the surroundings towns and cities. By 1849, Amritsar was fully a walled city and all the trade activities were carried on within the walls of city (Gauba, 1988). Maharaja Ranjit Singh took several initiatives for beautification of city and gave golden appearance to Darbar sahib (now popularly known as golden temple) (Gauba, 1988: 38). He desired to establish Amritsar as business centre and called fourteen most skilful business communities from their native land to Amritsar and gave them shops, land, community organization and many more facilities to establish business successfully. He took pains to provide protection to the traders by ensuring safe passage for carvans of traders and merchants, imposing lenient duties and encouraging trade with other countries. In the course of time, these business people decided to settle down permanently and engaged themselves in diverse type of business activities.

The spatial organization of the market indicates that in the past, trade activities were carried on in these congested lanes of the city, particularly within the walled city (core centre). The location of these bazaars was that one bazaar lead to another, forming continuous pockets. Each Katra had a main street and small streets were connected with the main street through small gates (Singh, 1977).

The residential areas 'Mohallas' and commercial centre 'Katra' were planned in such a way that the residents may have easy accessibility to places of worship, commercial centre and workplace etc. The whole city was based on pedestrian scale with zigzag streets and fortification was done to provide protection to the residents.

These areas, so called 'Katras' eventually developed as the wholesale business centre, became the hub of the city and acted as a source of employment for various castes (Sharma, 2010). The katras were also the social unit that relate to occupation, trade, language, religion, geographical origin of the residents.

The roads and streets were thickly populated, narrow, and irregular in shape with unhygienic streets, unequal in size, with irregular pattern of growth and temporary shops along the permanent shops and were planned to have compact development. The craftsmen of the city lived in these Katras having a very special work environment. The whole city was like a bazaar and large retail and wholesale outlets were concentrated in the primary streets while, bazaars on secondary streets specialized in single items.

Not only these katras were used as economic centres but also were used as open spaces and provided unique system of interrelationship between the residents (especially, those located in tertiary streets that tend to be closed. Long structured buildings with upper portion of the building were used as residential and lower as the godown. *'Thara'* (an additional sitting place usually on the entrance of the house, slightly on the street) outside godown with a window into narrow streets were used as *Hatti* (shop). The actual production and storage of all commodities occurred in interior courtyards and alley away from the primary streets. Production, storage and service centres were either immediately behind retail outlets or at short distance from the residential areas. Manufacturing was done on upper floor of houses and production accumulated in the courtyard was moved down the lane in hand drawn vehicles or on backs of men or animal to distribution centre along the secondary streets which filtered up to bazaars (Singh, 2006). The residential and market areas were also divided on the basis of castes i.e., Muslims and Dalits had their own localities and trade centres on the peripherals.

With the establishment of Amritsar as headquarter by British in 1849, wall was demolished from many areas of the city which encouraged growth of new areas in the city (Singh, 1994). Except for Rambagh gate, all gates built during the reign of Sikh ruler were reconstructed and names of some of the gates were also changed. A few new gates were also constructed such as Hall gate (in 1876), Beri Gate, Sheranwala Gate. With growing congestion becoming a concern within walled city, British initiated development of civil line areas which led to emergence of new economic zones in the city. From Town Hall to Hall Gate, a new market called 'Hall Bazaar' sprang up that catered to the needs of Europeans. The whole composition around the golden temple area changed. Up to close of nineteenth century more attention was being paid to development within the walled city. The streets which were originally zigzag were also broadened for easy movement of traffic.

Post independence, when Punjab became a ground for terrorism, the city of Amritsar became centre of terrorist activities and civil riots in 80s. Many of the businesses collapsed with heavy loss of life and property and many of the businessmen left the city and moved away to other cities. The entire event crippled the economy, trade and life of the city. As a result of government intervention, surroundings of the Golden Temple were de-congested followed by displacement and rehabilitation plans (Map 2) The settings of the city got disturbed under the Galiara scheme with the demographic changes. The Galiara Scheme was accorded approval on 8 April, 1988 at meeting held at prime ministerial level for de-congesting the localities in immediate vicinity of golden temple and for beautification of city in several rounds which interrupted business of the city several times Some of the markets in immediate vicinity of Golden Temple like Bazaar Muniaarian, Bazaar Kathian, Bazaar Kaulsar, Gali Bagh Wali and major portion of Bazaar Mai Sewan, Chownk Darbaar Sahib, Thara Sahib and Atta Mandi were razed down under Galiara project 1, 2, 3 phase in 1988. However, Mochi Bazaar and Jain Building in Bazaar Dhobian were axed under phase 4 and 5 of Galiara project in year 2003 and 2006 (Kalia, 2010). Katra Sher Singh, Katra Jaimal Singh, Qila Bhangian, Katra Moti Ram, Katra Mohar Singh, Ghee Mandi,

Lohgarh Gate, Bazaar Bakarwala, Ram Bagh, Katra Baggian, Kucha Acharjan, Chownk Carmon Deori and Katra Kanhaiya were badly hit (Singh, 2004-06). Therefore under this galiara scheme, many of popular and traditional bazaars and lanes were demolished. The local oustees were offered shops and residential areas in some other areas. Guru Nanak Market, IDH, Shaheed Bhagat Singh Market, Pink Plaza were some of the market which involved a collective shift of businesses..

Kalia (2010) states that the areas where oustees were offered new shops were areas in poor conditions. The shopkeepers of Bazaar Kathian, once a popular bazaar (retail/wholesale trade in readymade garments) where allotted shops at IDH market and Guru Nanak Market.

Kaulsar Market once dominated by cloth merchants was shifted to Golden Cloth Market near Sultanwind Gate by replacing Pattha Market (feed for horse). Thus, markets like Pink Plaza, Shaheed Bhagat Singh Market, IDH Market, Dashmesh Market, Guru Nanak Market and Golden Cloth Market were formed outside the four walls and came up over the filthy sewerage drains. Though, these additional shopping centres/ markets were created to meet the requirements under project yet it added to the problems of growing congestion in the city as walled city continued to be the core centre of business.

Sen (1983) highlighted the problem of congestion in these areas as a result of high density residential as well as market areas. Map 3 Earlier, the shopkeepers were in habit of parking vehicles on circular road for whole day but because of development of shops on circular road there has been a problem. Most of the large scale industry shifted to Chherrata which was beyond municipality but the problem of congestion within the walled city continues to be there. At present times the problem of parking is one of the major challenges for the traditional retailers within the walled city and for retailers of the city in general as businesses continue to be carried on in quite a similar manner within the walled city of Amritsar. From the above discussion, it can be inferred that from 1869 to1991 the city and its market had grown with marked fluctuations.

Business and Business Communities: Then and Now

Amritsar has remained for over a century, the first mart in Punjab and the commercial emporium of north India. The city has developed and prospered by having contacts with world outside. One reason for development of Amritsar as a commercial city is its religious character which has drawn pilgrims first from its neighbourhood and then from other parts of the country. Amritsar as we have read previously always remained an important centre of manufacture, trade and retail and entire trade was confined within walled city market. Coarse cloth, silk and fine shawls were manufactured in large quantities. The industry flourished by 1820s, with the immigration of Kashmiri's to Amritsar in large number. The city became a leading centre of silk manufacturing. About 900 weavers and 735 winders were engaged in silk manufacturing (Gauba, 1988:21). She also notes that by 1830, there were 2000 shops for manufacturing and trade of shawls and Khatris of Amritsar were very affluent who used to purchase raw silk and send it to weavers through their Brokers (Dalals). Pashmina Shawls were exported to Europe in a large number. Metal work was also popular in the city. Gold and Silver work in the form of Tila and Kandla (Tinsel and Wire drawing) of high standard was done in the city. Sunars (Hindus) and Zargars (mostly Muslims) specialised in trade of gold and had their different centre in interior of the city. Guru Bazaar was an important centre for jewellers.

Amritsar was most important centre of trade in kingdom of Lahore. Merchants of diverse backgrounds had trade contacts with the city and many of them thronged its bazaars and market. The essentiality of trade and commerce led to emergence of newly rich class that dominated the city life. The trade and commerce had come to be monopolized by certain castes and communities and many of them were migrants. Some of them were renowned and enormously rich merchants. Amritsar being a renowned economic centre attracted businessmen from all corners of the country. In the initial phase, much of the trade was in the hands of trading communities such as Aroras , Khatri and Baniyas among Hindus, Sikhs and non- Punjabi communities like Marwari, Sindhi, Gujarati, Afghans, Pathans and

Kashmiris among Muslims (Gauba, 1988:44). Among businessmen and traders the Khatris were considered best and the Kirars as the worst (Kaur, 1996). These communities started with small shops and business in congested lanes of the city originally designed for safety. The names of such communities (non Punjabi) were derived from their native places. Marwari came to Amritsar from Marwar (Rajasthan) during Maharaja Ranjit Singh's rule who gave them land for community organization and mandis. They belonged to three castes Maheshwari, Aggarwal and Oswal (Jains). Marwaris who had acquired mastery over business methods and organization largely exported commodities to Calcutta and Bombay. Also, Sindhi (inhabitants of Sindh region) established their business in the city after partition of India and settled as refugees. But many of them have already been living here prior partition. The migrated businessmen started capturing market by selling goods at cheaper rates than the local shopkeepers and slowly started dominating the retail and wholesale market. They started businesses at low level, low cost and widen up. Most of them also started businesses in which they were working as workers and took up diverse occupations.

In social terms, trading communities of Amritsar were next in importance only to the members of the ruling class, the Sardar and courtiers who had made Amritsar their home built impressive Havelis and developed Katras of their own. The streets were named after the professions and traders like Gali Loharan (blacksmiths), Gali Tarkhana (carpenters), Chownk Kumhara (potters), Galli Jattan, Gali Khairean, Gali Arorean, Gali Uppalan (Singh, 1988:39, Kaur, 1978:66). Montgomery (cited: Gauba 1988) notes that merchants of Amritsar belonged to old established houses and were wealthy and had correspondents in most of the principle towns in India, Afghanistan, Bukhara and Kashmir. Census of Punjab (1868) states that in Amritsar there were 658 merchants, 2115 bankers, 3463 money lenders and 12647 shopkeepers and so in economic terms traders and shopkeepers were most important section of the city population (C.f. Datta, 1967: 131-152).

Gauba (1988) notes that land around Amritsar which once belonged to Sikh nobility, passed into the hands of Khatri bourgeoisie.

Many of the Khatri also were the controllers of big mills (soap mills, carpet manufacturing). Next to their importance were the Aroras and Baniyas (who were originally the money lenders but later improved their position). Baniya dominated the piece goods business of Katra Ahluwalia. Baniya or his equivalent in status and position were common in the villages of Punjab who monopolized market. Their hereditary occupation was money lending and retailing. The influx of Baniya in the city started in 1930s and by 1947. A few of Baniyas became prominent members of municipality. Jains/ Bhabras were also important in trade though they were not numerically strong. Bhatias who were amongst the clans of Rajput coming from Jaisalmer and Rajputan desert also migrated from the villages to Amritsar also played an important role in the grain businesses and petty shop keeping.

The artisans in Amritsar outnumbered the agriculturalists. Some of important artisan caste of the city were Kharasi (wheat grinders), Thathears (potters), Sirkibandan (bamboo curtain makers), Julaha (weavers), Chamar (tanners and leather makers), Telli (oil extractors), Nai (barber) Chickndoz (embroiderer on cotton cloth) and dyers. Among Muslims, Khojas and Sheikhs were chief trading classes and were involved in diverse businesses (shawl trade, tanning and leather trade, carpet weaving). A few of them even established big business concerns during twentieth century at the close of 19th century (Bandhu, 1989). Amongst the most mobile business communities to enter into industries were the Khatri and Muslims while most of the shops were run by the Baniya community who continued to profess their traditional values and vocation. Therefore, business communities from different socio-religious groups residing in urban areas were engaged in collection and distribution of goods in the city.

The merchants of Amritsar had direct trade with those in British India, Afghanistan, Persia and Central Asia, Tibet and the far East, western Asia and Europe. Chief items of export were wheat, rice, cotton, sugar, poppy, indigo, salt, hides and skin and shawls. The important items of import were gold, silver, iron, steel, leather, fur, wool, piece goods, ivory, glass, spices, dry fruit, dyeing stuff and horses (Gauba, 1988). Likewise, from North- South, East- West of

Golden Temple trade activities were carried on in various katras for example- Bazaar Thathiaran was popular for utensil work, Katra Jaimal Singh was the famous cloth market, Ghee Mandi developed as butter and oil centre, Dhab Basti Ram became the biggest grain market, Bazaar Paparian specialized in household industry, Bazaar Kathian specialized in horse saddles. Guru Bazaar became the centre for gold ornaments, Katra Faizulla Purian was known for market for brass, steel and utensils. Bazaar Patrangan of Katra Hari Singh (Bhangi Misl) which was the oldest and most thickly populated Katra became the market for silk dyers. Raw silk was imported and dyed at this centre.

Likewise Bagh Rama Nand became a residential locality of traders. Katra Dullo had Bazaar Sirkibandan (curtain makers) as its shopping centre. Other than this, Katra Sant Singh, Katra Khazaana, Katra Safaid, Bazaar Mughal Darwaza,Bazaar Haria-Bahar, Bazaar Baghian/Kathian (horse saddles), Bazaar Nauhrian, Katra Ahluwalia, Katra Garba Singh, Namak Mandi (salt market), Lakarh Mandi (timber market), Atta Mandi (flour market), Majith Mandi (dying clothes), Kanak Mandi (grain market), were used as commercial centres. Majority of the shops within walled city dealt with the wholesale trade (nearly 80 per cent) and the businesses were established as old as 1840s (Sen, 1983).

Soon after the annexation of Punjab by the British, the city was marked by modernization and trade in Amritsar increased by one-third. Factors responsible for it were rationalisation of customs, construction of roads, establishment of peace and order after two Anglo-Sikh wars and new trade policy introduced by the British. Development of trade in Amritsar was closely connected with the trade development in India and in the world.

The traders of Amritsar responded well to the changing situations trying to make readjustments when possible and exploring altogether new possibilities at times. Amritsar ranked next to (second) Delhi in trade. In twentieth century, foreign exchange banks were introduced in Amritsar. The earlier ones were National Bank of India limited (1900), Chartered Bank of India, Australia, China (in 1908), Lloyds

Bank Limited (1930). Introduction of foreign banking system brought change in the economic system (Hundi) of traders in which the elite merchants of the city used to keep their money with Shahukars or bankers in the big towns as Amritsar, Lahore and Multan. With the outbreak of the world war II (1939-1945), 1940s experienced withdrawal of trade contacts with foreign countries. In the end of 1945, government lifted restrictions implanted and dumped goods started finding market in foreign countries and in return imported capital goods thus providing push to both, trade and industry (Gauba, 1988:103).

However, the economic prosperity could not be maintained for long as it got disturbed by the partition of India. As a result of partition, many of the skilful artisans (especially Muslim weavers, suniyars etc) left the country and moved to Pakistan and many other Hindu businessmen and artisans fled to other safer places in India out of fear of communal tension. The business and trade suffered heavily due to partition as there was loss of skilful business communities on one hand while on the other hand, some of the important industries were adversely affected as fertile regions such as raw jute and cotton growing areas went to East Pakistan. Partition of the country, resulted in loss of market by creating gap in production, demand as well as loss of skilled labour. Post partition, Amritsar city had been central to all the major events that took place in Punjab. However, Amritsar's industrialist were very sensitive to the changes and gave immediate response always. The industry of Amritsar was so stable that even great depression of 1929-1930 did not affect it that big as it did to the other parts of Punjab. Modern industrialization of Amritsar started in late quarter of nineteen century. The 1950s saw a huge expansion in the industrial sector of Amritsar with many new industries coming up and the old ones expanding at a fast rate. In the initial stage, cottage and small industries were established these require less space and started within the congested areas of the city. In between the years 1967-68, there were 27 large-scale industries and 5,500 small-scale industries in the city. The period 1997-98 saw an increase in small scale as well as medium and large scale industries i.e., 26844 and 59 respectively (Bawa, 2007).

Changing Businesses

As the city got matured over time, it got more defined in its pattern, structure and economic activities. Previously, the market was relatively restricted but due to the rapid urbanisation it expanded beyond the city covers. Due to the changing profile of the city, old features of city got replaced by newer ones. Today, the economic and residential zones are no more confined to the walled city rather have spread beyond the walls so much that there is a new city carved on the peripherals of the city called as New Amritsar. Presently, there has been an overlapping of the division of residential as well as market areas on the basis of caste and class, yet a tinge of class and caste can be seen from patterns of settlement. The city now presents duality in spatial pattern. Modern city (outside the walls) in contrast to traditional city (walled city) is new, clean and more spacious with modern built, infrastructure and architecture and provide attractive location for emerging markets.

Katras or businesses within walled city continue to cater to needs of people of Amritsar and around the city and continues to be central to commercial activity. Conversely, it is definite that these bazaars have lost their pristine beauty as compared to past as there has been a very little change in them and outer market has emerged as a strong parallel market. Bazaars within walled city continue to be unclean, having narrow roads and shops on both sides. Most of the shopsin deep interiors are facing severe threat which has hindered its growth due to inaccessibility. The size of some shops is so small that most of them do not even have enough space for even more than two people and for sitting. These traditional retail shops are very old, jointly owned, run by family members belonging to particular castes and are less educated. The shops are non-computerized and have been the source of income for majority. Traffic jams in the narrow lanes are frequent, all day long sans parking place (Singh, 1979). Also, frequent changing route to Golden Temple has affected the trade within the walled city. Amritsar market exhibits almost similar pattern of concentration of trading communities in the city. Among Hindus, the Khatri, Baniya, Arora, Brahmin and among non- Punjabi communities, the Marwari's dominate the market (Kaur, 1996) though some other non- business caste groups have also shown their prominence in business in Amritsar. Most of the trading communities continue to live within walled city. Retail in Amritsar is dominated by a large number of small and medium retailers consisting of the local kiryana shops, owner-manned general stores, chemists, footwear shops, apparel shops, paan and beedi shops, hand-cart hawkers, pavement vendors, etc (Appendix II) which together make up the so-called traditional retail in Amritsar. There are nearly sixteen thousand licensed shops and approximately thirty five thousand non licensed shops in the city. The licensed shops generated revenue of nearly ₹ 25 lakhs while, from the non licensed shops ₹ 17 crore was collected as revenue by the city revenue office (As per MTP records, till March, 2011). Most of the businessmen are involved in wholesale and retail trade in Amritsar, especially in cloth and blanket.

In recent years, Amritsar has attracted a number of developments in and around the city. Tourism, a major contributor to the city's economy has been aiding the financial well being of the city's residents and creating employment opportunities and influx of brands and malls into the city. With increasing prospects of trade with Pakistan, the city is now emerging as a cargo destination and also has an international airport. There is a lot of diversity in businesses or trade activities carried out in the city. Traditional bazaar of the city and outer market contrast in terms of their built and have their own specialities. The bazaars of Amritsar offer a colourful range of traditional and modern items. Modern markets developed so as to cater to the needs of growing population, to de-congest areas in vicinity of Golden Temple and to meet the changing needs of city dwellers. These new markets are more organized, well planned, spacious, with better parking facilities, newer formats (showroom) and owned by businessmen having modern outlook. Most of businessmen from walled city, seeing the better prospects of growth in modern markets, purchased shops, started their businesses there. It indicates outflow of capital from inner to outer city market.

The specialised bazaars (dealing in traditional items) like, *Guru Bazaar, Mochi Bazaar, Putligarh, Katra Jaimal Singh, IDH Market and Shastri Market* within walled city continue to maintain their identity and existence within the narrow lanes. While, *Lawrence Road, Ranjit Avenue, Mall Road, MM Malviya Road, Nehru Shopping Complex* have emerged as modern retail hub and are famous for contemporary shopping (See Map 3). Retail activity in both modern as well as traditional spaces is flourishing at equal pace. Every year nearly 100 shopping complexes are built and since 2007, the proposals for 287 shopping complexes have been approved by Municipal Town Planning department (Dainik Jagran, 15/1/2008). This indicates that the city has become a metropolis and retailers and developers are adding new dimensions to the business in the city. Giant shopping malls and branded stores have turned out to be an 'in-thing' in Amritsar and the culture is spreading like proverbial fire. With retail liberalisation policy of Indian government, modern retail formats are trying to focus on the new economic zones of the city than the traditional ones. With soaring land prices the promoters have taken a fancy for the suburban areas. The retail activities have also shown a parallel high rise in the city's development graph few of which are coming up in the famous *Lawrence, Green Avenue, Kennedy Avenue, Ranjit Avenue, Atari Road, Jallandhar-Amritsar highway and Mall Road.(Map 4)*

Due to the lack of large areas in the city a few cinemas are being converted into Malls and a few are coming up on the outskirts the *Batala Road* and the *GT Road* towards Jallandhar. Modern retailers are fast expanding their colossus chains on the outskirts of the city. The largest mall in the city is Alfa One; which is located adjacent to the emerging New Amritsar Economic-Zone. Amritsar represents a grand opportunity to retailers at large to exploit its huge consumption potential. These malls are roping in the leading brands in fashion, consumer, lifestyle, food and grocery products. For the city's booming middle class with increasing purchasing power, there are plenty of choices to shop from. Retail chains like Mark and Spencer, Blackberry, United Colours of Benetton, Vishal Mega Mart, Ebony, CTC, Kelvin Clian, Shoppers-Stop, Reliance are catering to the needs of people under one roof and have already become favourite shopping destinations. Few of the functional chains are: Celebration Mall, Ritu Wears, Ebony, V-Mart, Bharti Wall Mart, Reliance, Alpha One Mall.

On the contrary, many of the retail projects are lying deserted/ half constructed due to certain political and legal issues, these include Metropolitan Mall, Omaxe Novelty Mall, Splendor Gold, Collage Group, Ansal Plaza, Maiden Mall. Few projects are in the pipeline like Soul Mall, Big Bazaar. Many of the modern retail chains have also seen a shut down and these largely include food and grocery stores like 6Ten, Spencer, Subhiksha, More, More 4-U, KSO and Vishal retail (that has being overtaken by American retail Airplaza).

A total of 27 malls/stores were sanctioned in the city from 2008-10 (As per MTP records) but due to some or the other reason only a few mighty ones could make successful entries to the market. These retailers are trying out a variety of formats, ranging from discount stores, supermarkets, hypermarkets, specialty chains and malls (The Tribune, 12/1/ 2008) thereby heating up competition among the traditional as well as modern retailers and creating unrest among traditional retailers.

As a word of summation, it can be said that Amritsar city has evolved differently at different phases under specific requirements and is re-affirming its entrepreneurial status with the commotion caused in the retail market. The city as it exists today, presents a unique picture of modern and traditional which is a result of changing market organization, which is global in scope.

The market within the walled city represents and thrives on 'old economy' and caters to the traditional needs of people. Area outside the wall has emerged as hub for modern retail markets, thrives on 'new economy' and cater to the emerging needs of the city dwellers. The functioning, organization and structure of these retail markets is very different.

Rapid and uncertain segmental division of the market definitely will have certain implications for local business. Modern retailers with newer work practices, newer work places, promoting newer lifestyle and newer ways of doing business are attracting customers and giving traditional retailers no other chance than to compete in order to survive or die out. Though, modern retailers are not concentrating their business in the traditional markets of the city, yet impact of modern retail can be determined from raised concerns over concentration of wealth in the outer city area and outflow of customers and businesses thereof. Modern formats of retailing are largely roping up in posh localities or on outskirts of the city which provide ample space to their customers to shop and park their vehicles (which is a big problem the traditional bazaar is facing) and are trying to provide every facility and service to the customer which a local retailer cannot afford to provide. It can be said that enrichment of outer market has taken place at the improvishment of inner city or say it vice versa.

4

Socio- Economic Profile of Respondents

Market in India is largely controlled and organized by particular social groups or classes. Bruno's (2003) study of Indian entrepreneurship makes it clear that in India, few communities, regions, groups and families dominate the market. Thus, entrepreneurship in India is constricted around certain variables such as family, caste, community and regions. Traditionally, Vaishyas were the only merchant groups whose heridatry vocation was trade but with times, non-business caste groups have also proved their mettle in business and trade. For the present study, three sets of respondents (consisting of the traders, the employees and the consumers) were chosen so as to provide a broader overview to the issue.

I. Profile of Traditional Retailers

Shops have an important social role to play and have been catering to high frequency of customers having diverse needs and hailing from different background. Drawing a sociological profile of businessmen is quite a tricky task as the social identity of local businessman is often highly specific. They do not constitute a sociologically homogenous group in terms of power and networks. Social variables such as sex, caste, region and economic power are all significant to identify the businessman, their relevance may vary in specific markets, localities and professions. Kaur (1996) in her thesis on 'Non- Punjabi business communities in Amritsar city' states that among non Punjabi business communities in Amritsar, the Marwari, Sindhi and Gujarati were actively involved in business activities. These business communities hail from different socio- economic background and have their own values, cultures, tradition, unique skills, attitude and have contributed to economic development of the city. The present study aims at exploring the role and significance of the social determinants i.e., age, caste, religion, background of the respondents in shaping their entrepreneurial acumen.

Age

Age is an important factor that influences maturity of person and his aspirations. Young people are more energetic, progressive, innovative and prone to change than the old. They have attitude and interest different from the aged. Also, they are more adaptive to change and have more risk bearing attitude. Business is considered such an activity which requires time and maturity to acquire acumen, tricks and traits. Kaur's (1996) analysis of traditional Amritsari market showed that among Non-Punjabi business communities of Amritsar, the business was largely in the hands of middle aged and older generation. But, the data collected for the present study differs to some extent.

The age of respondents ranged from 21 to 90 years and the average age of retailers was found to be 39.2 years. Data represents prominence of young and middle population in retail business in Amritsar and indicate that a new wave of energetic young businessmen with different perception and cultural values have entered the market.

Gender and Marital Status

The pattern of gender inequality and submissive role of woman is visible in their participation in economy. On the basis of such sexual division of labour, woman have for quite a long time been disconnected from public sphere and participation in labour force.Woman's sphere was confined to home and men's to public life (Chafetz: Ebook). Gender roles are stereotypical based on relations of power and exploitation. Since long women were missing from the market as businesses involved transaction with males. Presently, women entrepreneurs have shown a visible presence in the maket but largely, the businesses lie in the hands of males. The findings of the study indicate that market thrives on unequal gender relations and business in Amritsar is predominantly dominated by males (92 per cent) thus wasting the human resource by confining woman to the four walls of house.

The business communities are traditional and still do not want their woman to go out for business or job (Bal, 1994). Also it was seen that women who were running shops constituted only eight per cent of the total respondents. They were either supporting their spouse in business or their sons and were not running their venture independently. Most of the respondents were married (73 per cent), a little more than one fifth of them were unmarried. A small number of them was of widowed (4 per cent) respondents and only a very few were divorcee (2 per cent) among them.

Religion and Caste

Religion is a system of beliefs, emotional attitudes and practices by which a group of people attempt to cope up with problems of life. It performs functions for both individuals and society and provides guidelines for human action and standard against which people's conduct is evaluated. Religion in Indian society defines social as well as economic life of people. Religious values impose a certain type of behaviour and act both as an inhibitor as well as facilitator.

It affects economic behaviour (eg: concept of Artha, i.e., righteous and honest pursuit of economic activities) as economic power is reinforced through the dominant position acquired in religious and family life that structures communities (Bruno: 2003). Religion also plays an important role in entrepreneurial activities of traditional as well as new communities. It is an important variable that shapes and transforms beliefs and attitude of an individual. Societies have always at some point of time been permissive. Where religion has moved with times, it has also advocated change. In present times, religion has to some extent ceased to play important role in determining the activities of individuals.

Table 4.1

Religion and Caste

Religion	**Respondents**	**Percentage**
Hindu	71	71.00
Sikh	29	29.00
Total	**100**	**100.00**
Caste		
Khatri	31	31.00
Arora	19	19.00
Brahmin	17	17.00
Baniya	12	12.00
Suniyar	8	8.00
Jatt	4	4.00
Ramgharia	4	4.00
Rajput	2	2.00
Cheemba	1	1.00
Chamar	1	1.00
Balmiki	1	1.00
Total	100	100.00

Table (4.1), present religion of the respondents. Largely, the respondents were Hindus (71 per cent) and others were Sikhs (29 per cent). The number of people belonging to Hindu religion is more than any other religion because mostly all trading caste groups are of Hindu religion.

Caste is another variable to understand Indian social reality. Caste structure is a pattern of social behaviour in which groups and individuals are guided by prescribed set of norms, values and sanctions. Individuals born into caste acquire roles and statuses associated with that caste identity. Sociologists like Ghurye (1969) and Hutton (1969) have defined caste as a hereditary endogamous group, having an association with an occupation and a particular position in the hierarchical settings. Caste system in India is linked with the 'Varna Model' which divides Hindu society into four orders, i.e., Brahmins (priests and scholars), Kshatriya (rulers, soldiers), Vaishyas (merchants) and Shudras (peasant, labourers and servants). Caste as it existed previously was highly closed/ restricted group.

Each caste had its own occupation and rules governing the behaviour of its members and mobility was not possible. For long, caste system was held responsible for India's backwardness as it played an important role in preserving hereditary values and promoting specialisation. Due to factors of social change like modernization, westernisation, globalisation, education and industrialization it has lost its extreme rigidity. Though, changes have been brought about in the occupational structure of caste, yet businesses predominately are still run by specific business communities. Hence, it is apt to highlight some space to the role of caste system in determining the entrepreneurial activities.

The Amritsar's market shows a predominant pattern of caste in entrepreneurial activities. Of the total respondents (Table 4.1), majority hailed from business castes like Khatri, Arora and Baniya. It was interesting to note that non- business castes such as Brahmins, Suniyar, Jat, Ramgharia, Cheemba, Balmiki and Rajputs also significantly contribute to businesses in Amritsar. The data, therefore, indicate that though, economic context of market has changed, yet businesses in Amritsar are still predominantly run by traditional business castes who dominated market in the past.

Education and Caste

Education is an important variable that defines one's attitudes and beliefs. Educational level of an individual is determinant of his life style. More the educational level is, more the modern values get incorporated into life style of people. Education plays a vital role in modification of behaviour and skill attainment. In India, caste in a certain way played an important role in determining performance of members through their influence to respond to economic opportunities, education, training, access to resources and social contacts. Business communities for long showed an indifferent attitude towards formal education. General attitude of the business communities was that there was no need for formal run a business (Appendix III). It was because of such an attitude that literacy rate was not so high among the business communities in the past and hence a vast majority of businessmen were uneducated and lacked refinement.

Table 4.2

Caste and Educational Qualifications

Qualification / Caste	Illiterate	Matric	10+2	Diplomaafter (+2)	Graduan	Post Graduatn	Total
Khatri	2(6.45)	2(6.45)	6(19.35	--	17(54.83)	4(12.90)	31(31.00
Arora	-	4(21.05)	1(5.26)	-	14(73.68)	-	19(19.00
Brahmin	–	2(11.76)	7(41.17	-	6(35.29)	2(11.76)	17(17.00
Baniya	-	2(16.66)	3(25.00	1(8.33)	6(50.00)	-	12(12.00
Suniyaar	-	4(50.00)	1(12.5)	-	2(25.00)	1(12.5)	8(8.00)
Jat	-	-	2(50.00	1(25.00)	1(25.00)	-	4(4.00)
Ramgharia	-	2(50.00)	-	-	1(25.00)	1(25.00)	4(4.00)
Rajput	1(50.00	-	-	-	-	1(50.00)	2(2.00)
Chemba	-	-	-	-	-	1(100.00)	1(1.00)
Chamar	-	-	-	-	1(100.00)	-	1(1.00)
Balmiki	-	-	-	-	1(100.0)	-	1(1.00)
Total	3(3.00)	16(16.00	20(20.0	2(2.00)	49(49.00	10(10.00	100(100.00)

Singh (1979) in his study on 'Traders of Mai Sewan Bazaar in Amritsar' found that book sellers within the walled city were either illiterate or had studied upto primary. A similar attitude of businessemen towards formal education was found in Kaur's (1996) study. As compared to the previous studies, an improving trend in education was seen in the present study. The number of graduates and post graduates together consisted of more than half of the respondents (Table, 4.2). While, very small number was found to be those of matriculates and illiterates. It was also seen that young were more receptive in gaining higher education, whereas, old contend that there was something innate in business skills and there was no need for formal education. It was seen that among Khatri (31%), most of the respondents were Graduates, one fifth of the respondents were 10+2 and less than one third were Post Gaduates. Only 6.45 per cent were found to be matriculates. Also among Aroras (19%), less than three fourth of respondents were Graduates. Among Brahmins (17 %), nearly 64 per cent were 10+2, more than one third were Graduates. Among Baniyas, half of respondents were Graduates. Among other castes such as Jat, Ramgharia, Chemba, Balmiki, Chamar and Suniyar improvement in educational qualification was seen. The data discerns increasing importance of education among different caste groups. Also, the data is evident of fact that all in all, there has been rise in the educational level. Today, educational qualification is seen as an indicator to learn and acquire skills and traits, which can help the businessmen in expansion of their business.

The earlier generation was much concerned about acquiring work skills informally through socialization process but now, businessmen (of various castes) have recognised the importance of formal education. As education contributes to widening of perspective, accommodating with changing times, modification of behaviour as well as help in learning social behaviour. The younger generation makes use of both formal and informal education to learn traits of business. They are educated, well equipped with the basic skills and ready to learn and orient themselves to varied situations. The cross table though does not suggests any significant relationship between caste and education but somehow brings that upper castes are more educated than others.

Business Acumen

By business acumen, the researcher means the tricks and traits of business. Every caste has its own minute details which are handed down from one generation to another generation (by elders to younger) through the process of socialization. Business skills are acquired either through formal and informal training or they are ascribed, by birth. Of recent, there has been increase in business schools and Entrepreneurial Development Programmes (since 1950s) that have been providing training to the entrepreneurs and helping them improving their skills. However, family continues to be an important institution for transmitting values and skill formation. It cannot be denied that certain common personality traits in members of communities are nurtured through socialization process in families. As far as business skills of the entrepreneurs are concerned, being surrounded in an environment full of business they were groomed to be an entrepreneur (Bal, 2006). Findings of the study revealed that more than half of the respondents (56 per cent) said that they hailed from business families and acquired business acumen through process of socialization and did not go for any sort of formal learning (Professional Business courses). Their skills and traits were hereditary and they acquired business values and ethics without any conscious efforts. Whereas, on the other hand, more than one-fourth of the respondents said they have acquired and learned business traits through training (formal and informal), i.e., skills attained from technical institution, training centre and from within the family. Whereas, 15 per cent said that they have acquired business skills on-the-job. From the above discussion, it can be said that socialization process continues to be the main source of acquiring business acumen.

Years Spent in Business:

For an entrepreneur each year spent in business is taken as an asset to acquire know-how of technicalities of the trade.

Table 4.3

Number of Year's Spent in Business

Years in Business	Response	Percentage
1- 10	33	33.00
11-20	24	24.00
21-30	16	16.00
31-40	13	13.00
41-50	8	8.00
51-60	2	2.00
More than 61	4	4.00
Total	**100**	**100.00**

The data collected on business details of the traders in Amritsar indicate that many of them were heirs to age-old family business whereas, others were self made men whose activities have flourished within a few years. The experience of respondents in business varied from 1 to 86 years. The average years spent by retailers of the selected sample area (Hall Bazaar, Putilgarh and Lawrence Road) were 22.60 years (Table 4.3). This means quite a number of respondents have spent a good time in their trade and are relying on retailing for their subsistence.

Type of Household and Businesses

Family is a universal social institution. Joint household is the first and the foremost classical Indian institution that many businessmen and industrialists still tend to follow. In Indian society, joint household was regarded as an ideal form as it fulfilled number of economic and emotional needs of an individual and acted as machinery for pooling funds in business. The adult male members had right to take important decisions in the joint family. However, changing patterns of life have resulted in nuclearisation of families. Joint households are disintegrating and becoming nuclear. In the present study also it was seen that half of the respondents had nuclear household. Whereas, more than one fourth of the respondents lived in joint household and one fifth lived in extended household which indicates that joint households are on decline. It was seen in the study that few of the respondents were migrants from other cities and only a few of them were commuter (from surrounding villages) while remaining were localities.

Businesses in India were nearly created by joint households who found it advantageous to remain so in the interest of the business, as joint property was regarded as an asset to keep aside any liability from outside. The sustenance of business depends upon the nature of one's family system (nuclear or joint), number of parties involved and strength of primordial ties. It also requires social networking. It was seen that though there has been increasing trend towards nuclearisation of families yet family owned business still follows, as more than four fifth of the respondent's business is family owned, followed by one sixth who have joint proprietorship (with secondary relatives or others).

Sales in Business

Business ventures are initiated by mobilising support (both financial resources and networks) through family and kinship.

Investment of capital in a venture depends upon size of business, profit earned, number of parties investing in business etc. The growth of business depends upon networking, information and a constant flow of capital. While inquiring about investments and income, research techniques such as observation and probing were also used to ensure validity of the responses by observing their gestures, unwillingness, the condition of their shop and number of employees. It can be inferred that responses were understated and might be to a certain extent non reliable. Nearly sixty per cent of the respondents didn't answered this question as general tendency of people to hide their income. The respondents interviewed together consist of heterogeneous population as they were from different lines of trading (as discussed earlier). Also, all sorts of traders were interviewed small, medium and upper class. The financial statement of the business of businessmen indicates that monthly sales of the respondents ranged from ₹ 1 lakh to ₹ 11 lakh and average monthly sales of the respondents was ₹ 3.82 Lakh. It can be inferred that Amritsar business is largely of small and medium size.

Pattern of Employment in Shop

Depending on the magnitude of the business, extra workforce is required for assistance in work at different levels as for the small businesses largely household labour (family members) is employed. Whereas, hired labour is employed for larger ventures.

Table 4.4

Pattern of Employment in Shops

Provided help in Business	Response	Percentage
Employee	66	66.00
Relative+ employee	13	13.00
Relative	6	6.00
Family member+ relative	4	4.00
Spouse	1	1.00
No one	10	10.00
Total	**100**	**100.00**

Majority (66 per cent) said that they are helped by their employees/ paid staff at different levels. While, 13 per cent said that their employees and relatives helped them in the business (Table 4.4). On the other hand, 10 per cent of the respondents said that they solely manage their business and did not seek any assistance from relatives/ employees or anyone else.

Data reveals that most of the respondents had 1 to 3 employees working at their shops while, others had 4 to 6 employees. Many of those who have small business or family owned business did not hire any employee at their shop. Those having bigger shops has 7 to 10 employees working at their shop and a few of them even had 13 employees.

These employees were largely hired as salesman, accountant, helper and security personnel and for managerial position. On an average, the employees were paid between ₹ 1500 to ₹ 5000 per month depending upon their experience and profits in business. Only a few of them are paid upto ₹ 8500, depending on experience and position. But, this is not the case with the petty shopkeepers as their business was largely run jointly by the family members than hired labour.

II. Profile of Employees At Modern Formats

The city of Amritsar has witnessed profound change in the past few years with retail development. Earlier, city dwellers were relying upon their own businesses in order to earn their livelihood till some call centres mushroomed up in the city and now modern retail formats have become the most sought after place for job seeking. Till 2007, the total number of skilled unemployed applicants in Amritsar district was 41843 and number of unskilled unemployed was 2225 in 2008. Also, the number of educated unemployed was 36059 and that of uneducated unemployed was 8009 (Punjab Statistical Abstract, 2009).

This part of the chapter, proposes that where market in traditional retail was run by middle aged and elderly, it is youngsters (18+ to 30 years) who dominate the modern retail formats. In contrast to a traditional market, that is gendered (with predominance of elderly male) the newer retailspaces are more egalitarian in the sense that increasing participation of woman in market and services is seen, which was never before. As modern retail format forms newer workplaces, the profile of the entrepreneurs is quite different from traditional businessmen.

Katakam (2007) and Gopptu (2009) have tried to highlight the socio- economic background of the employees in modern retail formats in India. Their studies make it clear that the employees working at these new formats hail from lower middle class working at the lower positions at malls/ stores and higher positions are occupied by the educated upper class. Largely, the employees at malls and stores are young with age range of 19 to 35 years. Woman are the most sought after human resource for these new formats as they are easy to hire at lower wages, and make these spaces a friendlier place, are easy to control, docile and honest.

These modern workplaces are egalitarian and based on achievement orientation of the actors. Working environment of these new retail formats is quite different from the traditional ones as sscribed statuses such as caste, religion play no role in employment of people. Retail jobs have flexibility of time and working in shift-system and contractual system of employment and so job- switching (i.e., changing job frequently) is a common practice among young employees. Most of the employees are unmarried men and woman who are working in retail as part timers in these formats and their salaries ranged from ₹ 3000 to ₹ 6000.

Though, salaries of the employees are less, yet earn though performances at work. The following discussion would focus upon socio- economic profile of modern retail employees in Amritsar city.

Age

Modern retail formats have emerged as a promising destination for job hunters. Youth has shown profound interest in modern retail than the elder generation. The age of employees working at modern stores/malls and marts ranges from 15 to 54 years. Average age of respondents was found to be 25.4 years. Less than half of the respondents were between the age 25-34 years and 45 per cent of respondents falled in age group of 15-24 years. Only 7 per cent of the employees working at malls were above 35 years. It can be said that modern retail formats have successfully provided young generation with avenues for employment.

Gender and Marital Status

Participation of woman in traditional retail was meagre as it was not thought of desirable for woman to work in public sphere (especially, where dealing with other men was involved). With the industrial revolution, the myths of public and private sphere were broken. The growing Employment of woman was generally marred by certain factors like- the type of family, i.e., woman living in joint family had fewer chances of entering into paid work. Similarly, the marital status of woman also affected the prospects of employment like, marriage meant withdrawal of woman from gainful employment for certain period which included dual responsibility and child care practices.

Whereas, for singles or unmarried woman there were relatively more job opportunities. With times, things have changed to quite an extent. Changing lifestyle and increasing opportunities required participation of woman for providing subsistence income (Singh, 1992). With modern retail expansion, demand for workforce has increased and women in particular have become the most sought after resource in retail sector. Reasons for more women being in retail space are that they are easy to hire at lower wages and are willing to be placed at any position (Katakam, 2007). Woman's high level of education has also contributed to the increase in female labour force participation. Modern retail jobs provide workers with abundant choices (working in shifts and part time working, easy contractual terms of employment and much more). It was noticed that most of the girls and boys working at malls and stores were unmarried (57 per cent), others were married (41 per cent) and only a few (one per cent each) were divorced and widowed.

Religion and Caste

Religion and caste in the past played an important role in determining economic choices of individual. Occupational choices of individual were earlier governed by ascribed characteristics such as caste, age, religion, sex etc. However, from time to time, caste barriers have weakened. Caste restrictions in India are today not as meticulously observed as they were some decades ago.

Social mobility has been important feature of caste system and it has always been present within the caste system. With the changes in traditional caste structure there has been increasing flexibility/openness in occupational structure. The growth of money economy has enabled relations to be governed by market conditions as opposed to inherited statuses. Modern market settings do not recognise the caste affiliations for employment of individuals rather; the employability is facilitated by the achievements of the individuals. Therefore, the modern market settings exhibit heterogeneity in terms of working population.

In this context, it can be said that where traditional businesses were largely run by a few traditional business communities and caste groups, the modern businesses are run by workforce hailing from different caste groups. The data collected for the present study indicates that most of the employees working at modern retail formats were Hindus (78 per cent).

While, others were Christians, Sikhs and Muslim. Modern market thrives on competitiveness, individual competency and achieved statuses than ascribed. This is evident from Table 4.5. It is seen, that respondents belong to different caste groups. Predominantly, they are the Khatris, Brahmins, Rajputs,

Table. 4.5 Caste of the Employees

Caste	Respondents	Percentage
Khatri	31	32.29
Brahmin	27	28.12
Rajput	10	10.42
Arora	8	8.33
Jat	4	4.17
Majabi/ Chamar	4	4.17
Mehrey	3	3.13
Mahajan/ Baniya	2	2.08
Ramgharia	2	2.08
Kamboj	2	2.08
Ghumiyar	1	1.04
Ramdasia	1	1.04
Suniyar	1	1.04
Total	**96***	**100.00**

* *Excluding 4 respondents, i.e, Sindhi and Muslim (1 each), Christian (2).*

On the basis of above findings, it can be said though people from different caste groups are involved in business activities but participation of business caste groups is higher as compared to other castes.

Household Type

Nuclear household is more independent social unit and is based on principle of social equality which is absent in joint household system. Also, nuclear household provide ample chances to woman to earn an additional income to support their families by participation in workforce.

Number of factors (economic, cultural and social) have led to reduction is family size in all the societies. Modern jobs require professionalism, formal codes of conduct and working and so requires several kinds of adjustments by the individual at family as well as professional level.

Therefore, there are varied patterns of family living and increasing trend of small family size is seen. This becomes clear from the data given that those who are working in such new formats of retailing largely hail from nuclear families (more than three-fourth).

While, a little less than one fifth of the respondents are from joint families and only five per cent are from extended families. It means number of respondents living in nuclear families is higher than those living in joint or extended families. As far as retail jobs are concerned, it requires long working hours, flexibility in personal domain which is possible in nuclear household (particularly in the case of woman).

Family Income and Monthly Salary

Economic class of an individual may determine his position in the occupational structure. Retail in India is in nascent stage and requires more workforce. Gopptu (2009), finds that majority of the people involved in modern retail formats hail from a similar socio-economic background, i.e., those on the top positions largely hail from upper classes, whereas, those from lower or lower middle are concentrated on the lower positions.

In the present study, it is found that average annual family income of the respondents is ₹ 17905.04 (Table 4.6). It is seen that half of the respondents family income ranged from ₹ 50,000 to ₹ 5,50,000 annually.

It can be said that most of the people working at modern formats hail from the lower- middle rung. Retail has emerged as a potential area for job seeking because of various advantages. People prefer to work in organized sector as they provide them with timely salary and at least better packages. Basic salaries in retail are very low but, far better than those provided by traditional shop owners. In this study, it was found that the salary of employees ranged from ₹ 2500 to ₹ 16500.

Monthly salaries of 72 per cent of the respondents ranged from ₹ 2500 to ₹ 8500. Some employees that were concentrated at higher positions got salary ranging from ₹ 8500 to ₹ 12500 and even as high as above ₹ 12500 per month (22 per cent) (Table 4.6).

The average monthly salary of store/mall/mart employees was ? 5440 per month. The salary given to the employees depend upon their performance and experience and positions at stores/ marts. It is seen that, those working on lower positions as security and housekeeping get ₹ 2500 to ₹ 4500 per month (such respondents comprised of 36%).

Table 4.6

Total Family Income (Annual) and Monthly Salary

Income ₹	Response	Percentage
Upto 50,000	8	8.00
50,001-1,50,000	28	28.00
1,50,001-2,50,000	27	27.00
2,50,001-3,50,000	5	5.00
3,50,001-4,50,000	3	3.00
Above 4,50,001	5	5.00
No response	24	24.00
Total	**100**	**100.00**
Monthly Salary (in ₹)		
2500-4500	36	36.00
4501-6500	20	20.00
6501-8500	16	16.00
8501-10500	9	9.00
10501-12500	4	4.00
Above 12501	9	9.00
No response	6	6.00
Total	**100**	**100.00**

While, a few (one fifth of the respondents) working as customer care executive, promoter, membership service representative gets a monthly salary between ₹ 4501 to ₹ 6500 depending upon the brand and profits earned by the store/mall. Those who were at managerial level were earning much higher. Other than the basic salaries the employees are given incentives for better performances in several ways such as promotions, incentives, getting discount coupons. The pay rule for retail jobs is higher the profits, higher the incentives given to employees.

Qualifications and Positions Held

Occupational position is an important factor in determination of individual prestige and in allocation of privileges (Caplow, 1970). People are placed in particular jobs depending upon different attributes required for the position they hold.

Table 4.7

Position Held and Qualification

Position / Education	Sales	Cashier	Supervisor/ Floor manager/ section head	Assistant manager	Manager/ Incharge	Promoter	Total
Matric	9 (100.00) (23.07)	--	--	-	--	--	9(9.00)
+2	11 (37.93) (28.20)	5 (17.24) (55.55)	3 (10.34) (30)	2 (6.87) (10.52)	8 (27.58) (36.36)	--	29(29.00)
Diploma +2	2 (66.66) (5.12)	--	1 (33.33) (10.00)	--	-	--	3(3.00)
Graduation	13 (27.65) (33.33)	3 (6.38) (33.33)	6 (12.76) (60.00)	14 (29.78) (73.68)	10 (21.27) (45.45)	1 (2.12) (100.00)	47(47.00)
PG	4 (33.33) (10.26)	1 (8.33) (11.11)	--	3 (25) (15.78)	4 (33.33) (18.18)	--	12(12.00)
Total	39(39.00	9(9.00)	10(10.00)	19(19.00)	22(22.00)	1(1.00)	100(100.00)

Higher occupational positions require a lot of innate talent and years of education and bring in the large salaries because these are what motivated talented individuals to devote themselves to years of arduous study. (Volti, 2008: 118). As per NABARD report (2011), top level employees (managers/ associate and assistant managers) in modern formats in India constitute 4 to 5 per cent of the total work force that comprise of people with higher degrees. Persons with matriculation or 10+2 account for more than half of the workforce (largely concentrated at customer service representative, sales associate position) in retail formats (www.nsdcindia.org). Herein, it was proposed to study relationship between educational qualifications of store/mall/mart employees and their rank at their respective stores.

Table 4.7, shows that, almost all of the respondents have basic qualifications necessary for retailing and are educated, equipped with the basic skill set, ready to learn and orient themselves to varied situations. Their placement on different positions depended upon the educational attainment and experience in retailing. There is a set organizational structure in modern retail formats though there may be difference in the hierarchical arrangement and positions at malls, stores and marts. A small store may have only two positions, i.e., store manager and sales executive. Whereas, a big mall or mart may have 10 to 12 different positions/ ranks. These positions (See, Appendix V) are assigned to the employees depending upon their age, qualification, experience in retailing and many a times gender also.

From the table, it can be seen that none of the Matriculate is appointed as manager or assistant manager in the stores/malls. Also it is seen, that out of 29 per cent of the 10 + 2 respondents, 55.17 per cent of them are working at a subordinate level whereas, the remaining were working as managers or assistant managers. Likewise, out of 47 per cent of the Graduates, more than half of the respondents are working as assistant manager and manager at stores and the remaining are at the lower positions. Likewise, 58.33 per cent of the Post Graduate respondents are working at managerial level and the remaining 42 per cent are at sales, cashier, floor supervisor or promoters positions The data reflect that majority of the respondents concentrated at top positions are those who hold higher degrees and expertise. Though, the employees are recruited on specific designations (Appendix V), yet they are also trained to do multi tasks at their stores. Job rotation is often limited because it is a potential threat to efficiency, but many a times, it is practiced.

Means of Commuting to Workplace

Commuting is a way of life for most workers, whose working day starts well before they arrive at work place and does not end till they return home. For many people, work related stress begins to set in as they get into their cars or board the buses that take them to their jobs (Volti, 2008: 235). To know the lifestyle of the employees, they were asked about the means of transport they use to come to their workplace. It was seen that a little more than half of the respondents said that they come by two-wheeler to their stores (Figure 3) and 19 per cent said that they came on foot. Whereas, 18 per cent said they used public transport as a means of coming to their workplace and a very few have a four wheeler.

III. Profile of the Consumers

Market is expanding unlike never before and so marketers are looking into patterns of consumer behaviour. More than half of the population is young in India. The median age in India was around 25 years in 2009 (www.nabard.org). Consumption pattern as compared to past has changed due to increasing number of young and urban professionals falling between 16 to 40 years of age. Generally youngsters (15 to 24 years old) have more time to shop than their older counterparts. Youth have great deal of authority in decision pertaining to selection of shopping location. Although, the popular belief was that youngsters buy products under impulse and were less rational in buying.

Many of the recent studies indicate that most respondents aged 14-25 compare prices and brands before buying (Loudan 2002, www.paggu.com). Apart from it, earlier studies on consumer profile indicate that woman enjoy shopping regardless of their social classes but shopping behaviour and motivations of woman of different social classes vary. Upper and middle class woman tend to be more focused and selective in their shopping, middle class woman exhibit more anxiety when purchasing non-food items and are much value conscious.

It can be said that consumer behaviour is a complex phenomenon and is influenced by various factors such as age, sex, income, occupation, class, education, lifestyle and geographical locations (Kumar, 2007). In this part of the chapter, an effort has been made to understand consumer characteristics so as to study its implications on various determinants of consumer behaviour.

Age

Age is related to level of maturity of an individual and affects his/ her activities. As a person ages, his decision making power increases but, there is a decline in ability to do strenuous physical tasks. Youngsters are highly energetic in performing even exhaustive activities and have ample time to spare for time consuming activities like shopping. Studies on consumer behaviour highlights that youngsters are most active shoppers. In the present study also, it was seen that more of the young and middle aged were involved in shopping activity. Half of the respondent falled in the middle age category. More than one third of the respondent's fall between the age group of 21 to 30 years. While, more than one sixth of the respondents were above 51 years. The average age of the respondents is 37.8 years.

Gender and Marital Status

The sex ratio at an All-India level has improved significantly since last few years. Even in Amritsar city, sex ratio has improved. In 1991, the sex ratio was 883, in 2001 it was recorded 864 and in 2011 (provisional) sex ratio was 893 (Town Directory Schedule, Amritsar 2011). In patriarchal societies, males are regarded as head of the family and role of women is reduced to negligible position at various levels in the family (Mishra, 1993). Patriarchal structure, social norms quite often inhibit woman from aspiring to decision making positions. Other inhibitors which do not let woman participate in decision making process are social conditioning, family influence in societal culture, masculine culture of organization, marginalisation, discrimination, multiple burden, lack of education, financial dependence and poverty (Jha, 2005).

As compared to men, is woman who is largely involved in shopping activity, as a homemaker. She participates in decision making at almost all the levels. However, some domains of decision making falls exclusively in her domain such as- buying household items (petty commodities, such as grocery, fruits, vegetables etc.). The findings of the study correspond with the above stated explanation.

It was seen that out of the total respondents, seventy four per cent of the respondents comprised of females while, male comprised of remaining 26 per cent.

Also, seventy five per cent of the respondents were married, more than one-fifth of the respondents were unmarried. Divorced (2 per cent) and widowed (1 per cent) comprised of a small proportion of the total respondents.

Religion and Caste

In Punjab, Sikhs comprise of 52.6 per cent, Hindu comprises of 43.3 per cent, Muslims comprise of 2.6 per cent and Christians form 0.9 per cent of the total population (Statistical Abstracts of Punjab, 2009). In the present study it is seen that Hindus comprised of a large proportion of the respondents (72 per cent) while Sikhs comprised of 27 per cent of the total respondents and a very small proportion of respondents were found to be Christians (1 per cent).

Though, the city exhibits diversity in residential areas. But somehow, the areas are divided on the basis of castes and classes. The sampled area were primarily trading centres hence, high concentration of Hindu castes may be due to the reason that these areas are market cum residential areas and more of Hindu are involved in business activity.

Caste in contemporary India is undergoing change and is transforming into classes through adaptive changes. Classes in India operate within the frameworks of castes and caste takes care of class interest (Sharma, 2007). Caste stratification carries consequences in terms of life style of the people. The families value their caste- class norms in adopting the various behaviour patterns, be it related to consumption. It was seen that one third of the respondents falling in the category of consumers were Brahmins. Khatris comprised of 17 per cent of the respondents. While, Aroras comprised of 19 per cent, Jats (10 per cent), Baniyas (8 per cent). On the other hand, Rajputs, Mehrey, Saini and Christians comprised of minority (Table 4.8).

Table 4.8

Caste of the Consumers

Caste	Response	Percentage
Brahmin	33	33.33
Arora	19	19.19
Khatri	17	17.17
Jat	10	10.10
Baniya	8	8.08
Rajput	4	4.04
Ramgharia	4	4.04
Mehrey	2	2.02
Saini	1	1.01
Balmiki	1	1.01
Total	**99***	**100.00**

* *Excluding 1 respondent who was Christian.*

Educational Qualifications

Literacy rate is one of the indicators of development. More the literacy rate is more the society progresses. The provisional Census 2011, highlights literacy rate of male and female in Punjab as 81.5 and 71.3 per cent, i.e., the overall literacy rate in Punjab is 71.3 per cent (Hindustan Times, 9 April: 2011). The data collected for the present study also shows a similar trend. It was found that quite a number of respondents were Graduates (41 per cent) and nearly 28 per cent of the respondents were Post Graduates. Number of Matriculates was 11 per cent, while of those who had passed 10+2 was 10 per cent. Four per cent of respondents were Diploma holders after attaining the Graduation degree. Whereas, 3 per cent were Diploma holders after completing their Post Graduation. The number of illiterates was very less (Table 4.9). The data hence is representative of the increasing literacy rate.

Table 4.9

Educational Qualifications

Qualification	Response	Percentage
Illiterate	1	1.00
Matric	11	11.00
10+2	10	10.00
Diploma +2	2	2.00
Graduation	41	41.00
Graduation +Diploma	4	4.00
Post Graduation	28	28.00
PG +diploma	3	3.00
Total	**100**	**100.00**

Annual Income

The ability of individual to buy is measured not only by the availability of goods and services but also by the amount of money they have to spend. It is proposed that income of an individual may be related to his expenditure, i.e., higher the income, more the consumption. For this, it is essential to know the income of the respondents. It was seen that majority of the respondents stated their annual income between ₹ 1 to ₹ 3 lakh. While 18 per cent said their annual income was upto ₹ 1 lakh and 16 per cent said their annual family income ranged from ₹ 4 to ₹ 9 Lakhs. The remaining twenty per cent of the respondents did not stated their income. The data discern that the respondents largely hail from middle income group. It can be said that as per Keynesian psychological law of consumption as income increases, the consumption expenditure also increases but less than the increase in income (Sacher, 2009: 11). Also, Friedman's permanent income hypothesis states that in long run consumption increases in proportion to change in permanent income which is independent of the size of income. Income levels of consumers are determinants of their expenditure.

Type of Household

In India, family system is in transition phase from joint to nuclear family. Woman are also playing important role in this direction as they are likely to find joint family less satisfactory than men. They are more receptive to idea of change in family living than men (Mishra, 1993). As a result of nuclearlisation of families, consumption pattern has also undergone change. There has been overall increase in per capita consumption patterns in families. Also increase in working woman population has led to disposable income and changes in consumption patterns in families. Growing trend towards nuclearisation of families was seen in Amritsar also. It was found that a large number of respondents hailed from nuclear household (75 per cent). While more than one fifth of the respondents hailed from joint household. While, a small number (3 per cent) of respondents hailed from extended families.

The chapter can be summed up saying that retail Globalisation can lead to both increase and decrease in employment. As traditional market places (Bazaars) have been a major source of employment for the masses, so with expansion of modern retail impact can be felt on family- businesses within walled city. On the contrary, modern formats of retail have generated employment for the youngster. A comparison of the socio- economic profile of traditional retailers and employees at modern retailers shows a contrast. Where traditional retail is dominated by young and middle aged men, modern retail formats are more egalitarian providing equal participation to both young men and woman. Though, Sikhs are a dominant caste group in Punjab, yet majority involved in business activities is that of Hindus (including non- Punjabi communities). Heterogeneity (in terms of caste and communities) was seen among traditional retailers but, predominantly it is people from traditional business groups who are largely involved in particular businesses.

It was also seen that modern retail sector thrives on competitiveness and achievement of an individual. Education, experience and technical skills play an important role in employability and recruitment of people in specific positions in modern retail as compared to traditional retail wherein socialization was considered as the only way to acquire business acumen. However, with the times, the traditional retailers are also recognising the worth of formal education and there has been increase in the educational level of younger generation. There has been increasing trend towards nuclearisation of families which was noticed even among the traditional business families. Though, nuclear households are on increase yet, family ventures are sustaining. Likewise, employees working at stores and malls largely hail from lower- middle income nuclear families. Finally, it is seen that youngsters and the middle aged are actively involved in shopping activity. As compared to men it is women who are largely involved in shopping activity. Caste and religion plays no role in determining the consumption pattern or shopping activities of people however, class and gender does. It was also found that respondents largely hail from nuclear households and middle income groups. Significant increase in educational level was also noticed.

5

Impact of Modern Retail on Traditional Business

From social as well as economic perspective, retailing plays an important role in lives of people. India predominantly houses traditional formats of retailing (local neighbourhood shop) which has played a significant role in structuring of its economy. India has highest density of retail outlets in the world pegged at Rs 12 lakh crore nearly Rs (66,000 crore traditional outlets inclusive) (The Tribune, 8/9/07). Traditional retail sector has been a major traditional employer to a large number of people. On an average, retail outlet in an unorganized sector feeds a household of six to seven members (www. andhracafe. com). Over past few years, modern retail has emerged as one of the sunrise sectors in Indian economy and has made India move from culture of traditional street retail markets to shopping centre culture (www.scribd.com).

Modern retail has played a significant role in the developed countries during their period of high growth and now, it is also contributing substantially to the growth of the developing countries. Of recent, there has been a huge growth in modern retail in India (since 2002-03) which is associated with the growth in the economy and the attendant rise in consumption spending. The recent debate over inclusion of corporate houses in retail sector and opening up of retail sector to foreign investors has led to unease among the traditional retailers and has raised the question of authenticity, equity, justice and re-employment of 40 million retailers (Sridhar, 2007). The issue of modern and traditional retail players is not as simple as monopolization of market by the big entities rather; it carries various socio- economic implications which cannot be undermined but needs to be explored.

It is also foreseen, that with an upsurge in modern retailing, local markets would go through a transmutation and local shops would soon become a thing of past. It is assumed that on one hand, entry of international players would be advantageous to India as enterprising players will generate market efficiency. On the other hand, it is feared that it will kill the traditional retail formats by putting majority at the potential risk of unemployment and closure of numerous enterprises. It is also feared that competition witll become more intense in the market as it would not be a two way competition between corporate houses and traditional retail, rather it would involve competition with various participants and at various levels such as local-local (Big V/s Small or Small v/s Small or Big v/s Big) and global- local (International V/s National V/s traditional). Raising competition by selling similar goods dearer is a common predatory strategy used by large players to drive out small players and disperse competition which the corporate houses will follow to wean away local retail. Wall-Mart, the world's biggest retail chain has become a model for analysis for studying implications of modern retailing on traditional retail in India. All in all, three major concerns have been raised over opening up of Indian retail sector to FDI:

(a) Market Efficiency

The fiercest argument against retail Globalisation is that in the name of increasing market efficiency, modern retail formats will destroy local businesses. This holds true when modern retailers enter new markets, inefficient players and some businesses will inevitably close their doors or in the meanwhile, will adjust and tailor their strategies to evolve into stronger businesses. For example, despite stiff foreign competition from the national as well as international players such as Reliance and Wal-Mart, domestic retailers in various parts of the country suffered heavy losses initially, but now are tailoring strategies to adapt themselves to changing business conditions.

Traditional retail has suffered due to the poor shopping experience, inability to offer wide range of products, lack of sourcing capabilities and lack of innovative business practices which traditional retailers are now well aware of with penetration of modern formats. The wave of modern retailing has brought in several changes in the market, both structural as well as functional. There were times, when neighbourhood shopkeepers would give things on credit to customers and keep an account of record of all the customers in their account ledger. Now, there has been a shift from credit towards cash transaction. Neither shopkeepers now prefer to give on credit, nor do many of the people want to buy on credit. In the past, families, friends and relatives were the primary sources for help in business, but now businessmen prefer to hire employees from outside the family. Traditional businesses are being diversified and innovation through imitation is being adopted by traditional retailers for business expansion. Intense competition would also mean a winning situation for consumers, who will be getting benefitted from improved selection, variety of goods at lower rates. It is certain that Globalisation creates efficacy in the market by encouraging competition.

(b) Labour Displacement

Displacement of labour is a major concern that has been raised over retail incursion. It is believed that as people move from traditional retail jobs to modern retail jobs, there would be more job loss in the traditional sector. Though, incoming of modern retail has brought profound changes in the society and lives of people, yet in the due process it has resulted in disenfranchisement of certain people within the society. The US/ European experience of retail policy shows that modern retail destroyed livelihood of small shopkeepers, who later became employees of such giant stores for paltry salaries (www.sprawlsbuster.com, www.cpasind.com). Mulhern (1998), in his work took reference of Shils Report in order to measure the impact of mega-retail discount chains on small businesses in various communities by interviewing hundreds of entrepreneurs throughout California, Illinois, New York and Pennsylvania. His main findings were that seventy-two per cent of respondents expected the mega-retail chains to negatively impact their businesses, 50 per cent believed a serious reduction in their work force was an inevitable consequence, and 80 per cent anticipated a major decline in sales.

It was anticipated by the Indian analysts that retail liberalisation would generate employment for nearly 180, 000 people in India, but would also dislocate eight million from their occupation and push vast number of families under the poverty line (Business Line, 2005). MNC's will bypass Mandis (wholesale markets) since no two supermarket chains will operate in the same domain and so, farmers will have no choice but to comply with the lower prices offered by the retailer. (www.planetretail.net).

As a result, these competitors will go out of business and the superstores will exercise their monopoly. An example of displacement is how modern retail has almost done away with the mediator and has centralized power in the hands of retailers.

(C) Job Creation

On the contrary, proponents of modern retail propose that modern retail might not be as big a threat to smaller retailers as it appears. A study by Global Insight reports that for every 100,000 square-foot Store, Wal-Mart creates 97 Retail jobs. However, about 30 local wholesale jobs are lost, leaving a net gain of about 67 jobs (www.ey.com/India, www.indiaretailing.com).

This indicates that it is not just that modern retail penetration will lead to dislocation of traditional retailers rather; it will reduce the rate of unemployment through gainful employment in retail. Likewise in India, supporters of retail policy argue that the business loss would not take place heavily in case of traditional retail as it is often located in residential areas where family-owned shops are generally an extension of the family home so the loss incurred will not be large.

It is anticipated, if MNCs, FDI and corporate houses were to take over 20 per cent of the retail trade in India, there would still be an employment of about 43,000 persons as surplus.

The Indian Retail Experience

Taking into consideration, the sraised concerns over such a significant policy move, several studies such as those conducted by Technopak Limited (www.csi.mckinsey.com), Indian Council for Research on International Economic Relations: 2008, India Retail Report: 2007, National Council of Applied Economic Research, NABARD: 2011(www.nabard.org), NSDC India (www.nsdcindia.org) and other studies conducted by individual researchers such as Sridhar: 2007, Kahlon: 2007, Chattopadhyay: 2007, Lal: 2005, Mulky and Nargundkar: 2003, Purohit: 2009 have been undertaken since 2006 to assess the impact of modern retail over traditional retail. Few of these studies (Sridhar: 2007) formed Wall Martian Experience as the basis for assessing the implications of modern retail.

Impact of Modern Retail (India)

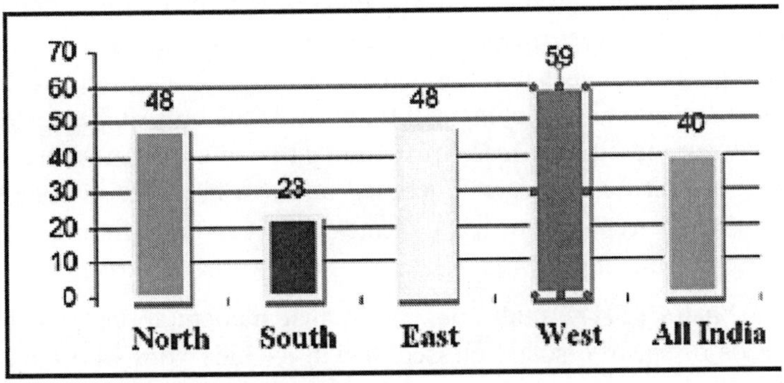

Source: ICRIER, 2008

Indian Council for Research on International Economic Relations (ICRIER 2008) presents a holistic picture to understand impact of modern retail on traditional retail sector throughout India. In this study, 40 per cent traditional businessmen at All-India level admitted that the opening of modern outlets in their vicinity had negatively affected their retail business. Region-wise, adverse impact of modern retail was admitted by as much as 59 per cent in the West, followed by 48 per cent both in the North and East, and only 23 per cent in the South. From the research, it can be said that incursion of modern retailers has definately affected business of traditional retailers at an All-India level.

Sridhar (2007), in his article 'Retail Invasion' highlights the problems, prospects and practices of modern retail stores and has raised concern over future of traditional retailers. Kahlon's (2007) article, 'Impact of Malls on Small Shops and Hawkers in Mumbai' points towards decline in sales of traditional retailers out of which 14 per cent of the retailers showed ability to cope up in intensive competition. Likewise, Sethi (2007) in his article 'Curious Practices' puts forward the work operation of India's retail giant 'Reliance'.

The researches brings forth that supply chain of vendors has been adversely affected and thrown out to low quality produce in India. Chattopadhyay's (2007) study of Kolkata highlights that oversupply of malls has been determinant to industry itself. In Kolkata, all malls/stores are though, not earning well, yet they have affected business of traditional retailers by their marketing strategies. Convenient access linked to price competitiveness and extended shopping experience at large chain stores suggests negative effect on the turnover and employment of traditional retailers (Mulhern, 1998). Likewise, he cites the case of Chandigarh and Gurgaon where only 50 per cent of malls are functional and rest have perished or still waiting for retailers which indicates that it is not defininte in the present compeitition who will survive and who will perish.

Shah's (2011) study, puts forth that modern formats cater to needs of specific social classes. It will exclude poor who have no purchasing power or who usually buy in small quantity and on informal credit basis, which will help in parallel expansion as well as strengthening of traditional retail.

Neilson (2011), study shows that no doubt, arrival of modern retail formats has negatively affected small grocers, but as a result of increasing competition, the sales of traditional retailers are also growing at a much lower rate (www.articles.economictimes.com). All in all, these researches indicate unique co-existence of modern retail as well as traditional retail in these cities and propose that it cannot in any way happen that modern formats would completely eliminate the traditional retail. What makes the issue of modern retail penetration debatable, is duality of Indian retail sector, i.e., a large number of small retailers catering to all the classes on one hand and a small number of big outlets catering to the needs of certain sections of the society on the other. It is assumed that due to surge in modern retailing, traditional retailers will be at a disadvantageous position.

For this, numbers of protests were raised in various parts of the country. Trader's organization in Mumbai, Thane and its neighbouring areas organized protest movements several times against entry of big companies in retail trade. Opponents of retail FDI inspect that entry of big chains would mean like in UK, about 10 retail chains control the entire market (The Tribune, 2007).

So far the situation has been peaceful in Punjab unlike the southern part of the country and other cities like Bhopal, Indore, Ranchi, Chennai and Delhi where maximum protests and violent attacks were made by CPI (M), small traders and farmers over opening up of modern food and grocery stores (that form the largest segment of Indian retail) to show anguish. There has been no voice from any corner over retail expansion in Punjab.

Other than, Mr. Prakash Singh Badal (Cheif Minister of Punjab) once said 'No' to entry of Reliance in Punjab. Therefore, the whole question of opening up of retail sector centres primarily on exclusion, i.e., Will expansion of modern retail formats result in mass unemployment of people who have been earning through retailing?

I. Impact on Traditional Business

The present study is based on premises that sudden changes in the market affect all participants and if the number of malls and retail chains multiply, the sales impact on small shops is likely to be intensified and earnings will keep falling and will result in dissonance and disequilibrium in the domestic market (Kahlon, 2007).

Modern retailers by using customer friendly strategies and influencing decision making power of consumers by advertising on large scale, offering schemes and other lucrative offers is adversely affecting the business of local retailers. Decline in sales is visible due to division of clientege that resulted in labour displacement and pauperisation of local retailers. There are two opinions on the issue related to impact of modern retailing on traditional retailing. Where on one hand, questions like- Will these newly emerged outlets be able to take over the age old business practices and foster their global values? Will modern retail take over the traditional retail? What are the prospects of both modern and traditional retail in city have become debatable.

The following part of the chapter would focus upon impact of modern retail incusion and strategies adopted by traditional retailers to survive in the intense competing environment.

Impact on Traditional Businesses

Indian retail business has been adversely affected at an All-India level due to modern retail incursion (ICRIER, 2008). Purohit's (2009) and NABARD (2011), study indicate that traditional retails did not fear that modern retail will negatively affect their businesses. Therefore, such studies show a mixed attitude of retailers over the competition between modern and traditional retailers.

In our study, the findings were also quite similar in this regard. Figure 1, reflects views of traders on impact of modern retail upsurge on business of traditional retailers. It was seen that 53 per cent of the respondents stated that their business had witnessed slow down due to modern retail invasion.

They put forward different reasons for decline in their business. Out of these, most of the respondents stated that due to rise in competition, with the entry of big players, their sales have gone down and the market has witnessed a slump. While, only a few of the respondents said that sometimes they have to suffer losses on selling dearer to the customers because malls/ stores throw tricky offers and schemes to wean away customers from shops to malls.

Hence, in order to compete with them they too have to follow their footsteps and sometime bear loss in order to survive.

Figure 1

Effect of Modern Retailing on Traditional Business

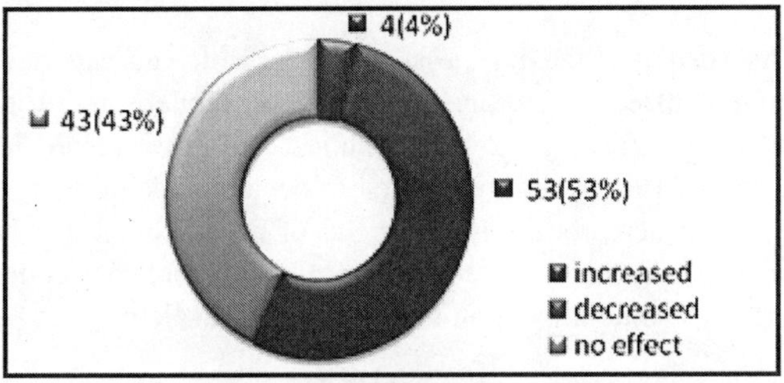

On the other hand, four per cent, said that their business has seen a spurred growth because of the retail invasion. Of these, more than half of the respondents said that in the initial stage local market went down slightly but now, market has reverted to normal, as it remained resilient in past. The customers are back to shops from stores/ malls. More than one third of the respondents said that their sales have improved with an increased flow of customers. Increasing affluence and burgeoning style of shopping has led to an increase in consumerism. Hence, people are shopping from everywhere (malls, shops, stores) like never before.

Likewise, almost forty three per cent of the respondents said that there has been no effect of modern retail on their business. They believe that in real sense, there exist no competition between traditional and modern retailers as both have their own competitors, clientele and limitations. It can be said, on the basis of ample studies (as discussed) that the traditional retail business has been affected in a great way in various parts of the country. Though in the initial phase, there was unrest among local retailers, yet with the passage of time the impact got lessened to some extent. This does not in any way mean that there has been no effect on the traditional business. Increasing number of malls/stores/ marts in the city and movement of customers from shops to modern formats are still posing a challenge for the traditional retailers. To further probe the enquiry, the pattern of procurement and sale of goods was taken as variable so as to cross check the response.

Trend of Procurement and Sales

As seen that the business of retailers of Amritsar have been negatively affected by the expansion of modern retail formats. Purohit's (2009) study shows that almost half of the respondents out of a total of 100 agreed that there has been decline in their sales. In order to further probe this, the trend of procurement and sale has been made as it was expected that the effect of increasing competition would have some impact on the purchase and sale of goods also.

Table 5.1

Trend of Procurement and Sales

Procurement / Sales	Increasing	Decreasing	Static	Total
Increasing	6(54.54) (42.85)	3(27.27) (7.31)	2(18.18) (4.44)	11(11.11)
Decreasing	3(16.66) (21.42)	9(50.00) (21.95)	6(33.33) (13.33)	18(18.18)
Static	5(7.04) (35.71)	29(40.84) (70.73)	37(52.11) (84.09)	71 (71.00)
Total	**14(14.00)**	**41(41.00)**	**44(44.00)**	**100(100.00)**

Table 5.1, represents the pattern of procurement of goods and sales of the respondents. The data given in table shows that a vast majority of the respondents (84.09 per cent) stated that because their sales were static, their procurements were also by and large static. More than half of respondents said that their businesses was neither going on very well nor was suffering heavy losses. Also, half of the respondents stated that because of several reasons there has been decline in the sales due to which they have adjusted their procurements accordingly, i.e., the stock procured was also on decline (as said by

50 per cent). On the contrary, nearly forty three per cent of the respondents said that their sales were improving and so were their procurements. Therefore, it can be said that there is a direct relationship between trend of sales and procurements. With the increase in sales, the procurements also increase and with the decline in sales, the procurements also decline sooner or later. Thus, the table shows that there were always fluctuations in sales and procurements but, it also remained static to a large extent. One possible reason for these fluctuations may be traced as the inflow and outflow of customers.

Geographical Settitng and Clientele: Impact Factor

Geographical settings of a venture have also been determinant of its success and failure. In earlier notions of market, a shop located on the fringe had lesser opportunity for flourishing than shop located in a densely populated area or centre as it was thought to attract more number of customers due to the easy accessibility. The newer trend of market settlement is that more of the retailers are concentrating their big box retail stores on the outskirts of the city so as to provide better facilities to the customer's like- parking sans traffic congestion, ample space for shopping, entertainment facilities and lavish buildings. In past, interior areas of the city were the trade hub but now peripheral areas of the city are fast becoming the most sought after market hubs. Modern formats of retailing have led to emergence of new economic zones in the city and are replacing the concept of convenient-shopping with comfort-shopping by providing numerous facilities to customers which are beyond the reach of traditional retailers. The respondents were also asked about location where they initiated their business. Majority of the respondents stated that they started their business at the same place (where it is today).

Whereas, few respondents commenced their business at some other place (outside the walled city, in exterior of the city, somewhere within the walled city, some in less developed area/ some at other place) and later moved to the present place. This shows that, majority of the respondents started their business at the same place and their business has been running efficiently till date, irrespective of the ups and downs in the market. However, it was seen that somehow vicinity of the shops to modern formats do affect the business, i.e., shops located near stores reported more severe impact as compared to those located at distance.

Since long, neighbourhood shops have been the only option available to the consumers and have been catering to the needs of all the sections of society. In the past, market relations between customers and retailers were very clear. Retailers knew of their definite clientele therefore, market relations were also informal. However, with more income in hands and better avenues for shopping locations (status seeking, convenience, trust etc) there has been dissolution of customer's loyalty towards shops. To ascertain the type of business and affect of retail invasion, the respondents were asked to characterize their clientele. It was seen that the prime effect of emergence of modern retail on exteriors of the city was noticed on the outsiders (villagers/ NRIs) who do not come to the city (interiors) for shopping purposes. Also, more likely the traders showed loss of their regular customers. While, a little impact was seen on last minute buyers, small stock buyers and those who buy on credit as they continue to shop from the most convenient locations in the neighbourhood.

Change in market is followed by change in social relationship and change in economic transaction also. Price is a very relative concept that helps consumers to establish their priorities and levels of acceptable need satisfaction. Traditional shopkeepers have always been accused of being dishonest, fraudulent and manipulating prices of goods. Earlier, it was a common practice among retailers to sell things by word of mouth or on credit and write down the name of customers and cost of goods sold in an account ledger. Now, there has been shift towards cash transaction. The shopkeepers now prefer to sell things on cash than credit. Almost all shops in the city have 'No Credit' stickers on their walls. It can be drawn that there has been an inclination towards cash sales and purchases. It may be due to the increasing formalism in social relationship, sans loyalty on the part of both buyer as well as seller.

Customer Slow Down

It is a general tendency of customers of various social classes to waver hither and theither andpurchase as per their needs and tase. Additional impact has been seen on traditional business withthe outflow of customers from shops to stores. Table 5.2, puts forth various reasons of customer slowdown as stated by respondents. Some, 24.27 per cent of the respondents said that there has been division of clientele with division of market.

Customers with better purchasing power prefer to buy from the stores/ malls. While, other classes prefer to buy from the traditional shops or once a while visit modern formats as they cannot afford to spend at malls and hesitate to be a part of elitist style of living. Some 18.44 per cent of respondents said that there has been slow down because people are ready to experience global shopping and are attracted towards advantages of one-stop shopping locations.

Whereas, 11.65 per cent of the respondents argued that customer slow down is primarily due to the fact that malls and stores sell goods at cheap prices during sale period and through promotional offers and schemes (like buy 1 get 1 free, 50+40 % off). Customers in a way think of being benefited through such schemes and desert their shopkeeper in lieu of strategies played on them by calculating retailers.

Table 5.2

Reasons for Customer Slowdown

Reasons	Response	Percentage
Customer divide (mushrooming up of franchise and showrooms)	25	24.27
One stop shopping and people's craze to gain global shopping experience	19	18.44
Marts/Stores sell cheap during sales/promos	12	11.65
Customer has become more demanding	10	9.71
More Quality, variety, brands available at Marts	10	9.71
Local and global competition	8	7.76
Development of nearby villages	6	5.82

Affluent and cash customers prefer to go to Malls	6	5.82
Western culture (jeans/brands)	4	3.89
Inflation	3	2.91
Total	**103***	**100.00**

* *Multiple Responses*

Nearly ten per cent of the respondent said that malls and stores provide people with a wide range of variety, quality and brands. So they prefer modern formats as they can get things of all sorts and all range of prices at one place which is time saving and hassle free. The customers have now become more demanding and conscious of everything around. Their choices have increased. A small shopkeeper cannot provide them with variety of things because they have limited pool of investment and hence are unable to meet the needs of their customers. Respondents also stated that another reason behind the customer slowdown is that retailers have to compete with both local and global players. Competing at a local front is still an easy task but competing with big companies is quite a difficult task as there is a wide difference between their investment and strategies.

Nearly, six per cent of the respondents said that there has been customer slow down because shopping from malls and luxurious branded stores have become a symbol of status and provides them with a class experience. People now prefer to shop from stores/ shops located in their own villages or nearby sub- urban areas rather than coming to the main city. Lifestyle changes and inflation were the other reasons stated by the respondents. On the other hand, 49 per cent of the respondents (Table, 4.2) disagreed that there has been any slowdown of customers to their shops. From the findings, it can be discerned that rate of outflow can vary in case there is an extension in modern retail activity.

Categorization of Customers on the basis of their Outflow

With booming economy and burgeoning middle class, shopping habits of people are changing fast. People have started preferring new formats of retailing and are deserting their traditional shopkeepers who are equally aware of the outflow of customers.

Table 5.3

Customers More likely to Move from Modern Formats than Shops

Category	Response	Percentage
High class	35	32.11
Customers buying on cash	18	16.51
Regular customers	1	0.92
Middle class	2	1.83
All	38	34.86
None	15	13.76
Total	**109***	**100.00**

**Multiple Responses*

The respondents were asked to enlist categories of customers who they think have deserted them for shopping at stores. It was anticipated that high class prefer to opt for shopping at modern formats than traditional.

Surprisingly, in our study, respondents stated that customer loyalty has become very unpredictable as all customers; waver hither and thither for shopping. One third of the respondents said that it is high class that deserts the shopkeeper because they have high purchasing power (Table 5.3).

They are more concerned about their social status and hence, prefer to purchase from the Hi-profile store/superstore which reflects their social status. Also, 16.51 per cent of the respondents said that the customers who buy purely on cash keep on trying new shops and stores. Whereas, nearly fourteen per cent said that none of the customers have stopped shopping at the traditional shops as it is the very nature of customers that they will buy a single thing after moving in and out of several shops. On the contrary, others said it was their regular customers and middle class who have ditched them.

The above stated arguments bring forth that markets have always been criticized for dissolving social bonds and reducing persons and goods to commodities.

Customers Prefer Modern Formats than Traditional: Opinion of Retailers

Modern retail formats have drawn attention of city dwellers. A great majority of the respondents (85 per cent) stated that customers desert their shopkeeper in favour of modern formats. Of these, nearly 21 per cent of the respondents said that it is the attitude of customers that they vacillate because they are inquisitive and do not feel satisfied with shopping at one place and are on look out for trying out new things and places. Ten and half per cent said that malls provide them with a good physical environment (spacious and lavish) free space to roam about and spend a quality time with family and friends and entertain oneself. Things are on display and so are the rates and their cut price so, people find it convenient to pick things as per their pocket and requirement. With increasing consciousness and interlinking of brands with status, people take shopping and brands as a signifier of their social status. Such view was held by 8.64 per cent of the respondents. Nearly seven per cent of the respondents said that customers prefer modern formats over traditional bazaars as the latter do not provide enough parking spaces and are located in congested streets of the city. Customers also abandon local shops primarily for air conditioned shopping stops. Modern jewellery showrooms were the first on to offer air conditioned ambience for shopping, while Raymond store was the first one to open chain stores with decor and ambience (Purohit, 2009). Also, rising income of people becoming a norm in urban areas, increased advertising and a jump in the number of working people have contributed towards an outflow of customers from shops to stores.

Table 5.4

Reasons for Preferring Modern Formats

Reasons	Response	Percentage
Attitude/inquisitiveness, craze for Malls/branded showroom	34	20.99
Quality, brand, variety, schemes, services, latest stuff, hassle free shopping	36	22.22

Physical Environment at Marts/Stores (free space to roam about, entertainment, rates and stocks displayed)	17	10.49
Brands and Malls have become a status symbol	14	8.64
People's choice have gone up and have become status conscious	15	9.25
Rates are Displayed, Are Uniform and can choose accordingly	11	6.79
Parking problem	11	6.79
Bulk purchase at low rates at Marts	11	6.79
Media promotes new lifestyle	5	3.09
People prefer to buy at the nearest, be it shop or store	4	2.47
Air conditioned shopping	4	2.47
Total	**162***	**100.00**

* *Multiple Responses*

Whereas, remaining said that people prefer to buy from the nearest possible locations (be it shop or store) as one cannot afford to go to a shpos/stores located several miles to buy frequent or small stock.

Benefits and Non Benefits of Modern Retail: Opinion of Retailers

It is natural when competition increases, it is a wining situation for consumer as they are the one who get maximum benefit out of competition between market players. Modern retailers adopt lucrative consumer friendly strategies to draw out customers from shops to stores. It was seen that nearly sixy per cent of respondents (59) were of the view that modern retail do not benefit customers. While, 26 per cent of respondents disagreed with them and were of the opinion that buying from marts and stores as beneficial because of availability of goods at discounted rates. On the other hand, 15 per cent held a neutral view. The respondents who responded in favour of modern retail gave arguments to support their views (Table 5.5).

Table 5.5

Benefits and Non Benefits of Big Retail to Customers, Reasons

Benefits	**Response**	**Percentage**
Sales and promos make things accessible so, people prefer to wait and buy on sale	23	24.73
One-stop shopping with entertainment	19	20.43
Only in readymade clothes	17	18.28
Branded products for status conscious class, better quality	10	10.75
Only some items are cheap (Fruits and Vegetable etc) not all	8	8.60
Friendly ambience	7	7.53
Give new stock/variety every week	6	6.45
For bulk purchase	2	2.15
Things are displayed, makes shopping easy	1	1.08
Total	**93***	**100.00**
Non Benefits	**Response**	**Percentage**
Deceptive offers/schemes/no bargaining	51	33.11
High investments lead to higher costs	46	29.89
Mixing of brands and inferior quality of goods, lacks exclusivity	24	15.59
Impersonal relationship (poor services/ credit)	12	7.79
Increase inflation and create superfluous wants (encourages consumerism)	7	4.54
Increase shortage by hoarding and cutting off supply in the market	7	4.54
Non availability of certain items	7	4.54
Total	**154***	**100.00**

* *Multiple Responses*

Of these 59 respondents, more than one-fifth respondents said that modern formats offer certain promotional offers, discounts and sales to customers to make things accessible by cutting the cost price. So, people prefer to wait and buy during sale period. Also, it helps them camouflage status as people get brands and other products at low prices which provide them with a sense of accomplishment and status consistency. Availability of goods under one roof and hassle free shopping is yet another advantage of shopping at malls/stores to the customers (20.43 per cent respectively). Alongwith shopping, malls/ stores have become a source of entertainment as it provides a clean and pleasant environment for shopping. Whereas, others said that only stores selling readymade garments are advantageous because they provide the customers with a greater transparency in prices and transaction and customers are not cheated in any way. They can shop for same brand anywhere in the city as there is uniformity in prices, transaction and products. Likewise, nearly eleven per cent of the respondents said that customers get benefit because global retailing provides them with branded products and a class feeling.

In a similar manner, 8.60 per cent of the respondents said that customers do not necessarily get benefited in all ways as only a few of items at malls/ stores are cheap such as Fruits and vegetables/ grocery. Offers like, buy 1 get 1 free, discount on evening purchase, better services, pleasant environment, friendly and formally dressed staffs with good communication skills provide ambience to customers which local shopkeeper cannot provide. A few of the respondents (2.15 per cent) modern retail as super saver locations both in terms of time and prices. Things are displayed, properly presented and are noticeable which makes shopping easy as one can pick as per one's need, liking and pocket.

Non-Beneficial Shopping at Modern Stores

Of more than half of respondents who stated modern formats as non beneficial, one third said that sales, offers and schemes are deceptive and manipulating (Tabe 5.5). The fixed-price stores deprive customers of their power of bargaining and compel them to buy at displayed prices. Less than one third of the respondents said higher investments of modern formats led to higher cost of the things. Malls/stores sell goods at high prices than MRP. Also, 15.59 per cent of the respondents said that there is no retail culture in the city as many of the stores adopt cheap techniques such as: mixing of brands and labels, selling inferior quality of goods at same prices to that of brands to mislead customers. Also, they lack exclusivity as they sell everything under one roof but there is nothing exclusive in variety.

In addition, 7.79 per cent added that malls/ stores do not provide better services than shopkeepers. They were of opinion that in modern markets, relationship between buyer and seller is impersonal. A local shopkeeper provides more personalised services as compared to malls/ store employees. The remaining respondents said non avialability of traditional kiryana items at malls/stores was another reason for preferring local shops. They were also of the opinion that corporate retailers create shortage in market by cutting off supply, and hoarding goods at their stores. These big retail houses buy in bulk from the local market at lower rates and sell them at their stores at higher prices. All in all, opinion of traditional retailers over modern formats was that stores and malls do not benefit customers in any way.

II. The Strategic Struggle For Inclusion

The current debate over exclusion of traditional retailers from the market as a result of inclusion of modern formats of retailing has become a prime concern for all. It is doubtless that traditional retailers will have to face tough competition from all angles in order to make their businesses survive. However, it may not be that easy for modern retailers to completely eliminate traditional retail market as traditional retailers are trying out number of ways to maintain their existence in the growing competition.

The retailers of Amritsar city are tying their best to compete with modern retailers which has brought a general slowdown in the local market. So in order to maintain themselves in ongoing competition they have devised number of strategies such as many have added more quantity, variety and brands to their shops. Some have also changed the physical environment of their shops, i.e., interior of the shop matching the new retail culture. Many of them got their shops air conditioned, have placed goods on stacks and rows. Some of them have even diversified their business or have changed business and have shifted their business / shop from a low developed area or from the interior of the city to posh area of the city to draw customers.

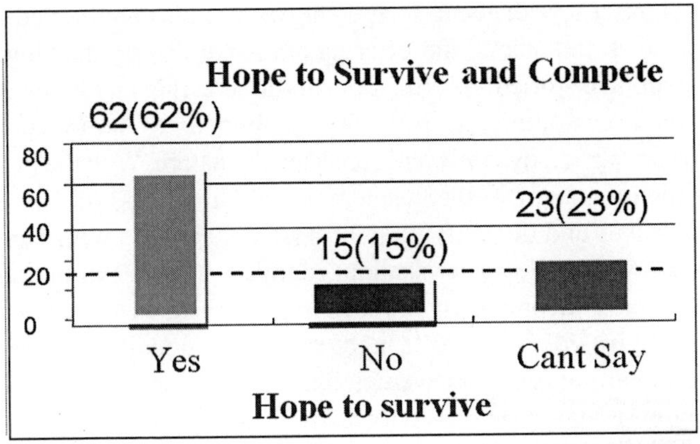

The data collected shows 'Never Say Die' attitude of businessmen of Amritsar as sixty two per cent of the respondents said that they hope to survive in the competition and are ready to compete with modern business tycoons. No opinion was held by 23 per cent as they were dwindling between what the situation offers. While, 15 per cent said that they had no hope of survival, but all the possibilities of shut down (Figure 2). Traditional retailers in Amritsar city are surely adjusting themselves with the changing business environment, but due to the uncertaininty in market fear of dislocation continues to haunt them.

Methods Adopted by Retailers

Those who showed optimism in such critical situation were adopting several strategies to keep themselves at pace with market trend. Table 5.6 shows that 49.27 per cent of respondents said that they now try to get latest variety, maintain quality of goods and provide better services to customers. Many of them (30.14 per cent), said they have lowered their rates in order to compete with malls/ stores which offer schemes and promotional offers to draw attention of customers. Thus, they have to lower their rates in order to make prices relative to market. Fifteen per cent said that they also offer sales and schemes to customers like modern retail formats. Remaining respondents stated that they also made some changes in their shops like converting an ordinary shop into a showroom, attaching a stylish name to the showroom, air conditioned interior with rows and stacks and offering attractive display, making simple shop double storied, offering door-to-door selling and home delivery to their customers. It reflects that people of Amritsar are an enterprising lot, dynamic and consistent by nature. With the increasing competition many of the businessmen are in process of restructuring themselves and diversifying their business activity. With increase in educational level, westernisation, adoption of more exhibitionist way of life and incoming of branded stores, there has been increased desirability for soft skills and business etiquettes. In the past, traditional shopkeepers were looked down upon because of their dishonest and rude behaviour, use of impolite slang and their inattentiveness to customer's needs. But now, with change in market, traditional retailers are recognising that behavioural skills and mannerism play an important role in shaping ones business.

Table 5.6

Strategies Used to Survive and Compete

Strategies	Response	Percentage
Keeping with the trend/ maintaining quality/ services/ variety	67	49.26
Lowering rates	41	30.15
Selling on offers/sale/discounts	20	14.71
Adopting store style (stacks/rows etc..)	4	2.94
Home delivery/ door to door selling	3	2.21
All of the above	1	0.73
Total	**136***	**100.00**

**Multiple responses.*

Today, a retailer cannot afford to miss out such a general way of conduct to maintain efficacy of business. The jargons like 'customer is always right', 'customer satisfaction' have become popular among businessmen. Retailers are mending their erroneous practices by replacing them with new values like honesty, trustworthiness, reliability, dependability and are imitating modern retail practices to survive.

Liking for Modern Formats: Opinion as Consumers

There is quite a hustle and bustle in showrooms, malls, and stores in Amritsar. Everyone likes to go to malls for different purposes and traditional retailers are no exception to it. As a consumer, they too are interested in experiencing new spaces of consumption and new lifestyle. Interestingly, it was seen that many of the shopkeepers go to malls for shopping (nearly, 51 per cent) and others go to spend their leisure time with their family, friends or sometimes go alone for window-shopping (24.5 per cent). Some of them even go to malls for business purpose (18.6 per cent), i.e., to see the latest trend, design and prices in order to keep in touch with the business world and also purchase goods in bulk for business purpose (5.89 per cent). It indicates that even local businessmen are interested in new consumption lifestyle.

Along with this, shopkeepers were asked to express their liking at modern formats (Table 5.7). Nearly, forty eight per cent of the respondents said that luxurious, well designed and planned interiors with A/C, false ceiling, wall painting, stacks and rows, sitting arrangement, restaurant at malls/ stores and marts attract them. Huge variety of the goods/ products and range and availability of everything under one roof was liked by 26.13 per cent. People can make purchase according to their taste, range and requirement which is one of the main advantages of stores. Inescapable eye-catching schemes and services (10.22 per cent), quality products (7.95 per cent) make customers stay at a distance from any ordinary shop. Also, 2.27 per cent said that they like the dealings of attendants at malls and stores who talk so politely and help them in all the ways, well dressed staff having good communication skill gives them a sense of classy shopping.

Table. 5.7 : Liking at Malls/Marts

Category	Response	Percentage
Interior	42	47.72
Variety	23	26.13
Schemes and services	9	10.22
Quality of products	7	7.95
Dealings	2	2.27
All of the above	5	5.70
Total	**88***	**100.00**

**Multiple responses*

From the above arguments, it can be said that malls/ marts are the in-things, as they provide customers with variety of products, prices, brands, physical environment, quality. attractive schemes, offers and other advantages such as: shopping under one roof and provision of parking lots. They are regarded as a super saver location which saves time and money as well. One need not carry shopping cart as everything is displayed and one can choose as per his own choice. It can be said shopkeepers as consumers gave a welcoming response to the modern retail formats.

Opinion on Allowing FDI in Retail

As it is feared that FDI in retail will devastate traditional retail market the issue of allowing complete FDI in retail sector has been still under consideration by government.

Figure 3

Opinion on Allowing FDI in Retail

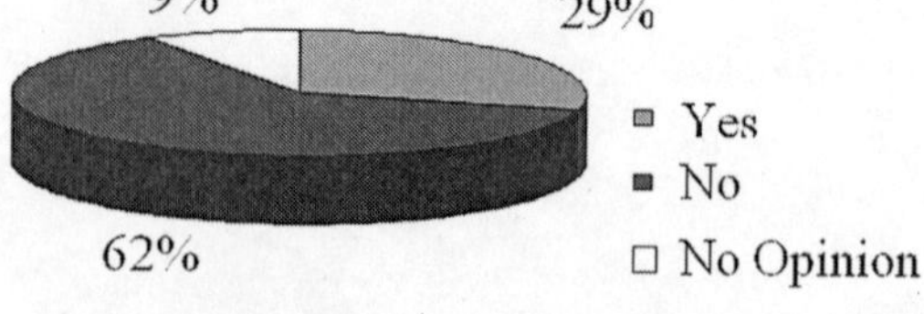

Respondents expressed their views on government's decision on allowing complete FDI in retail sector (Figure 3). Majority condemned government's decision on allowing FDI in retail sector. They were of opinion that FDI in retail is fundamentally different from that of manufacturing as it is anticipated that FDI in retail trade may create severe job losses and exclude traditional supply chains. Only few of them (29 per cent), favoured FDI in Indian retail market. It shows that traditional retailers are though competing in order to sustain their business, yet they fear unfettered growth of big box sellers in Indian market.

Views of Opponents and Proponents on FDI in Retail

The views of the respondents (Table 5.8) depict that the opening up of complete FDIs would negatively hit local retail sector and exclude traditional retailer from the market. Out of the total respondents (62 per cent, Figure 3) who opposed FDI in retail, 44.44 per cent of them (Table 5.8) were of the opinion that allowing FDI in retail would aggravate market crises. There will be loss to local business and national brands as people will prefer to buy from international retailers. One-fifth of? respondents said that allowing FDI would mean unemployment and dislocation of already employed businessmen. The strongest argument raised against retail Globalisation is that FDI will wipe away businesses who cannot hold on the might of big corporate entities. It will destroy the traditional business. Many of the respondents (nearly fifteen per cent) were of the opinion that Indian businessmen cannot compete with the foreign competitors not because they are inefficient but due to certain deprivations such as lack of superior resources, sound economic push, hi-tech skills.

Table. 5.8 : Views of Opponents and Proponents on FDI

Views of Opponents	**Response**	**Percentage**
Market crises will aggravate, loss to local business and brands	48	44.44
Un- employment and dislocation of already employed businessman (merger and acquisition)	26	24.07
Indian businessmen cannot compete with big corporates, Indian companies should be given chances and not MNCs	16	14.81
Lead to hegemonic relation and monopoly of the mighty	11	10.19
Hike in estate prices, inflation, shortage of supply, poverty increase	7	6.49
Total	**108***	**100.00**
Views of Proponets		
Globalism/development	20	25.00
Increase competition/consumer/consumerism	18	22.50
Generate employment/increase salary	15	18.75
Improve quality, services and efficiency	11	13.75
Innovation, to change oneself	6	7.50
50% should be opened	6	7.50
Fair trade practices	4	5.00
Total	**80***	**100.00**

**Multiple Responses*

They (10.19 per cent respondents) feared that FDI will bring monopoly in market. In addition to this, 6.49 per cent reasoned that more FDI means increase in conspicuous consumption that will result in hike in estate prices, lead to inflation and shortage of supply as retailers will purchase in bulk from market and create shortage which will increase poverty and widen the economic disparities.

Proponents of FDI

Where a large number of respondents view retail Globalisation as a threat to their survival, others view it as an opportunity for business expansion and innovation. Table 5.8, presents the view of proponents of FDI (nearly 30 per cent, Figure 3). Of these, one fourth of the respondents said that FDI should be encouraged as FDIs are an asset for the nation and would result in improvement of market structure by generating employment for masses (the opinion was held by 18.75 per cent of the respondents). Standard of living of people will improve and the nature of market will undergo a change. Nearly, fourteen per cent of respondents said that with retail Globalisation there will an improvement in quality of products, human resources, management and work culture as the inflow of FDI does not only mean inflow of capital, but also imbibing new ways of acting, thinking and behaving which will result in market efficiency. Local retailers will learn and acquire new technological methods, strategies and skills in order to adapt themselves to changing environment. Similarly, 7.5 per cent of the respondents said FDIs are the facilitators for growth of an economy. Government should not hesitate in opening retail, but should determine how much to allow taking into account the issue of subsistence of millions involved in businesses.

Respondents too suggested that fifty per cent should be opened at initial stage. Five per cent respondents said that inclusion of FDI to Indian economy will result in fair trade practices and a transparent system of networking which will be beneficial for consumers and retailers (both national and international). They were also of opinion that there was no competition between modern and traditional retailers as the powers of both are incomparable. They held the opinion that there is no alternative to make Indian market more efficient and globally competitive, but to globalise. Hence, retail globalism must be viewed as an opportunity and conditions must be created to make India an attractive destination for foreign investments (Siddharthan, 1999, 2004).

Future of Shops, Malls and Stores

The structure of Indian retail is developing rapidly with shopping malls becoming increasingly common in urban and rural landscape. With more disposable income in hands, investors have been seeking avenues to do so thereby, fuelling retail boom in the city. Sudden increase in closure, merger and acquisition of underperforming stores all over the country has given a new dimension to competition in market, i.e., competition is not only confined to modern and traditional but also is happening in diverse manner. Table 5.9, reflects views of respondents on future of modern retailers. It was seen that 18.13 per cent of respondents said that malls would not survive, as they sell goods at unaffordable prices. Modern formats in city have lesser turnover and are lowly maintained, only a few of them are doing well in the city while, others have become a place to spend leisure time with family and friends. Also, 9.30 per cent said modern formats are unaffordable, therefore these formats will only survive, if they lower their prices and come down to market.

Table 5.9

Future of Malls/Stores/Marts

Gloomy	**Response**	**Percentage**
Tough to survive (expensive, low maintenance and less turnover)	39	18.14
Malls and shops will co-exist	37	17.20
Malls have become a Source of entertainment and shopping (face-lift the city, indicator of development)	31	14.42
Malls/ Stores will have to come down to market level and lower their prices in order to survive	20	9.30
Only malls will go on, as they provide people s with brands at cheap rate	19	8.83
Will not work well as people's purchasing power is low, population is limited	17	7.91
Bright		
Market will undergo metamorphosis (increase efficiency, consumerism and improvement in quality	17	7.91
Stores /Malls will spread and hit local business	9	4.19
Malls/Stores will be at competition with each other, shops will survive	9	4.19
Extra burden on city-no parking, congestion on streets	9	4.19
Single brands will work well than Malls	8	3.72
Total	**215***	**100.00**

* *Multiple Responses*

Nearly 7.90 per cent said it would not work well as people in the city have low purchasing power, and population of the city is also limited. Few of the respondents (4.19 per cent) were of the opinion that malls would spread in the coming years and hit local business and also anticipated that single branded stores would do better than malls. They further added that traditional retailers always cater to needs of lower-income groups and all other sections of the society. In contrast, large outlets cater to the need of a particular section of the society, i.e., high class and upper middle class customers, hence their clientele remains defined. Also, what traditional retailers can provide with their age old understanding of local culture cannot be provided by the foreign entrants. Therefore, it is assumed that big challenge which these modern stores/malls will have to cater to the needs of heterogeneous market.

For many others, future of modern formats seems to be bright. Almost, 17.20 per cent (Table 5.9) believe that there will be a unique co-existence of both malls/stores and shops, as their clientele are different and there is no competition between the two. Malls have become a source of entertainment and shopping for the city dwellers (in the opinion of 14.41per cent). People like to spend their leisure time at malls, stores which have added to beautification of the city and are indicator of development. On the other hand, 8.83 per cent of the respondents said malls would do well as people like to visit and shop from malls as they provide people with brands at cheap rates. Market will undergo the metamorphosis and become more efficient and improve quality of goods and services. Other than this, 4.19 per cent said that malls/stores will be at competition with each other and in the due process small traders will be able to carve a niche for themselves.

Apart from it, additional information was collected on the functioning of traders association in the city. Each bazaar has its own trade association and there are association of various trade activities. All shopkeepers were members of these trade associations, i.e., each association has approx 50 to 2000 members. The meetings are held occasionally and sometimes quarterly. The associations have played an important role in management of trade related activities in bazaars in the past but, due to politicization of these associations and conflicts within the members they are not so fruitfully contributing in encouraging the local business, which is one of the main reasons for slump. Many of the shopkeepers are though members of various market associations but they hardly possess any knowledge about activities of such committees. Many of them do not even know whether these associations are registered or not. They have more or less knowledge about the working of these trade associations. The meetings are restricted to few of the members who attend them and discuss the issues related to parking, Tax, VAT, drainage problems, neatness of the bazaar, inflation and mall invasion. Many respondents stated, these meetings have become a sort of get-together than professional meetings. Hence, these serve no purpose in their life and business and are dormant bodies such status is evident from the fact that modern retailers have entered local market without much resistance from the trade organizations.

As a word of summation it can be said that traditional retailers of Amritsar have spent quite a good time in their businesses. A near to fifty-fifty effect on the traditional retailers with the expansion of modern formats was seen. Nearly, half of the respondents said that they have witnessed customer slowdown followed by decline in sales due to division of clientele. As a result, their sales were static and so were their procurements. On the other hand, near to half of the respondents stated that there was no effect on their business due to modern formats as there exists no competition between the two. Both modern as well as traditional retail formats have their different competitors and clientege. They were of the opinion that traditional retail is embedded in social relationships which cannot be broken so easily and so are hopeful enough to sustain their businesses by adopting innovative means and emulating the strategies of modern formats. They themselves, as consumers are also not completely rejecting the new retail but opposed the government's decision of further extending retail policy.

6

Worklife of Employees at Modern Retail Formats

Work occupies a significant proportion of ones lives. At the basic level, work is seen as carrying out tasks whether remunerative or not that enables people to make a living with environment in which they find themselves (Watson, 1980). Macarov (1980) defines it as any activity in which people engage in order to acquire material necessities and luxuries. Indian census defines work as participation (may be physical or mental) in any economically productive activity. Work not only involves actual physical work but also effective supervision and direction of work, unpaid work on farm or in family enterprise. The concept of work has undergone change with the times everywhere. In the early history of human race, no difference was made between work and non work activities. In the pre industrial societies, no pretense was made that work was anything but a necessity, to be avoided in so far as the consequences were not too unpleasant.

As per ancient Greeks and primitive Christianity, work was frowned upon, denigrated and seen as a punishment. Men were classified as 'gentlemen' and 'non gentlemen' because of the work they performed. It was assumed and accepted that no 'Gentlemen' would sully his hand with work (particularly, physical work) or even enter 'Trade'. A number of factors led to the change in the role of work in the world such as the advent of money economy, improvement of means of transportation, emergence of feudal society, changes in inheritance laws, advent of factory system, mercantilism and the laissez-faire conception of economy. The most important attitudinal changes regarding work took place in the west with the spread of protestant ethics. Lutherism and Calvinistic tenets became a driving force for motivating people to work. Protestantism supplanted Catholicism's idea of good work by adding religious motivation to its human relations motivations (Chakarborty, 1991).

In contrast to the western notion of work, Indian religious ethics have been radically different. Chakarborty (1991) discusses the philosophical basis of work in India and how traditional religious ethics have been both a motivator as well as inhibitor to work culture, i.e., there is greater integration of work and workplaces within sphere of religion. Work is treated as one of the goals and preconditions for attaining 'Moksha' and he who performs his assigned duty without seeking a reward make way to achieve salvation. According to Hindu religion, one must work within his ascribed statuses to glorify one's future.

Working lives have undergone enormous change. Work now relates to quality of work life which is often been taken as a symbol of personal identity, status, economic reward and a means to realise full potential (http://books.google.co.in/books/the/sociology/of/work). On an average, a person spends one-third of entire life at his workplace and it does influence the overall quality of life. The workplace is thus not only a place to do a job but it also serves as a kind of school where new abilities and skills are developed as well as a social club from which one draws friends and acquaintances (Volti, 2008).

Work relates to the capacity to produce pleasure, self identity, satisfaction and self fulfilment rather than mere means of meeting economic needs. It is an individualised experience and imposes specific time- place restrictions on the freedom of individuals. Volti (2008) presented views of Maslow who defines working as instinctual, i.e., work performs certain psychological functions, i.e., it fulfils our different needs. When one need is satisfied, people move on to needs of higher order for self-actualisation. Therefore, people derive sense of fulfillment through their experience both on and off-the-job. For this, governments all over the world have been working extensively for improving the quality of working life of people.

The concept of work culture has been changing ever since realised and a major contribution has been of the industrial revolution that has introduced new work methods and conditions which were undreamt of by the pre-industrial generations. By work culture it is meant, work related activities and meanings attached to such activities in the framework of norms and values regarding work contextualised in an organization having its own boundaries, goals, objectives, technology, material and human resources as well as constraints and employees having skills, knowledge, needs and expectations (Sinha, 1990). The notion of 'quality of working life' and 'quality of life' are used quite inter related. In broader sense, International Labour Organization defines quality of life as the sum total of values (material and non material) attained by worker, throughout life as a wage or salary earner. Quality of life includes all aspects of work related life such as wages and hours, work environment, occupational health, safety, job security, fair treatment, benefits and services, career prospects and human relations for work satisfaction and motivation. It therefore, refers to workers need for meaningful and satisfying work and for participation in decisions that affect work and their situation. Under ILO (1976) Programme for the Improvement of Working Conditions and Environment (PIACT), occupational health and safety, flexibility of working hours, job security, fair treatment at work, participation in decision making were given to priority (Delamontte, 1984).

Taking into consideration the ILOs conventions, governments all over have taken steps to prioritise safety and health at workplaces so as to improve working environment and prevent accidents. The law also places workers right to inform the labour inspector of any violation of law and forbid discriminatory practices against the worker. This notion of equal treatment of workers was recognised at ILOs discrimination convention of 1950 (employment and occupation). It also recognised that night work negatively affects female workers but at the same time banning night work for woman also reduces their career development prospects and puts break on mobility of woman and compel them into poorly paid jobs with inferior work conditions. Likewise, long working hours affect both private life as well as leisure time of individuals and result in frustration and loose bonding of relationship. Many countries have tackled this problem by reduction of working week by many ways, such as; providing more paid vacations to employees, flexible working hours and encouraging part time work (especially among woman).

Earlier, provision related to job security and good working conditions were of less value to a worker, who were exposed at risk of loosing his/her job. Now, with ample availability of part time jobs the workers prefer to exercise their choice in selection of employment as well as suitable workplace. There has been an increasing demand for better quality of services and growing need for individual's choices and privacy. Fortunately, fast developing industries are recognising the fact that success and failure of an organization are directly related to the worker's quality of life and labour management relations (ILO, 1984). It is so, modern employers make it sure to provide their employees with good work environment so as to check the human resource wastage as well as to maintain efficiency in their organization (Davis, 1975).

Modern Retail Jobs and Quality of Work Life

Work and work lives in India have undergone significant change with times. In the Indian context, contributions of colonial rule in India cannot be missed out which brought about great transformation that hitched Indian society to a new path. Britishers were the first to introduce the western type of public administration in India. The organizational structure, administrative procedures and work methods were all patterned after British. Later, in the second half of nineteen century, number of Indian-owned companies increased rapidly but management remained in the hands of Europeans as a result of which Indians inherited an authoritarian western corporate culture from the British which transformed work and work culture in India. The second phase of changes brought about in the work and working lives of individuals can be attributed to the economic reforms of 1991. With the adoption of new entrepreneurial culture and the change in economic attitude there has been change in economic lifestyle of workers which has also transformed the Indian work values. In this context, Sinha (1982) identified three typical values in the Indian work culture a) peace of mind b) comforts of life c) dependency (to seek help from others in personal matters). Lastly, as a result of globalisation, dissemination of western values there has been transition from the economic ethic of traditional capitalism to the economic ethic of modern capitalism in India (Swedberg, 2004). Many of changes in the Indian economic values had not been possible without the New Economic Policy which India adopted for restructuring of its economy.

Rise of service sector as a dominant source of employment represents one of the most significant transformations of life and work in human history. Change in the occupational structure can be illustrated from the shift in employment from primary sector (which dominated pre-industrial societies) to secondary and tertiary sector (which dominates the industrial capitalist societies) (Edgell, 2006:11). Kambhampti (2004) in this regard states that structural changes towards industrial sector can be measured by looking at changes in composition of both output as well as employment i.e., between 1970 and 1993, there was increase in the share of manufacturing and services in GDP relative to share of agriculture in most developing countries. At the same time, medium and high income economies saw stagnation in manufacturing but, increase in productive services.

Service sector covers a wider range of activities such as trading, banking, finance, info-tainment, real estate, transportation, security, management and technical consultancy etc (http://www.iloveindia.com). Service sector is playing a vital role in upward mobility for aspiring class as it is free from grip of bureaucracy that provides opportunities for emergence of new class of entrepreneurs. Today, India is one of the few markets in the world that offers high prospects for growth and earning potential in practically all areas of business.

The emerging service sector has become quite appealing for the job hunters as it is labour intensive and gender friendly. With the adoption of LPG Policy, Indian economy has passed through metamorphosis of occupational patterns with it there has been eclipsing of primary sector to secondary and tertiary sector, creating newer kinds of jobs.

Of recent, the share of services in GDP has rose sharply from 45.2 per cent in 1993-94 to 53.7 per cent in 2004-05, but its share in employment has grown somewhat slowly from 23.1 per cent to 28.5 per cent during the same period. Within the services sector, the share of trade (both retail and wholesale) in GDP has risen from 11.9 per cent in 1993-94 to 14.9 per cent in 2004-05, but its share in employment has grown marginally from 7.7 per cent to 8.4 per cent during the same period (www.scribed.com, Ray 2003). Service sector in India accounts for more than half of India's GDP, i.e., nearly 43.5 million people are involved in service sector in India (www.itftindia.com). A similar pattern of sectoral shift is seen in economy of Punjab. The growth rate of primary sector has been noted as insignificant since 2005 until 2009, i.e., in 2005-2006 it was 1.94 per cent; in 2006-2007 it was 2.78 per cent; 3.89 per cent in 2007-2008; 2.40 per cent in 2008-2009 respectively. Likewise, manufacturing or secondary sector has grown with leaps and bounds i.e., the growth rate was 7.77 per cent in 2005-2006; 11.22 per cent in 2006-2007 and 17.20 per cent in 2007-2008. Whereas, tertiary or service sector is another rapidly emerging sector in Punjab i.e., the growth rate was 4.73 per cent in 2005-2006; 8.45 per cent in 2006-2007; 7.63 per cent in 2007-2008 and 9.31 per cent in 2008-2009 (www.punjabgovt.nic.in). This indicates that while agriculture continues to be major contributor to GDP at national level. The share of service sector and employment in tertiary sector is growing rapidly and is bringing transformation in the worklives and quality of life.

Newer businesses involve political, economic, social as well as cultural networking as a result of which there is dissemination of new ideas and values. New entrepreneurial network therefore requires skilled, well trained and flexible workers who can adjust well within the global as well as local networks. Castells (2000), notion of network society rightly fits here, in explaining the process of inclusion and exclusion of actors from the networks. For him, the ability of an actor to be in the network is determined by degree to which he can contribute to the goals of network. The people at bottom are those who with nothing to offer to the network are excluded. His ideas can be applied to see how the sectoral shift from primary and secondary to tertiary is consequential in terms that it excludes those who do not have those skills or abilities which are required in services.

Growth of modern retail has enhanced the employment potential of the Indian economy by providing direct employment in retail and driving the growth of number of activities in the market. Secondly, most distinctive characteristics of economic system of modern societies is that work has become divided into enormous number of occupations in which people specialize. The jobs that modern retail displaced are the low-end, low-quality, underproductive ones with the new jobs that are of high quality and more productive ones. The modern retail has generated number of jobs for unskilled labour for the menial tasks of sorting, grading, and labelling but, at a same time, demands individuals to be intact with the employability demands in order to survive in the market. Employees in modern retail formats are required to enhance their employability by cultivating enterprising personality traits as well as development of soft skills of self presentation and communication, which are now much valued in the job market particularly in service sector.

Modern retail job involves multiple positions which involve front end (store operation) and back end operation (merchandising, logistics and distribution, marketing, procurement and purchase and corporate services (www.nsdcindia.org). More than seventy per cent of the employees are involved in store operation and are responsible for day to day management of store. Multi- skilling or multi- tasking rather than narrow specialisation has become a major focus for mall employer as it is believed that people with multi skills can be trained to develop new skills on job. This is one of the reasons that most of the store employees who are concentrated at the lower positions involving multi tasking hail from lower or middle income classes. Whereas, higher positions involve specialized people who hail from the higher class having better qualifications, technical knowhow and better interpersonal skills. These new retail formats also symbolise modern organizations promoting corporate culture with multiplicity of positions and designations to the employees than treating them as mere servants which provide employees with a sense of self esteem. It has directly affected individual identity, subjective attitudes and perceptions regarding the way they work, the family life, social relationships, leisure time activities, the products, and services used and the demand for workforce. With the intermingling of markets, the notion of work, work practices, organizations and attitude of people towards work has also undergone change. Where earlier, work was seen as a mere means of earning livelihood, it now relates to capacity to produce pleasure, satisfaction, self fulfilment and identity formation. Many of these changes would not have been possible without changes in retailing.

New entrepreneurial culture, ethics, practices have led to change in worklives and lifestyles of people. Family businesses are being replaced by big business houses that adopt new techniques, knowledge of new markets, modern management skills, have non-sluggish attitude, are well versed in soft-skill management and have formal training from technical institutes. This has broken away long held assumptions that entrepreneurial qualities are not available among few gifted individuals, but are created. Modern retail jobs require higer levels of skills and expertise and prior training. The retail companies prefer to train their staff through workshops and training programmes that lasts for a few days or weeks. It can be said that employment generated by modern retail is building a quality labour class that is gaining vocational training in skilled and unskilled jobs so as to meet the growing demand of trained professionals in retail industry.

Occupations which were earlier regarded exclusively for males (like those involving strenuous tasks and demanding high skills) are now also been occupied by woman (Rahman, 2005). If we look post-1970s, scenario of woman's work has changed. By 1976, woman accounted for approximately 30% per cent of total workforce, by 1990 they constituted 45 per cent and presently, it forms more than half of the total workforce. India has world's largest number of professionally qualified woman and has more working woman than any other nation. The modern working woman who have broken away from beaten track are exploring new vistas of economic participation and so have become much sought after in many emerging areas of work. Mitra (1997), in this context adds that with removal of work setting from home to factory, the concept of work changed dramatically but at the same time negatively affected woman's employment. He makes use of contingency approach to study why some occupations are regarded as fit for men and others for woman and how woman makes her employment choices. This approach to career choices restricts woman to certain sphere of professional activity and discourages aggressive pursuits of career in competitive sphere. Woman chooses occupations that are flexible and can respond with any contingency like marriage, childbirth.

With retail industry witnessing a spurt in growth, demand for female labour force has increased and as the requirement of this sector is depends on interpersonal skills, management, communication and housekeeping. Woman have become the most sought after human resource in this sector as they are easy to hire and are willing to be placed in any position. Even mall managements believe that woman make malls a friendlier place and shoppers feel more comfortable with woman around. On the other hand, it is noteworthy that despite the fact that woman make up nearly half of the labour force, inequality persists between men and woman in labour market, woman are still paid less than their male counterparts for comparable jobs. Modern retail formats are totally in contrast with traditional retail and so the people are showing much interest in seeking employment in these modern formats.

Opponents of modern retail formats in contrast accuse modern retail as more inhumane in practice. Employee experiences at Wall Mart (world's largest employer) with 1.3 million employees in the United States indicate that modern retail is equally exploitative (www.wakeupwallMart.com, www.atkearny.com). Global Insight reports points that for every 1,00,000 square-foot store, Wal-Mart creates 97 retail jobs however, loss of about 30 local wholesale jobs leaving a net gain of about 67 jobs (http: //www.ey.com/India) (www.indiaretailing.com/retail). Thousands of complaints are filled everyday on Wall Mart labour practices related to violation of Fair Labour Standards Act over workers being denied overtime, income discrepancy and over overtime pay, equal wages regardless of gender and race, and a minimum wage, denial of workers rights for their federally mandated breaks, forcing employees to work off-the-clock, to work without breaks, and in some cases, locking employees in the store overnight to perform work off-the-clock and shaming as a large part of disciplining workers at Wal-Mart. This is the reason that more than half of Wal-Mart employees leave each year as it also opposes unionization of its associates. It points out that modern retail monopoly might aggravate labour problems if unchecked.

Indian retail saga is little different. In Indian market which largely comprises of informal sector, workers and labourers suffers from similar problems which go much beyond the low wages to insecurity of jobs, long and unregulated hours of work, absence of accident and other insurances. The modern retail (formal) is a new concept in India, hence constitutes an extremely new area of interest and investigation and the work culture is still nascent. No labour issue has come up as prominent in India as in case of US. Though, not much has been done to study the work life of store employees beyond shelves except few studies and articles (Gopptu: 2009, Katakam: 2007) have very briefly touched upon the various aspects of mall management in India. Gopptu (2009) and Katakam (2007) analyzed work life of employees at modern formats in Mumbai and Kolkata in their respective articles. Katakam (2007), in her study discusses how modern retail formats have encouraged woman's employment in retail sector which was earlier male dominated and discusses various reasons for more women in retail space. Her study brings forth that women working at modern formats largely hail from lower income classes and are placed at lower positions. Higher positions are occupied by the highly educated upper class employees (largely males). Along with it, she also highligthts problems faced by them at their workplaces (wage discrepancy, alienation, gender discrimination, workplace harassment) and how they are treated indifferently by the management. The studies point out that modern retail provides a better quality of life to their employees with regard to labour practices, quality employment and provision to their employees. Most importantly, employment generated by modern retail is building a quality labour class that is gaining vocational training in skilled and unskilled jobs. Foreseeing the demand for trained staff, leading retailers are creating their captive human resources pool through internal training and programmes and tie-ups with Retail Management Institutes. Following part of the chapter seeks to address to the issue of work and employment in new work places in Amritsar city.

Work Life of Employesss at Modern Retail Formats

Amritsar has witnessed growth of modern formats recently. It has been 7-8 years when first mini mart 'Ebony' opened in the city. Modern formats are fast replacing the old features of the city, the way of life of people and have set in new trend of employment and job seekers. Modern retail jobs have become popular within a short span of time and have provided employment to significant number of people from diverse social classes.

Work Status

Modern retail jobs involve both full time as well as part time working so as to suit to the needs of both employer as well as employee. Part time working is regarded as a non standardised form of employment and a means to earn some income while maintaining a share of family responsibilities. Part time work entails working week of less than thirty five hours (Volti, 2008). Part timers are usually hired during the peak season or on voluntary retirement after a short term contract. Part time work suits both the requirement of the employer as well as the workers. Gopptu (2009) and Katakam (2007) found that significant proportions of people employed in retailing are working as full timers and woman forms majority as part time workers in retail formats as they find it more suitable to their personal life and provides them with an additional income to support their families. Part time work is a recent trend in the city. In our study more of respondents were working on full time basis and only 5 per cent of respondents were working as part timers. Though, part time working is not yet as popular in the city, yet these formats do provide strategic employment through part time working so as to fulfil their demands of seasonal workforce.

Motivation to Work at Mart/Store

Work performs number of purposes, not all of which are monetary. Many things such as status, autonomy, authority, amiable settings, competent fellow workers and opportunity for advancement go into making a job worth having. Modern retail is characterized by formal labour contracts and employment benefits which is one of the main reasons as opposed to informal working at local shops. Prestige of an occupation is usually reflected by the wages or salaries attached to it, the kind of responsibilities discharged by the people and its work environment.Table 6.1, reflects pull factors of joining modern retail formats. It was seen, apart from fulfilling the need, money provides a sense of security and motivation to work. Of the total respondents, more than one-third of respondents work at malls and stores because of economic reasons and incentives. For the remaining respondents, working with brands signifies their status. Better and freer environment, part time working and timely salary were other reasons stated by respondents.

Table 6.1

Motivation to Work at Modern Retail Formats

Motivation	Response	Percentage
Economic reasons and incentives given	62	36.05
Brand/ prestige	55	31.98
Gain Retail experience/ Avenues for growth	30	17.44
Short duration of job/ free to do side work	11	6.40
Timely salary	9	5.23
Independence/autonomy and comfortable	3	1.74
Safe environment	2	1.16
Total	**172***	**99.97**

* *Multiple Responses*

On the whole, it can be said that respondents are differently motivated to work at modern formats and work is seen as a source of economic independence,means to improve their lifestyle and consumption habits, acquire valuable skills and gain experience for improving future prospects.

Discriminatory Practices at Malls/Store

Occupational segregation by sex is seen everywhere causing labour market rigidity, economic inefficiency, wastage of human resources, preventing change, disadvantaging woman and perpetuating gender inequalities. Modern store employers follow discriminatory practices at different levels (Katakam, 2007).

In this study, it was seen that depending upon size of modern formats the number of total employees ranged from 4 to 60 (approx). Women didnot even contributed to half of the total employees. Our study could not bring extreme indices of practice of gender discrimination at malls/ store because data was collected in 2008 and malls and stores were newer to the city and a large number of respondents stated modern retail as egalitarian. Only a small number i.e., five per cent respondents pointed out that discrimination was practiced at their respective formats in form of assignment of duties to male and female employees. For instance, at many of the stores, cash counter duties were mostly assigned to male employees and woman were largely hired for customer care services, and assigned general work shifts. During data collection, it was also observed that most of the higher (managerial) positions were occupied by males and concentration of females was lesser at high positions.

In non traditional areas of female employment, sexual harassment of woman by their male colleagues was the reason for exclusion of woman from male dominated domains. However, implementation of Vishakha Guidelines, has helped in maintaining fair work environment at workplaces. Sexual Harassment at workplaces as defined under Vishakha Guidelines includes any kind of unwelcomed sexually determined behaviour (whether directly or by implication) at workplaces (www.legalservicesindia.com). Sexual harassment also encompass having to work in a hostile work environment which encompasses behaviour, remarks or the display of the objects that are offensive to co workers and interfere with the performance of their work (Volti, 2007). In leiu of this, majority said that there was no incident of sexual harassment at malls/ marts, except the use of derogatory remarks and rough language by their counterparts. It is generally seen that woman do not come up openly in reporting such issues as they regard it as mundane activity.

Criteria for Recruitment of Staff

To get a job in some traditional shop, education of job seeker may not be an issue but technical education and professional skills are key preconditions for seeking employment at modern retail formats. Modern retail jobs adopt several criterias such as educational qualifications, experience in retailing, work skills when recruiting staff. Many of retail companies even take verbal and written test of candidates and then train them to acquire retail acumen.

Interviewing has become one of the most efficient ways of recruiting staff. Other than formal methods, social network continues to be a preferred way of recruiting people to jobs. Most of stores employ staff on contract basis with a probation period of a minimum of six months. If the performance is found to be satisfactory, he or she is given an official offer of employment with a defined starting salary and position.

With employment opportunities for young people in sales, finance and marketing, packing, loading, cleaning, security and parking, the retail sector provides employment to men and woman with diverse socio- economic background depending upon the different criteria of selection for the right candidate. Most of the stores employ workers on the contract basis with a probation period of about minimum of six months.

The recruitment criterion of employees varies depending upon size and brand concerned. Respondents were asked about criteria of recruitment at their respective stores. A great majority said that the selection depended upon qualification (Matric to higher) and experience in retailing.

Whereas, 9 per cent said interview and written test, educational qualification and work experience was also considered. Lastly, 6 per cent said recruitment was done on the basis of educational qualification, retail experience and interview methods.

Active Shopping Sections at Modern Formats

Modern retail has become the most sought after place in the city for people of all classes, caste and gender. Respondents were asked to list active shopping sections to their respective shops and stores. Out of the total respondents, 39.42 per cent of respondents said it was difficult to determine as everyone visits modern formats these days. Less than one third of respondents said it was youngsters who visit store/ mall more.

Whereas, 18.27 per cent said woman were the most active shoppers. Nearly ten per cent said it was middle aged (men and woman) who come to their store/ mall/mart as they find it comfortable to shop at one place.

Remaining respondents said it was NRIs who come to their stores/mall. It can be inferred that modern formats of retailing have drawn attention of all sections of society as it offers something for everyone (Table 6.2).

Table 6.2

Active Shopping Sections

Active Shoppers	Response	Percentage
All	41	39.42
Young	32	30.77
Woman	19	18.27
Middle aged (men + woman)	10	9.61
NRI	2	1.92
Total	**104***	**100.0**

* *Multiple Responses*

Best Selling Section of the Store/Mall/Mart

Amritsar has more of multi-assortment retail formats. The respondents were also asked about best selling section at their retail formats.

Table 6.3

Best Selling Sections at Malls/Stores

Best Sellers	Response	Percentage
Apparels	45	44.00
Grocery	24	24.00
Electronics	9	9.00
Sports/Toys	8	8.00
Fashion /Optical	5	5.00
Cosmetics/Jewellery	4	4.00
Home Décor	4	4.00
Shoes	1	1.00
Total	**100**	**100.00**

Table 6.3, reveals that fourty five per cent listed apparels as best selling section of their mall/store. On the other hand, 24 per cent said that it was grocery (excluding, fruits and vegetables) and nine per cent of the respondents listed electronics as the best sellers. Eight per cent said it was sports and toys.

Fashion and opticals, home decoration, cosmetics, jewellery, footwear were also listed by some. The findings correspond to the overall consumption pattern of Punjab as well as India i.e., expenditure on clothing is more than grocery.

Services Provided to Customers

Services provided by modern retail formats are one of the factors that has drawn attention of customers. Of the total respondents, majority said that malls and stores provide their customers with facility of paying through credit card (Table 6.4) which provides a sort of ease to customers as they don't have to carry heavy cash alongwith them.

They stated that most of luxury items are purchased by customers through credit cards as in the entire transaction heavy expenditure does not seems to be painful to customer.

Table 6.4
Services Provided to Customers

Services	Response	Percentage
Credit card	92	65.25
Home delivery	29	20.57
E-shop/	13	9.22
Insurance+ Recharge	6	4.26
Membership card+ Bonus point	1	0.70
Total	**141***	**100.00**

* *Multiple Responses*

Also, 20.57 per cent of respondents said that delivery of goods at door steps of customers is a prevailing trend to make shopping easier and more comfortable and many of the stores/ marts provide home delivery services to their customers at a phone call. E-shopping was another service provided by some retail chains. Another, 4.26 per cent of respondents said that they provide their customers with membership card, earning bonus points through purchase for next shopping which is way of establishing good relationship with customer. Moreover, the customers feel honoured of their purchases. Modern retail is not all about shopping but serving customers at the best and making shopping an exciting experience for them.

Strengthening Relationship with Customers

Sales person serves as the last link in marketing chain and affects consumer's decision on purchases. Of the total respondent's, majority said that they helped their customers in all possible ways whereas the remaining said that they do not interfere much as things are displayed properly and customers prefer to walk around and select as per his own choice. They provide them with trolleys to put their goods, help them in locating the things, attend them efficiently, tell about the schemes and offers available and make announcements to their customers. On the other hand, a few said that they do not provide unasked services, as customers do not like unwanted indulgence of employees while shopping whenever they are asked for help by the customers only then go. Number of people visit malls/stores daily and come in contact with employees working there that lead to establishment of new social relationship. Where some employees take it as a chance to widen their chain of acknowledgement and extend social ties others try to keep the acquaintances to the work place only and not personal. The customer and employees relationship is more formalised at modern settings.

Trend of Monthly Sales

Within a notice of few months, difference has been seen in the performance of stores, malls and local shops. A few months back there was quite a hustle and bustle at modern formats. Though, modern formats continue to apeeal different sections but not all stores and marts are doing well in the city and many of them have more or less become a place of entertainment. It is generally assumed that there exists a relationship between conditions of shopping place and the output i.e., the more conducive the physical condition of shopping place is, more will be the output. Corporate retailers spend huge money on the outlook of their stores so as to gain attention of the masses but in such a compeititve environment it is very difficult to survive only on facelifts. The current sales of the stores/ malls in the city may be estimated half the sales during the introductory months/ years (as stated by respondents). People of Amritsar have very abruptly responded to increasing competition and incoming of modern formats. Though, managers of stores and malls did not want to share economic indices of their store and mall, yet information was extracted in approximation. It was found that monthly income of stores/ malls and marts in Amritsar city ranged from ₹ 1 lakh to ₹ 40 lakh. Nearly, 48 per cent did not disclose their store income due to fear of managers and head.

Malls/ Stores: Catering to Needs of all Classes

A retailer's most fundamental task is to identify and satisfy profitable target market, i.e., group of consumers. Intense competition and wide variety of consumers make it impossible for a single retailer to be 'all things to all people'. An effective retailer concentrates on satisfying a profitable set of need held in common by a certain group of customers within a reasonable geographical proximity (Marquardt, 1979). Stores are set up at different locations taking into consideration the patronage of particular area. In the light of this proposition, i.e., modern formats do not cater to the needs of all classes, proved false.

Figure 4

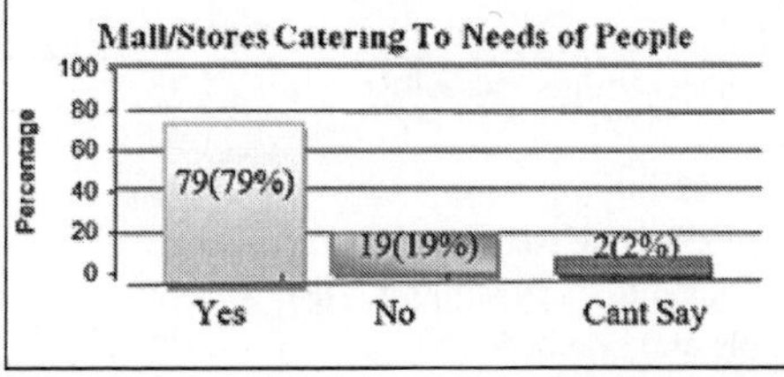

Out of the total respondents, more than half of the respondents (Figure 4) said that malls cater to the needs of all classes and, 19 per cent of respondents disagreed with the above held view. Promoters claim that the stores fufil requirements of people of all classes as their prices are affordable and they provide a huge range of variety of goods and prices.

Strategies Used to Cater to the Needs of all Classes

Of those who were of the opinion that modern formats cater to needs of all, less than one-third of the respondents said that their store/ mart offer schemes/ sales/ offers which are real money saver and bring down value of products by making things accessible to every class (Table 6.5). While, 25.64 per cent of respondents said that stores/ marts provide ample variety and ample range of products to customers. One can pick goods as per requirement and price. More than one-fifth of respondents stated one stop shopping, i.e., availability of all items under one roof as another strategy to save time of shoppers. Things are well displayed on rows and stacks so people prefer to purchase as per their needs and pocket and there is no need to carry shopping lists along. Provision of quality products, branded stuff, durable goods and easy going services like home delivery were other mechanisms adopted by the store and malls. Malls, marts and stores do not restrict entry to anyone and are open to people of all classes.

Of the 19 per cent of respondents who disagreed with the above stated views some 52.17 per cent respondents said that modern retail was class centric , i.e., they target higher class, upper middle class and young population. On the other hand, 30.43 per cent said that malls are unaffordable as they sell goods at higher prices.

Table 6.5

Mechanisms Adopted to Cater to the Needs of Different Classes

Mechanism Adopted	**Response**	**Percentage**
Schemes/ sales/ offers makes things accessible	48	30.77
Variety for all	40	25.64
One stop shopping/ availability of items	33	21.15
Items are displayed , people purchase according to need and pocket, no need to carry shopping list	18	11.53
Quality product, durable and branded	14	8.97
Home Delivery	2	1.29
Open to all classes	1	0.64
Total	**156***	**100.00**

**Multiple Responses*

The schemes and offers they provide are deceptive and are means to overpower shopping decisions of customers. Lastly, 17.39 per cent respondents were of the opinion that all formats do not fulfil requirememnts of all as they dealt with specific variety of goods. From both the arguments, it can be drawn that modern retailers are leaving no stone unturn to win over customers of all sections to their stores by adopting lucrative strategies.

Traditional Retail v/s Modern Retail

Respondents were asked their opinion on competition between modern and traditional retail formats. Of the total respondents, more than half of respondents expressed fear of elimination of traditional retail formats. The remaining disagreed with them (Figure 5). Of 57 per cent respondents, nearly 20.54 per cent of respondents (Table 6.6) said that with availability of goods under one roof and hassle free environment people's dream of easy shopping has come true but has affected the business of traditional retailers.

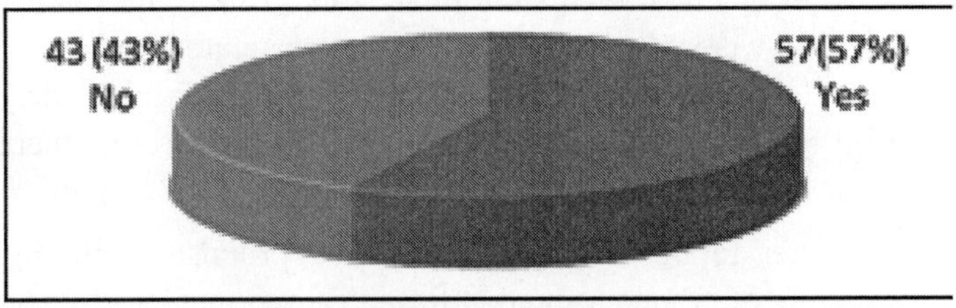

Fig. Taking over the Traditional Retail

Shopping no longer is a hectic experience rather, entertaining. Another, one fifth of respondents said that there has been division of customers and polarisation of market. Sales, schemes and offers that malls provide to their customers are strategies to wipe the traditional retail out from market as they will not be able to hold strategies of modern retailers.

Table 6.6

Modern Formats will Takeover Traditional Formats of Retailing

Reasons Stated	Response	Percentage
Availability of all items under one roof (hassle free shopping) and variety	23	20.54
Division of customers, sales and schemes will wipe out local traders	23	20.54
Quality and brands at cheaper rates	19	16.96
Malls, Marts and brands have become status symbol	15	13.39
Fascinate/ monopoly, market structure is changing Malls, Stores are the in-things today	12	10.71
Reliable and durable products at Marts/ Store / awareness among people for brands	10	8.93
Comfortable environment	5	4.46
Cater to needs of specific classes	4	3.57
Adjust to change to survive	1	0.89
Total	**112***	**100.00**

* *Multiple Responses*

Nearly 17 per cent respondents said that modern formats provide goods of better quality and brands at cheaper rates which is not the case with traditional retail. In addition, 13.39 per cent mentioned that malls/marts and brands have become a signifier of status so people prefer to shop from a mall than an ordinary shop. Nearly, eleven per cent respondents were of opinion that market structure is changing today with malls and stores are 'in-thing' and people are fascinated by such beautifully built and spacious shopping plazas. As a result, there has been a movement of people from traditional to modern formats.

People prefer to buy from locations that promise durability, reliability, quality of products and comfortable environment. With an increasing awareness of quality and prices people prefer transparent shopping. There is no way out for traditional businessmen but to modify their work practices in order to survive and co-exist.

Traditional Retail will Survive: Opinion

Those who disagreed (43 per cent, fig 5) with the above stated arguments forwarded their views. Less than one third of respondents (Table 6.7) were of opinion that mall mania will have timely effect on the business of local business and in future there will be unique co-existence of modern and traditiona retail as both cater to diverse needs of diverse population. Other than this, 12.98 per cent of the respondents said that customers prefer to buy from the nearest possible locations as it is not viable to go again and again to a mall located several kilometres away from home to buy a small stock on discounted price nor can one afford to visit it frequently.

Therefore, neighbourhood shops will continue to be preferred location for purchasing goods. A same number of respondents said that people of Amritsar city are not so brand conscious as they hail from different classes hence, not everyone can afford to buy brands. Others were of the opinion that malls provide poor services, deteriorated quality of goods and there was not much difference in standard of things and work practices at malls than shops.

Whereas, 10.39 per cent respondents said customers do not necessarily shop from malls. Customers are more concerned about getting value of his hard earned money and are not much concerned about who sells the goods but, prefer to buy cheap and best wherever available from.

Traditional retailers will learn and acquire newer ways of doing business and improve their business practices and will be able to survive (9.09 per cent). The respondents were also of the opinion that malls/stores do not provide customers with all kinds of things which means people will continue to rely upon both forms of retail for metting their diverse needs.

Table 6.7

Modern Formats will not Takeover Traditional Business

Reasons Stated	Response	Percentage
Timely effect, Malls and Stores and shops will co exist	23	29.87
People can not go to Malls to buy small stock	10	12.99
People in the city are not much brand conscious	10	12.99
Malls provide poor servicesa and quality, all items are same as shops	9	11.69
Customer prefer cheap and best, no matter who sells it	8	10.39
Small retail will do well as people prefer Malls for spending freetime	7	9.09
All things are not available (traditional are out of stock)	4	5.19
Only particular class of people shop from Malls	3	3.89
Modern Retail is not as per global standard	3	3.89
Total	**77***	**99.95**

* *Multiple Responses*

Further, they stated that modern retail is not really organized the way it should have been. Though modern retailers have successfully adopted global modern formats of retailing, yet in actual have not been able to adopt global business skills and acumen.

Most of the times, things are out of stock, outdated, expired not in good condition which is one of the reason of footfall of modern retail.

Lastly, 3.89 per cent respondents said that modern formats cater to needs of particular section (higher class/ cash customers/ youngster). From both the views it can be inferred that many of respondents were of the opinion that modern retailers will take over and result in heavy loss to the traditional retail.

Workplace Problems

Work can give an individual a sense of fulfilment but at the same time, it can also be source of psychological stress, problems and harassment.

Some employees may find themselves at ease with their work roles, whereas others may feel detached from their jobs. Working at malls/ stores is a great experience on one hand but, at the same time, employees face certain problems. The respondents discussed their workplace problems and dissatisfaction with their current job and management.

These problems discussed in Table 6.8, indicate that 23.63 per cent respondents find that because entry to malls/ stores for all, customers with different temperaments visit these formats. Many a times, they have to encounter rough and notorious customers who are rude and complaining by nature.

As the primary interest of modern stores is to take care of the needs of customers, employees are ranked much low than customers by the management and are treated differently. Many a times, they are scolded and have to repent for no fault.

More than one-fifth of respondents complained that their present job does not provide them with any scope of promotion or increase in salary.

They joined stores with a hope that it will increase their job prospects and promote good earning but there has been no such enhancement. Full day standing job, which is a hectic and tiresome task was another problem stated by 16.36 per cent respondents. They were of opinion that though this trend is global, yet employees must be given a provision to sit when no customers is there at desk.

They complained of such strictness in work practices as inhumane. The employees have to work under strict surveillance of their managers with Closed Circuit Cameras (CCCs) enclosed everywhere and they do not feel free to work. It is one of the reasons behind lack of coordination and discord between managers and subordinates.

Table 6.8

Problems Faced at Stores/Malls

Problems faced by Respondents	Response	Percentage
Complaining and rough customers	13	23.63
No scope for promotion/ increase in salary	12	21.81
Standing job (CCC enclosed)	9	16.36
Time consuming process of online payment	7	12.72
Behavioural problems with manager	6	10.90
Problematic work shifts	4	7.27
Lack of rules/ codes	4	7.27
Total	**55***	**99.95**

**Multiple Responses*

A few of them, i.e., 13 per cent respondents said they did not like online system of payments as it is far more time consuming and tedious task. Rude behaviour of managers and restrictions imposed upon give them a sense of estrangement from their fellow beings and work. Such view was held by 10.90 per cent of respondents). Stores/ malls lack good organization in their work practices. A same number of respondents (male respondents) said that they found the shift system problematic as woman were given only general shifts and men were assigned late evening shifts. There is lack of fairness and equity at stores and malls.

Apart from the above stated problems, it was also observed that modern stores practice strict duty hours for employees. They cannot step out before the dispersal time and also do not get a fixed time break for lunch or relaxation i.e., at the most they get fifteen minutes to one hour break in the whole day. The malls and store donot even provide any refreshment to the staff except a few who were provided tea as refreshment from their stores. It can be said that malls/ stores in the city are not well equipped in human resource practices. For them, the main focus is to provide better services to customers and not employees. All in all, low pay, long working hours, monotony, physical exhaustion, lack of career advancement, absence of future prospects and promotions were the major problems listed by respondents. They think of themselves as commodities displayed like the goods they sell. Despite their many grievances and a sense of exploitation, workers exercise restraint and refrain from venting discontent or complaints at work. When they do feel outraged, they simply choose to quit.

Quality of Work Life at Modern Formats

The changing economy not only transforms economic lives of people but also their lifestyle. Such change is possible only through the occupation one chooses, i.e., more prestigious and rewarding an occupation is, more are the chances of improving ones lifestyle. With better avenues of employment and better income in hand, aspiring classes try to adopt the lifestyle of the affluent by changing their consumption habits, extending social network and camouflaging their status.

Retail malls and stores offer best to its employee's and so they have become an attractive destination for job seekers. Those coming from different backgrounds expressed gratification at availability of variety of experiences, entertainment, recreation, consumption practices and habits (Gopptu, 2009). Working in a professional environment with brands has become a signifier of status and accomplishment.

There is a great difference of life style and the quality of life of employees working at these stores/marts than those working in traditional shops. The occupation reflects ones social status, identity and thereby shapes lifestyle.

The work place is not only a place for job related tasks and earning a living but also is a depot of values, attitudes, norms, accepted procedures and forming new social relationship. Most kinds of work require constant and sometimes forceful interactions with the people and other co-workers. Some of these can be unpleasant and a source of stress but it often happens that work place serves as a prime site for socialising with fellow workers and forming strong bonds of friendship with some of them (Volti, 2008:

186). Working at modern retail formats is full of glamour and has lots of secrets to unveil. In between the shelves, one can discover romance, humour and other realities of life (www.ifibeam.com). The employees are different; they unite against demanding customers and try to amuse each other until punch- out time.

As we have seen that the employees working at malls/stores are largely youngsters hence they find themselves more comfortable working together, sharing each others problems, playing pranks on customers secretly and making their day enliven by sharing their thoughts and experiences with each other (Gopptu, 2009). Friendships are more likely to form when the work environment requires or encourages interaction and interdependence alongwith a lack of competition. In contrast, the possibility of forming friendships may be inhibited in work situation where workers are separated from one another by physical and spatial barriers. Social barriers in the form of rigid hierarchies also inhibit informal interactions and the opportunity to form friendship (Volti, 2008). The workplace acts as a source of forming newer social relationship on one hand while on the other hand; it may be stressful to existing social relationship (Gopptu, 2009).

Work Environment Provided at Malls/ Stores/ Marts

Ambience and size of an enterprise always has some influence on the roles of its members (Caplow, 1970: 47). Work environment at modern retail is different from that of traditional retail as modern sector is marked by professionalism and formalism. It was seen that 24.16 per cent of the respondents said that their malls/ stores provide them with good work environment, friendly atmosphere, good staff and classy customers as compared to any ordinary shop (Table 6.9).

Table. 6.9 : Work Environment Provided

Work Environment	Response	Percentage
Friendly Atmosphere/Staff, Good Customers	36	24.16
Professionalism, Brand	23	15.44
Good Variety/Range/Quality and Services	23	15.44
Good Physical Environment	17	11.41
Nothing Unusual	15	10.07
Self Dependent	14	9.39
Status Enhancing and positive	10	6.71
Avenues for Growth	11	7.38
Total	**149***	**100.00**

**Multiple Responses*

Also, 15.44 per cent said that malls/ stores provide a professional environment and dealing in brands. Another 15.44 per cent said they also derive feeling of contentment while working in a standardised showroom. Other elements that workers stated as appealing about their job are range and variety of interaction with customers and colleagues, the challenge and excitement of winning over customers with polished conversation. Corporate style workplace that are physically and comfortable clean, usually air conditioned, western dress code and English as the medium of conversation were the other appealing things for them as it had something to do with status enhancement.

Working with a branded store also was stated as a means of status enhancement that gives them a sense of fulfilment. Others (11.18 per cent) stated that modern formats them with a pleasant/ good physical environment, amenities like air- conditioner and music system to enjoy along with work. Others stated that modern retail provided themwith better opportunity for growth. Hard work pays in the form of increase in salary, added incentives and other benefits such as upward mobility of rank and freedom to quit job on volition. Therefore, youth derives a sense of both self-esteem and pride working at modern retail formats.

Management and Employee Relationship

Management plays a vital role in efficacy of the business and role of managers is very important in performance of an organization. To motivate employees and performance the management attempts to develop a close relationship with workers. Myer's (1960) study of Indian managers highlight that Indian managers are more authoritarian by nature. With the expansion of industrial activities, large number of managers were drawn from broader spectrum of the society. In the initial phase, only sons of elite and businessmen were seen at management positions. They were college educated, socialised in english medium schools, urbanised, sons of white collar workers and cherish elitist values (Dhingra and Pathak, 1972), (Jain, 1971). But now, Indian managers hail from lower- middle class. Modern organisations focus much upon the management issues as they recognise that productivity can be hindred if management fails to function effectively.

In the present study, it was seen that 46 per cent of respondents said that they have good and active management. The respondents mentioned that there are various forms of regular interaction between employees and managers. The managers and other employees are quite young and of almost equal age so they have close, informal relationship with each other. However, 29 per cent said that it was fair and the remaining 25 per cent regretted poor management at malls/stores. They were of opinion that store head/ managers have a bully attitude and were indifferent to the problems of the subordinates.

As modern retail is in nascent stage, employees are not so enlightened about their rights and issues. There has been no anti-mall response from those working at malls and stores. There may be number of reasons behind this as for insance, employees are very happy with their management and job as they are paid well and on time and work in better workplace or they don't need a union as they don't have a say at management level.

Delay in salary is usually seen as one of the main problems among workers that result in strained relationship among workers and management. In modern retail, delay in salary is not an issue. A very small number of the respondents stated delay in salary.

Most of the employees are found to be content with their salary as they hail from lower income group. New market structure has performance oriented approach, i.e., harder the worker works, the more he gets paid. Hence, workers are willing to work hard to achieve surplus targets based on performance rather than subjective evaluations.

Satisfaction and dissatisfaction with a job is not solely driven by levels of remuneration. People work for self gratification and in the absence of that instinct, work would lose purpose for them. Respondents were asked if they would continue to work at the same store in future. It was asked to know if they were satisfied with their job or not. It was seen that almost half of the respondents said they wish to continue serve at their respective stores. The remaining showed dissatisfaction with their present job and expressed openness for mobility. It was found that there was only one store/ mall employee union in the past named AHIRA which got vanished away within sometime as it was discouraged by managers and failed to work effectively.

Work Schedule

Labour regulations of retail sector fall under the jurisdiction of state governments and are contained in the Shops and Establishments Acts (SEA) which contains various laws related to working conditions of employees (Amin, 2008). In Amritsar city, late night shopping is not a practice therefore, there is no trend of graveyard working (night shifts) at malls/ stores. The respondents were asked about the total time spent (in a day, on an average) by them working at their respective retail chains. A few of the stores/ malls have shift systems. The duration of working hour varies from 6-12 hours. Though, employees do not work overtime at malls and stores, yet many times they have to spend extra hours for finishing up their tasks when asked for. They are not paid in any way for overtime working which is regarded as a part of normal working hours by management. The time people spend on the job reflects the kind of work that they do. Employees in the broad occupational categories of managers and salesmen work for longer hours on an average than those employed at lower ranks. Those who work on shift basis do not have a flexible shift system. Woman are usually assigned general shifts (morning and afternoon) whereas, late evening shifts are reserved for males.

Respondents were also asked if they found their work tiresome and hectic as the work involves extensive working hours and hectic schedule. It was interesting to find that majority (70 per cent) was content with their job and found retail job entertaining. Less than one third of the respondents said that their work was hectic and many a times monotonous.

Withering Relationship

Work is not sum total of human life. No matter how committed one is to his work, one needs to spend quality time on family and personal relationship. Work can be extremely a positive experience and an essential part of satisfying life, but many a times, it becomes a source of considerable stress and unhappiness when, it overcrowds family and relationship. As we know, a major source of stress in contemporary society is for not having enough time to adequately fulfil the roles defined by work and family responsibilities.

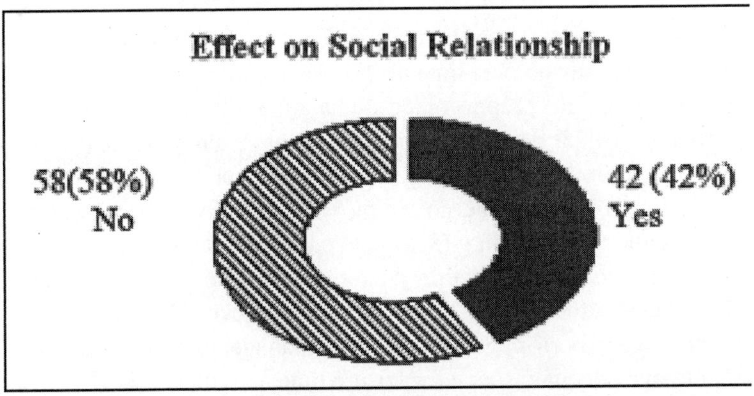

Fig. Effect on Social Relationship

Respondents were asked, if long work schedule was affecting their family and relationship in any way. More than half of respondents (figure 6) said that it was not affecting their life in any way. Whereas, 42 per cent respondents said that such long working hours affected their family and relationship negatively. Long working hours and fewer holidays interrupted their social life.

The respondents addressed their problem of reconciling family and work by saying that many a times they have to work on weekend and get a very less time to spend with their family, friends and relatives and barely for themselves. They regretted for being socially cut off. Largely, when workers get lesser time for themselves and their families they think about their work place as being a family but seniors or the mangers are not included in this family (Gopptu, 2009: 52). The employees discuss their problems and issues with each other taking workplace and co-workers as their workplace family.

Leisure Time Activities at Workplace

As retail job entails long working hours and uninterrupted communication with untimely customers, it is natural that job gets monotonous many a times and so it is necessary to provide the employees with recreational activities to increase their efficiency and decrease work pressure. Respondents were asked to give a note of the leisure time activities at malls/ stores, i.e., activities they perform during their free hours.

It was seen that almost half of respondents just managed their store whenever they get free time i.e. they do cleaning, book keeping, arranging things at proper places, changing display etc. Other respondents (18.25 per cent) said that they listen music/ watch Television and do internet surfing. Some (17.46 per cent) also stated that they like to spend time gossiping with their friends and other employees and the remaining (8.73 per cent) said that they just stand idle waiting for customers as they do not have any provision of TV or music system at their store. It can be said that even during leisure time, employees perform duty tasks i.e., management of store and does not have adequate scope for leisure time activities.

Maintaining Presentation

Retailing involves more of soft skills, along with assertiveness and public speaking, smartness and a clever ability to persuade customers. Jobs in modern retail as opposed to traditional retailing are ranked as of higher status. Modern retail employees see themselves as a part of corporate culture than mere servants (as in case of traditional retail). Job titles such as, customer care executive, store head and executive gives them a sense of being a part of corporate world and so becomes a mean to derive accomplishment.

Employees try to acquire and enhance desirable characteristic required for their job by grooming their appearance, learning and enhancing interpersonal communication skills, and working hard. Gopptu (2009) puts that shopping malls are playing decisive part in crafting suitable workers and citizens and in shaping individual subjectivity, consonant with the needs of markets. Modern retail formats follow corporate style of organization and work practices for which employees have to maintain certain kinds of behavioural as well as physical standards.

The employees in the present study were asked how they maintained their on-job presentation. It was seen that half of the respondents said that they use their interpersonal skills to make themselves presentable, i.e., good communication skills, provide better services to customers and deal tactfully with customers. Further, 16 per cent said that they pay more attention to their grooming in order to make themselves presentable, i.e., they dress up well, get a nice hairstyling. Others said they pay equal attention to grooming and their work skills because in retailing both grooming and skills are essential. Employee's mode of dress is of particular importance in case of high quality retail, since the total image of the store can be lowered by even one employee. In the west, McDonald attempted to control the behaviour of employees, their appearance and interaction with customers by standardising it with compulsory wearing of uniforms and scripted sentences (Edgell, 2006). Most of the modern stores/malls practice such strategies to create uniformity among employees by assigning dress code for them. In this study, it was seen that store managers prefer their sales personnel to dress in work clothes for practical as well as image building purpose and provide them with the dress code and uniforms.

It was seen that company provided 1-2 uniforms to their employees at the most that included T- Shirts and trousers/ saris. The consignment was delivered by headquarter through request sent by store/mall manager via mail or telephonic conversation. This may be a mode of practicing uniformity for management but, at the same time, it is a source of tension among employees. A few respondents said they do not have any uniform and many of them who have got their uniforms do not like to wear them. Many of the females discussed their problems of wearing uniforms from home to store. They said that many of them were not used to wear western dresses, but being a part of retail culture they have to wear jeans and top/ T-shirts on duty which they would not have been wearing otherwise. Some respondents stated that they feel good to wear jeans and tops but prefer to get ready in their store dressing room rather than wearing it from home to store as they were not allowed to wear it by their family members. Their family find it hard to re-assimilate with the westernized dress code and their changed lifestyle. Many of female employees find it good to wear western clothes that otherwise, they would not have been able to wear or allowed by their families. It was also observed that the problem of dressing below the image of the store was the commonest among employees in the city as people of different classes are working in these retail chains.

Compulsive Consumerism

Brand culture and the new shopping culture have hit upon the pocket of everyone and employees working at modern formats are no exception to it. Being surrounded by brands, quality products and latent knowledge of advantages and disadvantages of the products they are more prone to compulsive buying. Respondents were asked whether working at modern formats have hit their pocket. Of the total respondents, 54 per cent respondents said that working at marts/ branded stores have not hit their pocket in any way. Whereas, 46 per cent of the respondents said that it has hit their pocket as they have become more brand conscious and they have a good knowledge of brands working with them. Malls and stores have become favourite locations for shopping today due to various reasons. Majority (66 per cent) said that they shop from the stores/ malls they are working in. On the other hand, 28 per cent said that they do not purchase things from their stores or malls due to unaffordable prices. Remaining respondents said that they occasionally purchase from the malls/stores, i.e., during sale season as they don't find time to go for shopping elsewhere.

On the whole, it can be inferred that modern retail formats have turn out to be most sought after places for job seeking especially for young men and woman. Employers prefer to hire young men and woman more than the elderly because they are malleable and can be trained easily. Most of the employees are working as full timers at these formats and are differently motivated to work at modern formats. Working in a professional environment and in their dealing with brands, quality products and services have become a signifier of status and accomplishment for young employees. It is seen as an instrument to gain access to better, freer life and consumption. Likewise, working at modern formats is both positive as well as negative experience, as many a times it becomes a source of considerable stress and unhappiness when it crowds out family life. Respondents work at stores/ malls usually for 6-12 hours everyday. Overtime is not practiced normally. There has been no anti-mall response from those working at these formats. Staff member are paid timely and are found to be content with their salary as majority hails from lower income group. Overall, it can be said that modern capitalist formats have emerged as prosperous organizational system in which employees remains satisfied with the work culture and so remain passive. The employees working at these formats do not completely find themselves out of place when they see themselves surrounded by luxurious goods as their desire to make more money gets fulfilled by earning more wages through reward system. Many times they do feel out of place while behaving as a part of class to which they belong superficially. They have to what Goffman (1956) calls as 'maintain a Public-Self', which is different from their 'Private Self'. Everyday, they have to present themselves to others, not the way they are actually. Hence, they try to present it in a manner that appears to be more real and actual which is required in modern retail. Modern retail jobs are to what Goffman calls as all about 'Impression Management'

7

The Social Context of 'Things': Consumption and Consumer Behaviour

Large scale restructuring of capitalism in US and elsewhere, and increasing numerical strength of middle class having more purchasing power, in past several decades, has placed consumption indisputably at the centre of economic subjecthood. Consumption has increasingly become a means of leading sophisticated, refined life so as to advance socially and economically. It has replaced the normal desire for an adequate supply of life's necessities, community life, a stable family and healthy relationship, with an artificial ongoing and insatiable quest for things and the money to buy them and sets each person against themselves in endless quest for attainment of material things (www.verdant.net/). From a sociological perspective, the study of consumption and its cultural and social significance in life is imperative. Economic and cultural integration is fast transforming the socio-economic scape which is visible in the form of development and expansion of modern retail formats such as malls, stores, super marts and hyper marts that have emerged as new social as well as economic spaces. These modern formats perform numerous social as well as cultural functions.

Shopping is no longer limited to mere buying activity rather, has become synonymous with splurging time, money and comfort. At the same time, it also produces structural changes in society by promoting growth of middle classes, who would always aspire for material pursuits. Liberals see role of middle class as essential in attracting retailers from everywhere and in production of affluent consumers in societies. In contrast, others see it negatively and condemn middle class for its vulnerability to excesses of consumerism. Sociologists like Gramsci and Habermas have written quite richly on middle classes (C.f. Giddens, 2006). Gramsci sees significance of middle classes in bringing social transformation by viewing them as symbols of power. In his observation, power is exercised by privileged groups or classes in two ways, i.e., through domination and hegemony. It influences subordinate groups who are influenced to internalise the value system and world view of privileged groups thus to consent their own marginalisation. The shift towards new economy represents validation of new patterns of consumption associated with aspiring middle class that has become a model for social progress whereby aspiring classes contribute to realtering of power structure.

In India, there is great complexity in conceptually defining middle classes as definition of middle class has undergone significant change with times. Vital parameters adopted to define middle classes are economic position, status, caste background, lifestyle pattern, consumption level of goods and services, education and occupational aspirations and political contribution as intelligentsia. In the contemporary that is post-1990s, middle class woke up with changes taking place in socio- economic scenario in India brought in by LPG. In 1991, the Indian middle class came into new prominence with expansion of service sector of economy and of professional white collar employment within private sector, particularly in MNC (Pandey, 2009).

Characteristics of Income Classes of India

Income classes	Houshold income (Rs per annum at 2004-05 prices)	Estimated household in '000s			Distribution of household (%)		
		All India	Urban	Rural	All India	Urban	Rural
Deprived	< 1,20,000	1,14,394	18,049	96,345	51.5	26.1	63.1
Aspirers	1,20,000-2,50,000	75,304	29,249	46,055	33.9	42.3	30.2
Middle class	2,50,000-10,00,000	28,441	18,942	9,499	12.8	27.4	6.2
Rich	Over 10,00,000	3,806	2,963	846	1.7	4.3	0.6
Total		2,21,946	69,202	1,52,745	100	100	100

Source: *(C.f., National Bank for Agriculture and Rural Development:2011)*

New middle class is today seen as prosperous and major beneficiaries of liberalisation, privatisation and globalisation. NCAER survey (C.f. Pandey, 2009) titled, 'The consumer classes' reveals that the annual household income in India ranged from ?45000 to ? 215000. Very rich comprises of above 6 million people or million household. Below them middle class consist of three segments-consuming class (30 million households and 180 million people), climbers (50 million household and 275 million people) and aspiring (275 million people).

These figures indicate towards expansion of middle class in India. With shift from rural to urban consumption, India will witness rapid growth from middle class household with disposable income from ₹ 2,00,000 to ₹ 10,00,000 per year.

The trend indicates that India will become fifth largest consumer economy by 2050 up from 12th now. Mc Kinsey Report, 2011 (C.f. The Tribune 14/1/2011) on urbanising India too estimates that 91 million urban household will belong to middle class by 2030. There would be 270 million net-increase in working age population.

Keeping into mind the increasing number of aspiring and climbing middle class Indian consumers, it is assumed that spending will shift substantially from informal economy to the more efficient formal economy of modern businesses. Also, earlier it was believed that middle class and upper class shopped more frequently than lower class, but with change in market and class composition, the pattern of consumption has also undergone change.

Consumer market research of National Institute of Applied Economic Research (NIAER) brings forth that spending power of low income and high income household was more or less uniform in all the four zones (North, East, South, West of India) in relation to Fast Moving Consumer Goods (FMCG) market by income in 1998-99.

The trends also indicate that number of middle class has been on increase since 1995-96, which means that the base of lower income class is shrinking and people are consuming more than before.

Redefining Consumption and Consumer Behaviour

Function of market has undergone change over a period of time and so has the meaning of consumption. The relationship between the economy and contemporary consumption culture is indivisible. Since the end of 1980s, scholars have become aware of how transnational cultural flows as a result of Globalisation transform local cultures (Derne, 2008). Lencher (2005), notes that with integration of markets, world is intimately being converted in complex ways with the rise of global culture. Such cultural interaction can be viewed as transaction or exchanges of symbolic or material goods within an economic framework (Nadarajah, 2007). Sklair (1995: 60) calls it as 'culture- ideology of global capitalist system'. To him, in such a freer world, MNCs produce commodities and services necessary to manufacture and then sell them to eager consumers of other countries. Such integration involves not mere economic exchange but also, culture ideology of consumerism produces values and attitudes that create and sustain the needs for products by infusing typical culture- ideological transnational practices. Tomlinson (1999), uses examples of supermarkets in western cities to illustrate how Globalisation defined as complex connectivity turns the world into a single social and cultural setting (ibid: 10). In such settings, the customers experience becomes de-territorialized as they are no longer limited to local produce. By the sheer variety supermarkets offer, they symbolises the absence of a single dominated style, i.e., there is heterogeneity in the market of goods, buyers and sellers.

Modern consumption is mediated by market relations and takes form of consumption of commodities (www.ukgeocities.com). In contemporary times, consumption is important not just for economic reasons but also has emerged as a primary site for identity formation within the economic system by which goods are eroticised and social distanciation are created and communicated in society. Bourdieu and Veblen (C.f. Merton: 1968), Smelser: 1965, Bucholtz: 2007 (C.f. Singh, 2001) also explicate that 'things' have ability tocarry and communicatecultural meanings. Modern consumer culture has become a means of negotiating status and identity with which one makes his social appearance, social networks and structure of social values (www.uk.geocities.com). Core social practices, cultural values, ideas, aspirations and identities are defined and oriented in relation to consumption. Likewise, cultural values shape consumption choices to a certain extent by interacting with our emotional needs to influence our behaviour and cause us to select the products we choose, distinctive way of life and their complete design for living (Loudan, 2002: 101).

Sociologists such as Marcuse (1968) and Bauman (c.f. Singh, 2001) have interpreted consumerist logic negatively. For them, consumption is a system of domination that produces gap between needs and wants. Marcuse (1968), in his 'One Dimensional Man' thesis explains how economic, political and technical institutions work in modern capitalist society in collaboration so as to determine the needs of people (to what he calls as true needs and false needs). Such a system of domination destroys the mental ability of man to reason out making him one dimensional by super imposing false needs in mind. They see function of modern market as exploitative, i.e., it creates inequality and engender a sense of inadequacy and incompleteness in personality of individuals by display of new goods and commodities, which can be overcome only by the use or consumption of those goods. For both the scholars, modern consumption functions in a way that individual's autonomy and choices thereby get controlled and determined by market oriented consumer choices that results in 'loss of self'. Therefore, their perspective is harshly negative as they view market as a system that generates unhappiness, fear, anxiety and sufferings of personal adequacy.

In contrast, cultural dimension to consumerism presents the functional role of goods, i.e., goods carry a symbolic value. In modern consumerist society, differences in consumption (tastes, habits and consumption pattern) have become means for identity formation and also means for gratification and value formation. Dominant values in society are not only organized through consumption practices but, also in some way derived from them. From the functionalist perspective, 'Goods' perform two functions: manifest and latent. On one hand, it is a means to fulfil one's needs (manifest function) while, on the other hand, goods have symbolic meaning that is goods perform latent functions (Smelser, 1965 and Merton, 1968). Veblen (C.f., Merton, 1968) on the symbolic or latent function of the goods of argues that people buy expensive goods not because they are superior but, because they are expensive and enhance their status. Costliness as per consumerist logic is held as a mark of higher social status. His concept of 'Conspicuous Consumption' apparently describes irrational and confounding form of economic behaviour in which display of expensive items is regarded as 'honorific', symbols of power and self and failure to consume/ buy becomes a mark of inferiority and demerit. Subsumption (colonization of social life) has become an integral part of modern- consumerist societies (Singh, 2003) and consumption itself has become a power in its own sense. Development, if we say thrive on production, the other parallel strand of it is consumption, which saves the system from breaking down through the creation of false needs. Demonstrative consumption is the core of modern societies, but remains confined to minority.

Urban space, amenity and urban cultures have become valuable commodities for sale in the global marketplace and have become sites for identity formation. The role of business can never be underestimated in popularising this urban culture agenda. 'Places' have now become important markers of internationally recognizable symbols of identity, and sophistication. Modern shopping places in the form of modern retail formats have redefined the urban culture and consumer culture. These privately owned leisure cum shopping places are fast replacing traditional places such as 'main street' where once people of different social classes and backgrounds mingled freely and consumed more of less similar kinds of goods. Modern retail formats in contrast to traditional marketspace offers and suits to the contemporary culture of consumption in which consumption has a vogue life.

Modern retail formats have emerged as large indoor places with controlled environment where large crowds are formed and serve interest of particular groups. They offer high degree of security (detection booths, be frisked with body scanners, bag searches, food stuffs are prohibited) as well as leisure and new environment for retail activity. These new formats are fast replacing the role of community gathering places and provide new form of public space, a sensual environment that is sensitised, secure, carefully planned, selectively accessed and privately operated. They commodify new social aspirations, prioritising cleanliness, safety, congeniality and providing environment that distances the well off consumers from immediate past of fear, discomfort and scarcity in public space. It is so, modern retail format becomes a place for identity formation and class segregation. Earlier, austerity was regarded as the basis of social life in traditional societies but now, consumption has become central to the social life. This development is at variance with the values of our culture which puts premium on curtailment of needs. People look for objects/ places which help them in segregating themselves from the class above or below their own. It becomes clear that same goods and services may have a very different effect on different people under varying circumstances. Giddens (2006), rightly notes that these malls, stores and other super shopping locations are more exclusive, i.e., poor do not have adequate resources to participate in the dazzling world of flamboyant consumerism. He substantiates his opinion by putting that of the 5.5 billion people who make up the world's population, 3.5 lacks cash and credit to buy any consumer goods. It indicates that the modern market culture is deprives a vast majority from consumption process, so that distnciation is maintained.

Other than consumption, people patronise modern retail formats for status seeking, comfort seeking, class segregation and hedonism. Expansion of modern retail has simultaneously led to change in the consumer values too. 'Feel good factor' and notion of 'good life' has led to rise in lifestyle spending amongst Indian consumers. With availability of goods at low prices (as they claim through offers), there has been excessive indulgence in buying and abandoning goods which has re-defined the notion of successful life and status that is equated with having everything. The spread of consumer culture has replaced the traditional notion of self- sufficiency, self reliance, anti materialism and austerity which were high held ideals in Indian value system. There has been a shift from 'need based' to 'want based' consumption (www.financialexpress.com). People desire a combination of comfort and suitability which these malls cater to by providing various amenities such as restaurant, multiplex, shopping under one roof to customers. The mass appeal for malls and stores lies in the fact that it has something on offer for everyone. There is a wide range of shopping experiences, bargains and discounts, amusement facilities for kids, a large choice of cuisines for family meals, and multiplex theatres.

Mall/ store culture has also led to changes in lifestyle of rich, middle classes and youth, largely followed by changes in food habits, selection of goods, recreational activities etc. The target of modern market is creation of mass culture that requires standardisation of perception about fun, lifestyle, behaviour pattern, choices of product for daily use. In addition, modern retail has changed the lifestyle and psyche of Indian consumers dramatically. People have become aware of value of their hard earned money so they are well versed with the concepts about quality, products and services. The non-food sector, comprising apparel, accessories, fashion, and lifestyle have felt significant change with the emergence of new stores formats. Food retailing has become an important retail business in the national arena. Concept of packed foods and fast foods chain has changed the food habits of people. Malls have taken place of shopping complexes and are giving best to the customers with food, entertainment and shopping under one roof. With increasing competition in market, customers now expect better services from traditional retailers as well as great bargains at modern retail stores.

Retail transmutation has brought in significant change in consumer goods, brands and their consumption. Despite the fact that goods are available at international prices, people are ready to buy them. Middle class's desire to imbibe an elitist style of living and their readiness and potential to spend on the commodities and services is one of the reasons for surge in modern retailing. Other than this, malls are also bringing in profound change in the way mass affluent household spends. It is common to find many families doing their monthly grocery shopping at malls and paying by cards. A few years back, the same was done at neighbourhood shops through cash and credit transactions which is now looked down upon. Rajagopal (2001) notices that people today are faced with a plethora of goods so they like to spend more time at malls than anywhere else besides work and home. They are limited with time and loaded with incomes and need shopping places where they can get everything and their search ends at shopping malls. It can be said that consumption has taken centre stage as far as human lives are concerned and the market has increasingly become a sole locus of power in determining social trends thereby excluding majority from consumption of goods and services which are sold at these modern formats (Nayyar, 2008). In many ways, malls reflect the state of our society and act as agents of change.

Shopping Behaviour of Respondents

Shopping is an important activity in our lives. It does not necessarily involve spending of money and purchase of goods in fact, purchase of goods may be incidental to experience of shopping. Consumers shop for experimental and emotional reasons as well as for goods, services and information. Kaul (2007), analyzed shopping behaviour of people from cultural perspective, and found that shopping carries some symbolic, emotional and cognitive association and these meanings differ across cultures and keep on changing. Likewise, shopping activity is influenced by both personal and social motives (Loudan, 2002). Personal motives to shopping include diversion from routine of daily life and shopping for recreation and self gratification. Whereas, social role includes part of role playing, i.e., shopping activities are learned behaviour and are expected or accepted as a part of one's position or role.

Social motives to shopping include opportunities for seeking new acquaintances, encounters with friends, communication with others having a similar interest and peer group attraction. Shopping also provides an opportunity to obtain a feeling of status and power. Other than this shopping also offers enjoyment of gaining a lower price through bargaining, companion shopping or visiting special sales (www.oppaers.com). Shopping also provide sensory benefits such as looking at and handling merchandise, listening to the sounds (silence, soft background music) and smelling the scents. Kaul (2007) examined several studies (Carmen: 1978, Mc Cracken: 1986 and Yau: 1988) and from them drew strong impact of cultural values in shaping consumers motivation and product choices. The recreational or hedonic aspects of shopping he finds are increasingly important to consumers. Shopper's attention is more focused on fun, emotions, fantasy, amusement elements as well as on the goods they buy for consumption.

The process of shopping is not individual activity but, socially embedded and begins from decision making process within family. The purchasing decision depends upon and is affected by certain factors such as role structure, power structure stage in decision making process, family specific characteristics, social environment, culture and media (Mathur, 2010). Cultural values interact with our emotional needs to influence our behaviour and cause us to select the products we choose. For example in India, where we have patriarchal system of family, the father (or any other elder male member) is the head of the family and the main decision maker, woman are consulted for petty issues and children were not much involved in decision making process. Similarly, there were not many options available for shopping so the shopping activity largely took place in the most convenient and nearest locations. Consumer had certain evaluative selection criteria established in their mind. Several other factors influenced consumer choice behaviour such as physical design, assortment, prices, advertising, sales promotion, personnel and services.

With incoming of modern retail formats consumer choice has surely expanded (www.business.mapsofindia.com). Johnson (2009) brings forward different typologies and orientation of shoppers to shop. Some shoppers pay more attention to merchandise, price and quality. Some seek personal relationship with a sales person. Some shop out of necessity. Some shop for recreation. Some shop for novelty seeking. It can be sadid that purchase decision is also affected by orientation of shoppers. If a shopper shops for novelty seeking one would prefer to go to some hi- profile store. If one is shopping for necessity or out of compulsion, he would prefer to buy it from the nearest possible and convenient locations. The motivation of shoppers also depends upon their social class. Despite this, people of all the classes enjoy shopping. Where earlier, men were predominantly decision makers pertaining to buying high priced commodities, women were decision makers in petty shopping. With the incoming of modern formats, shopping pattern has undergone change.

In this study, it was seen that process of decision making varies as per the product, for example, decision for buying grocery has now become more of a family decision with expansion of stores. Earlier, woman played role of homemaker and so used to exercise her will for managing grocery for family and men played the role of payee. With change in lifestyle and within family domain, the whole family is involved in buying grocery and go together to select amongst wide variety. Everyone (young and old) in the family works out with on prices and products. More important decisions pertaining to buying heavy goods still lie in the hand of male members. Whilst, woman are consulted for looks and colours. This suggests that some kinds of changes have taken place in decision making at family level. Keeping these changes in mind, the chapter seeks to build a better understanding of how consumers make their purchases and how expansion of modern retail stores in Amritsar has affected consumer behaviour.

The Process of Shopping

Prior to change in retail market customers had a limited choice in selecting a place to shop. The entry of modern retail has brought diversity in the market. Consumers make choice over shopping location on the basis of demographic characteristics, lifestyle characteristics and general perception of store/shop. Respondents were asked to state their preferred place for shopping. Not much of difference in the customer's preference for shopping place was found as respondents preferred both traditional as well as modern stores for shopping (Table 7.1). As mall/store culture is new to the city, people are gradually adjusting themselves to the changing market environment and there is likelihood that there will be the transition of people from shops to malls and stores in the coming years. Convenience of location was another crucial store or shop selection criterion, i.e., 26.05 per cent of respondents said that they prefered to shop at place near to their residence, be it store or shop. Also, 3.52 per cent stated that they prefer to shop from wherever they get things at cheaper prices. Nearly one per cent of the respondents said that they prefer to buy from the one with better quality of products. The data is indicative of the fact that with the incoming of modern retail formats there has been a division of clientege into three categories broadly, i.e., shop customers, store customers and casual customers. Data discern that traditional retail and modern stores are growing parallel and there is still a scope to increase mall visit of consumers through engraining habit of mall going in the mass culture.

Table 7.1

Preferred Place for Shopping

Preferred place	Response	Percentage
Shop	50	35.21
Store	49	34.50
Nearest to residence	37	26.05
Who ever seels cheapest	5	3.52
Who ever sells quality	1	0.70
Total	**142***	**99.98**

* *Multiple Responses*

In addition, it was seen that on an average, a respondent largely goes on weekly basis to buy from neighbourhood retail. Whereas, visit to store and mall were on monthly basis as malls/ store are located at different locations of the city so one has to spare time for paying visit to them. The findings correspond with Sinha's (2003) study of shopping orientation of Indian consumers that shopper's preference for a store/ shop that is nearer and visited frequently poses a major challenge in current retail environment. From the above findings, it can be said that Amritsari's have not yet fully integrated mall culture into their lives but have not also remained unaffected from it. They patronise shopping centres as per their diverse orientation.

Orientation of Going to Malls/Stores

Sinha's (2003), study of shopping orientation of Indian shoppers highlights that orientation of Indian shoppers is based on entertainment derived out of shopping. As per his findings, Indians sought emotional value more than functional value of shopping. Malls and stores are not only places for shopping, but also are places of recreation and solve both purposes of shoppers, i.e., shopping and entertainment. People visit these modern formats with different purposes.

Figure 7

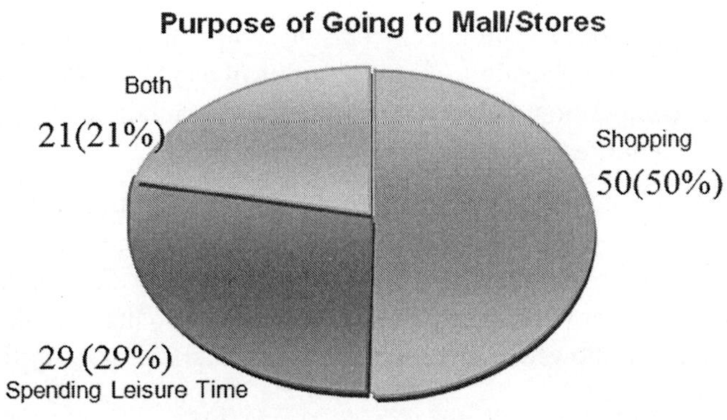

The respondents gave reasons for preferring modern retail. Half of respondents said that they go to malls exclusively for shopping (Figure 7). Twenty nine per cent of respondents said that they patronise them for spending leisure time and window shopping. Remaining respondents said that they go to malls/ stores for both windows shopping as well as shopping. From the above findings, it can be said that shoppers go to malls and stores not solely for spending money but also for recreational purposes.

Accompanying Persons

The city of Amritsar doesnot offer much to people who want to spend quality time wih family and friends. New retail is fulfilling this requirement of city dweller by providing a mixed space (shopping and entertainment) for shopping, eating, participating in cultural events, cinema and shopping. Quite a good number of respondents in our study preferred going with family to stores/malls. Sixteen per cent preferred to go with friends and 13 per cent preferred to go alone. It means people go to malls and stores to spend a quality time with their families. Research conducted by Jaitley (2010) also brings out that people like to go collectively with friends and family to these modern formats. From this it can be said that these shopping places are playing a major role in integrating families and strengthening relationships.

Shopping Time

Baneerjee (2001), states that increasing competition among retail players is consumer friendly. Sales, promotion in retail are induced by increased competition because of which these retail stores are becoming favourite places for shoppers.

The trend of offers and schemes is becoming so popular that even local retailers have started following it. It was seen that more than half of the respondents said that now they do not wait for offers and sale and prefer to shop anytime (Table 7.2). More than one-fifth of respondents showed inclination towards shopping only during sales.

They said, other than necessities many a time they wait for good offers and sale to buy branded products. Schemes/ lucrative offers now play an essential part in forming decision of shoppers to shop but due to excessive number of sales/ offers going all throughout the year customers prefer to shop as per their need and time. The respondents were also asked to enlist their preferences for commodities they buy from modern stores. It was seen that people largely shop for grocery items and apparels and showed less interest in purchasing electronics, home décor from stores and malls. Modern shopping has facilitated buying through various modes, i.e., buying on credit card and E-Shopping to make shopping easier and comfortable but the preferred way of buying continues to be cash and carry at modern stores.

Table 7.2

Shopping Time

Time	Response	Total
Any time	69	67.64
During Sale/ Discount period	33	32.36
Total	**102***	**100.00**

**Multiple Responses*

Most of the respondents stated that their mode of shopping is purely on cash basis. Whereas, others stated that they buy luxury items through credit card as heavy expenditure is not painful this way. Where earlier buying on credit from a local shopkeeper is looked down upon today, buying through credit card has become a means of status enhancement and convenient shopping at stores. This indicates how our perception of things undergoes change with the trend or fashion.

Sources of Information

A customer derives information of sales and offers through several sources that makes an impact on buying activity of consumers (a) Personal sources- shared by friends, family, colleagues (b) Commercial sources- newspaper, other media. (c) Experimental sources- practical demonstration, handling, examining and using the product (Loudan, 2002).

Consumerism is driven by huge sums spent on advertising which has become a major instrument to persuade people to buy goods that they do not even need. Frankfurt school emphasises role of advertisement in preservation of capitalist society by creating false needs in people who are seduced by flow of goods. It can be said that advertisement has a cultural role to play as it creates particular societal culture, i.e., consumerism in which consumers look for positional goods that help in establishing an identity (Kapoor, 2007). Effective advertising always play an important role in modifying consumer choices.

Earlier sources like TV, newspaper were used for effective selling; today new sources such as information through mobile phones, internet, FM are used to disseminate information.

Other than this, social network has always remained as source of gaining information as well for advertisingIn our study it was seen that nearly thirty seven per cent of the respondents said that they come to know of the offers through media.

This indicates the effective role media plays in advertising and dissemination of information. More than one-fifth of respondents said that they receive a call/ SMS from the store/mart about offers. Whereas, for others networking is an essential part of lives as people talk to each other, discuss and exchange the information.

Less than one- fifth of respondents said that they come to know of offers/sale through hoardings. Remaining nine per cent said that they come to know of offers when they pay visit to the malls/store or through the announcements made. It shows that consumers are informed through various sources.

Monthly Ration and Preference for Traditional Retail Shop

With ample choices to shop from, consumers are actively participating in flamboyant world of consumerism. As discussed previously, new retail chains are roping up largely in food and grocery and clothing segment.

Among the food and grocery stores, not all are performing well. Initially, people started buying fruits and vegetables from stores and marts but, got disappointed with the quality supplied at these formats. As a result, many of the food and grocery stores got shut down.

The closure of such stores reflects the attitude of consumers of Amritsar towards grocery stores that they would not compromise quality for cheaper rates. Respondents were also asked about their preferred place for buying monthly ration / grocery.

Figure 8

Place for Buying Monthly Ration

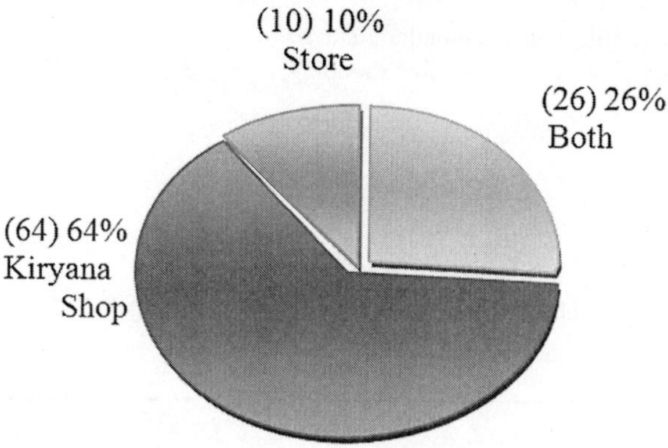

Sixty per cent of respondents said that they preferred to buy ration from traditional kiryana shop (Figure 8). While, 26 per cent of the respondents preferred to buy monthly ration from modern store and remaining said they preferred to shop from both kiryana shop as well as stores or from wherever they find products of good quality and cheap rates. This data shows, kiryana stores continue to be a preferred place for buying grocery for people. This shows that neighbourhood traditional shops continue to maintain their niche despite increasing competition.

Table. 7.3 : Reasons for Preferring Retail Formats

Traditional Format	Response	Percentage
In case of emergency	47	26.86
Acquaintance/ Traditional Link	34	19.43
Loyal/ Honest/ Reliable	28	16.00
Home Delivery	24	13.71
Good Quality	22	12.57
Credit	10	5.71
Cheaper rate	10	5.71
Total	**175***	**99.97**

Modern Formats		
Poor quality at shops, expired and duplicate goods on Stacks	16	23.53
Quality, services, offers, atmosphere, ample variety, entertainment	11	16.18
Cheap rates at Malls, savings on bulk purchase	11	16.18
Availability under one roof/hassle free shopping, displayed goods	8	11.76
Dishonest and dis-loyal shopkeeper, and their rude behaviour	6	8.82
Brands at Store/Malls	6	8.82
Billing facility at Store/Malls	3	4.41
For change, comfort, and standard	3	4.41
Uniform prices and schemes at Malls/Stores	2	2.94
Children prefer to go	1	1.47
Status symbol	1	1.47
Total	**68***	**99.96**

* *Multiple Responses*

Reasons for Preferring Different Formats

Respondents were asked to state the reasons for preferring traditional retail in contrast to modern formats for monthly shopping.

More than one-fourth of respondents prefered shops because they are located it their vicinity which means they are easy to approach especially, during emergency and is time saving than stores located in different corners of city (Table 7.3). The assumption; farther the place of shopping, greater is the number of intervening alternatives holds true. In traditional market, there exists informal relationship between buyers and sellers as they hail from a common setting. So people also preferred to buy from local retailers simply because they had some kind of acquaintace (19.43 per cent). Sixteen per cent of the respondents said that reliability, honesty and loyalty of shopkeeper drew them to traditional retail. Nearly, fourteen per cent respondents said that traditional retailers provide them with better facility of home delivery. Others said shops provide better quality of goods and facility of credit. Another 5.71 per cent of respondents said malls and stores sell goods at heavy prices so they prefer shops.

From the findings, it can be drawn that easy approachability of traditional shops can be a challange for modern retail.

Reasons for Preferring Modern Formats

Changes in retail environment have also been accompanied by significant changes in shopping behaviour. Today it is difficult to talk of traits of partcular shopping segment because shoppers engage in cross shopping. Johnson (et.al., 2009) notes that this phenomenon is more prevalent among youth as they have more time and money at their disposal and are more inclined towards experimenting different locations and products. In this study, respondents stated number of reasons for preferring modern formats (Table, 7.3). Some 23.52 per cent of respondents held the opinion that traditional businessmen were responsible for the outflow of customers from shops to stores as they maintained low business practices like selling poor quality, expired, duplicate goods to the consumers. Some 16.18 per cent of respondents favoured malls and store as they provide better quality, services, offers, variety, shopping atmosphere and entertainment facilities to the customers. A same number of respondents said that these stores sell goods cheaper than the shops and one can save money by making bulk purchases at stores. They also stated that because of added advantages of shopping alongwith entertainment they preferred stores over shops. Nearly, twelve per cent of the respondents said that shopping at malls and marts is more comfortable due to availability of all kinds of goods under one roof. Goods are well displayed and categorized in rows and stacks and makes shopping easy and hassle free. Whereas, nine per cent of the respondents said that they have stopped shopping at traditional shops because of dishonest and rude behaviour of shopkeepers. Incoming of modern stores and increasing competition will shortly end local businessmen's autonomy.

Other respondents said there has been increased trend and liking towards buying brands at stores as they provide customers with an authentic billing which local shopkeeper does not provide. Also they said that they haven't completely abandoned the relationship with local shops rather have moved to stores for change, comfort and standard. Malls and stores sell goods at uniform prices hence there is lesser deception and one can find the same brands in stores located at different locations. Increasing bent of youngsters towards stores was said to be another reason given by 1.47 per cent of the respondents. Status seeking through shopping at high profile store and mall was another reason stated by the respondents. From both the arguments, it can be drawn that as people hail from different economic classes and have different requirements, hence their preferences for the place of shopping vary. However, there has not been complete disowning of traditional retail by consumers as they prefer both modern as well as traditional retail for shopping.

Culture of 'Fixed Price'

Earlier bargaining (a technique adopted by customer over price reduction by arguing with the seller) was regarded as the right of customers by which price consensus could be reached with the neighbourhood retailer. Bargaining formed a part of shopping culture. Consumers try their best to bargain at traditional shops while, malls deprive them of their power to bargain by compelling them to buy on fixed prices. Modern retailing has made certain business concepts common to local markets too. Traditional retailers are imitating modern retail in many ways. They have also followed culture of selling at fixed prices. This culture of fixed price selling has grown out of compulsive consumerism as people want to buy what they want irrespective of the cost.

Respondents were asked if they missed their power to bargain while shopping at stores. It was seen that more than half of respondents said that they did not miss their power of bargaining while shopping at store and malls. They were of the opinion that fixed rates make shopping easier as one does not have to end up with a bad conversation or fight over with seller for a small amount. While, remaining respondents said they missed their power of bargaining while shopping at stores. It can be said that transformation in the market has introduced the culture of shopping at fixed prices. For some people, it has made shopping more convenient by saving time and energy. For others, it has deprived them of power to bargain with seller.

Deception at Stores

Malls/ stores aim at making shopping easier and comfortable by providing numerous facilities to customer's like online payments, lucrative offers and sales. As discussed previously, traditional retail is accused of deception and non transparency, and modern retail is thought of to be more transparent in terms of transaction and sales. It was assumed that the customers would find greter satisfaction in shopping at modern formats with minimal chances of deception. For this, the respondents were asked if they ever had been or felt cheated while shopping at malls/stores. It was found that more than half of the respondents said that they found themselves cheated on in some or the other way while shopping at malls and stores. For instance, some said they found goods bought lesser in quantity, poor quality of goods, cheated on at non refundable and non returnable policies. The remaining forty eight per cent said they were never cheated on at stores while shopping. Whatever be the case, people prefer to buy from both shops and stores/malls. With roads lined up with hoardings of branded products people are shopping like never before at moder retail formats.

Why Malls have an Appeal?

There has been a strategic rise in demand for commodities, brands and services as a means for securing upward mobility and upgrading position in society. People prefer to patron modern retail formats because they serve different sections of society having diverse needs and choices.

Table 7.4

Appeal of Malls/Stores, Reasons

Appeals	Reasons	Percentage
Display, environment, easy to locate, no carts, interior/neatness	36	21.43
Exclusive variety/fashionable items, ample choice	29	17.26
Low rates and services	21	12.5
Brands, quality, freshness/packed	20	11.90
Availability under one roof	19	11.31

Apparels	8	4.76
Grocery	7	4.17
Attendants/professionalism	6	3.57
Hassle free shopping/comfortable	5	2.97
Class feeling/good mob around	3	1.78
Leisure/time pass place	2	1.19
Modern shopping	2	1.19
Fruits and vegetables	2	1.19
Everything	8	4.76
Total	**168***	**100.00**

* *Multiple Responses*

There are diverse opinions on liking and disliking for mall and stores. The respondents were asked to list things liked by them at stores. It was seen that 21.43 per cent of the respondents said that it is easy to locate things at malls and stores as they are displayed in a systematic way (Table 7.4). The physical environment, i.e., interior of store, neatness and cart-free shopping appeals them more. Likewise, 17.26 per cent of respondents said that malls and stores provide them with exclusive and fashionable items, ample choice and variety of things.

Some respondents said that it is the low rates and services provided at malls that appeal them. Brands, quality, freshness, packing of things, availability of goods under one roof and apparels were stated as more appealing by others.

Similarly, 4.17 per cent of respondents said that they exclusively like grocery at malls and stores. Professionalism and dealings of attendants were stated as appealing by 3.57 per cent of respondents. Others said that hassle free, comfortable environment, and fruits and vegetables were liked by them. The remaining respondents liked to see a class of people around them as for them shopping at stores involved class distanciation and status enhancement.

Lacking Appeal

On the contrary, respondents expressed their disliking at modern formats. Quite a number of respondents i.e., 41.06 per cent of respondents said that stores sell goods at very high prices sans bargaining and do not refund money if customer tries to return back defected goods even a minute after payment (Table 7.5). Also, 16.56 per cent of the respondents expressed disliking for poor quality of goods sold at stores (not malls) in particular. They were of opinion that stores in the city fall below standards as they were selling poor quality goods. Many a times things displayed at stacks were long expired, out of stock and sale. Similarly, 15.23 per cent of respondents said that mall and store employees do not attend customers properly; rather customers have to help themselves in shopping. Some of respondents said that they did not like variety at malls and stores as things are dumped in bulk and there is no exclusivity in products. They pointed towards clothing section, in particular that the stock doesn't fit well with the physical statistics of Punjabi people as clothing is largely of small and medium size. Also, fruits and vegetables at stores were of poor quality (10.59 per cent).

Table 7.5

Not So Appealing Stores and Malls, Reasons.

Does Not appeal	**Response**	**Percentage**
High rates/fixed rates/no bargains, non refundable	62	41.06
Stale/poor quality/expired products, shortage of stock, all items are not available	25	16.56
Lack of services/poor services/self services	23	15.23
Bulk of commodities	20	13.25
Fruits and Vegetables	16	10.59
Poor online billing and frisking	3	1.99
Deceptive sales	2	1.32
Total	**151***	**100.00**

* *Multiple Responses*

Many of the stores keep on sticking 'fresh stock' tag on fruits and vegetable sections even when they look rotten and stale. A few respondents also said that poor online billing system and checking of shopping bags by security men during disperse were not liked by them. For them, frisking was against dignity of customers and further suggested self-scan system instead of checking system. Lastly, 1.32 per cent showed their disliking for lucrative but deceptive sales at stores.

Mall/ Stores as Signifier of Status

Uberoi (2008), discusses three lives of 'Things', i.e., Things have a Machine Life (use value), Market Life (exchange value) and Vogue Life (social value). In post modern society, vogue life of things has overtaken the market life of objects that are being symbolically used for display of power and self and are valued for the non utilitarian reasons such as status seeking, envy provocation and novelty seeking. Commercial brands, high tagged commodities have today become signifier of status and the basis of assessing positional distinctions in society. Consumption of commodities and store choices for maintaining style other than utility is the new mantra for enhancing ones social status. Modern formats have emerged as a site, for indulging in convenient shopping on one hand. On the other hand, represent class of its own as people patronise them for status seeking. In our study, it was seen that for 47 per cent of respondents, shopping at malls and stores has become a status symbol (Figure 9).

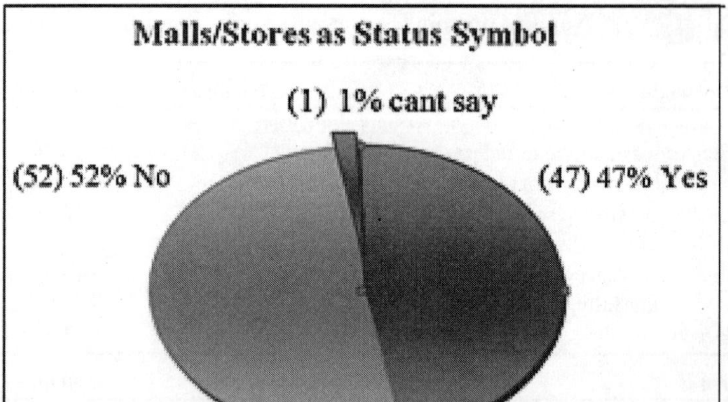

Store/ mall preference has something to do with class membership as they provide customers with a sense of class, value for money, comfort and help to adopt an exhibitionist way of life by indulging themselves in restricted shopping centres. For others, it is a means to camouflage status by buying discounted items at high profile stores so as to feel as a part of selected crowd.

The remaining respondents disagreed that malls have become a status symbol for them. Therefore, not a very significant difference was seen in the opinion of respondents.

It can be said that status symbolisation and status consciousness of material items, remain important aspect of consumer culture i.e., things consumer buy become symbols, telling others who they are what their social status is. This substantiates Smelser's (1965) argument that goods not only have economic value but also have symbolic meanings.

Preference for Brands

Role of Multinational Corporations has become very important in bringing cultural as well as economic change in societies. These multinationals constantly seek out new or under-exploited markets to create new needs and new market among different target groups. The commodity form of Globalisation has increasingly become central to the life of young, for constructing their identities, relationships, their emotional and social worlds.

Today, Brands have become an integral part of consumer culture and so there has been an inclination of people towards buying brands. Brand consciousness is more than simply an awareness or preference for brand names.

It is a general perception that brands carry a functional and symbolic value.

Brands are most desired now days and so there are number of branded chains in city. It was expected that more of people will show preference for branded goods.

Likely, a very high number of respondents showed their preference for brands (Figure, 10). Only eighteen per cent did not showed inclination towards branded goods. Remaining respondents showed a mixed taste in buying branded as well as non branded products.

Figure 10

Showing Preference for Brands

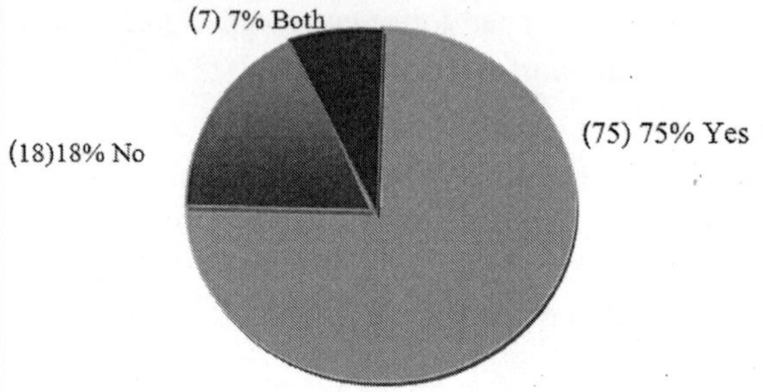

It was interesting to see that almost half of respondents prefered to buy brands for quality sake and not for status enhancement (Table 7.6). The use value of the branded products was valued more by the respondents.

Table 7.6

Reasons for Preferring Brands

Preference	Response	Percentage
Quality, value for money	53	51.45
Durable, reliable, refundable	24	23.30
Trend/name, fashionable/looks good/status symbol	9	8.74
Comfort, satisfaction	6	5.83
Uniform rates/ no deception/authentic	5	4.85
Brands are good	3	2.91
Children prefer	2	1.94
All brands are not good	1	0.97
Total	**103***	**99.97**

* *Multiple Responses*

Also, 23.30 per cent of the respondents said that they prefer brands because of durability, reliability and refundability (i.e., branded products offer returnable policies). Almost nine per cent of respondents said that they prefer brands as they are fashionable, trendy, good looking and are signifier of status. Branded products have uniform rates in all the stores so there are fewer chances of deception. Authenticity of prices was another reason stated by 4.85 per cent. Others said that it is generally presumed that branded goods are best choice. So, youngsters and children prefer to buy brands. They also replied that they are selective in brands as all the brands are not good and does not carry an equal quality. The use value of branded goods was valued more by respondents.

Changes in Consumer Behaviour

Retail Globalisation has brought about major transformation in access to consumer goods, consumption patterns and spending. The population of working woman has increased from 12 per cent in 1991 to 18 per cent in 2005 in India. As a result of increase in number of working woman, it is seen that working woman tend to spend more than housewives which also means that kitchen is getting redefined. There has been increasing demand for processed and semi- processed food, convenience seeking, time saving recipes as they value time, space and privacy (www.nabard.org). Globalisation and increasing role of media (advertisement) has played an important role in socialization of consumers and making them aware and conscious of products they use.

Table 7.7

Showing Consciousness

Conscious for	Response	Percentage
Quality	84	46.40
Expiry and date of manufacturing	58	32.04
Rates	39	21.54
Total	**181***	**99.98**

* *Multiple Responses*

It is not that people are just buying from the market, rather with increasing options, people are becoming conscious. It was seen that more of the respondents laid stress upon qualitative aspect of goods. While, 32.04 per cent said that they were now more aware about expiry and date of manufacturing of all products, which earlier they did not. Remaining respondents replied that they are more rate conscious than quality or anything else (Table 7.7). As people have become more quality conscious it can be one reason that they prefer to buy branded products.

II. Views on Competition Between Traditional and Modern Retail Formats

Malls and stores are pouring in one after another with multi assortment, heavy investment, huge buildings, and variety of goods to target spending capacities of people of various strata in society. How far stores and malls cater to needs of various sections of society remains debateable. In the previous section, it was found that customers tend to shop at different shopping locations and their criteria of selection of the shopping place, depends on various factors and the varied orientations. The modern retailers keep on trying their best to win over masses by adapting themselves to the local culture by understanding the needs of different segments. For example, McDonald which is one of the largest food chain entered Indian market in the mid- nineties and it deviated from its general global menu recognising the fact that it was entering a Hindu society where beef eating was prohibited. As Mc Donanld adapted itself to the cultural and religious pattern of Indians, it is equally a success in India as it is worldwide. With such strategic moves, modern retailers are trying their best draw more customers towards them.

In the initial stage, expansion of modern retail formats signalled transition of customers from shops to stores as they adopted lucrative strategies to popularise mall culture among different social classes by providing them almost everything under one roof. From a consumer perspective, it was seen found that more than half of the respondents (54 per cent) said that malls and stores in the city were not catering to the needs people of all classes.

Only, fourty per cent of respondents were of the opinion that modern retail formats cater to nneds of all the sections of society. Remaining six respondents did not give any opinion.

Of the fifty four per cent respondents, nearly forty four per cent of respondents said that prices of goods available at malls/ stores are high and beyond the reach of middle and lower classes (Table 7.8). This points towards a general rule of business, higher the investments in a venture, higher is the cost of goods. Malls and stores were found to be largely catering to needs of upper and upper middle class (40.24 per cent) and people from other classes hesitate to shop from stores and marts selling goods at higher prices. Some 6.10 per cent of respondents said that rates at malls /stores are high, fixed and beyond the reach of all the classes. Shopping at stores and malls also deprives consumers of their power of bargaining and sales and offers are deceptive tricks to lure customers. Nearly five per cent of respondents said that malls and stores do not provide customers with credit facility unlike the local shopkeepers. The transactions are purely on cash basis which means that only people who have ready cash in hand can buy or those having debit card facility. So the mall culture excludes poor sections of society. A same number of respondents said that malls and stores have poor quality of goods and many a times goods are out of stock and not available.

Table 7.8

Reasons for Malls/Stores not Catering to Needs

Reasons	**Responses**	**Percentage**
Higher investments lead to higher costs	36	43.90
Class centric(high and upper middle class)/ people hesitate to go to Malls	33	40.24
Tricky and deceptive schemes and prices, fixed rates	5	6.10
No credit facility for poor or other customers	4	4.88
Non availability of items, poor quality	4	4.88
Total	**82***	**100.00**

**Multiple Responses*

In contrast, nearly thirty one per cent of respondents were of the opinion that modern retail formats were catering to needs of all, i.e., entry to malls is not restricted to anyone (Table 7.9). While, 29.23 per cent of respondents said that there is ample variety and range of goods available at malls /storeso that people can buy as per their pocket and need without any hesitation. Similarly, 18.46 per cent of respondents said that malls and stores sell goods at lower rates than shops. People get all sorts of brands under single roof which makes shopping hassle free and easy as all the things are available at one location. There is no restriction for buyers in terms of time and choice. They can stay inside store/ mall for as long as they wish. Apart from it, few respondents also differentiated between malls and stores to express their opinion.

Table 7.9

Malls/Stores Cater to Needs of People

Reasons	Response	Percentage
Open to all	20	30.77
Purchase according to need without hesitation/ ample variety and range	19	29.23
Lower rates/sales and offers/brands/other facilities like credit card shopping	12	18.46
Hassle free/easy/one roof shopping	6	9.23
Entertainment/window shopping, no restriction (open time/choice), self service	3	4.61
Store caters to the needs of people Malls do not	2	3.08
Good quality at Malls not Stores	2	3.08
Youngsters Prefer Malls/Stores	1	1.53
Total	**65***	**100.00**

**Multiple Responses*

It was seen that 3.08 per cent of respondents stated stores as cheaper than malls. It can be true to some extent as malls involve heavy investments than stores which are of smaller size and involve comparatively lesser investment. Another 3.08 per cent of respondents said that malls cater to needs of people of all classes by providing them quality products while stores have slightly inferior quality of goods. Other respondents said that malls and stores largely cater to need of youngsters. It can be said that people believe that the new market structure is not catering to the needs of all the sections of the society rather, it is depriving the vast majority from the consumption process thereby sharpening the gulf between rich and the poor. In any way it cannot be denied that modern retail formats appear to be customer friendly.

Future of Modern Formats

National as well as international retailers have entered Amritsar market on the strength of rising affluence of the city dwellers, changing lifestyle and fashion consciousness. The local market remained silent for a few months as there was a craze among people over experiencing modern formats of retailing offering schemes and offers for everyone. Initially, they became favourite locations for shopping for everyone. But of recent, with increase in stores/ mall penetration in Amritsari market on one hand and poor response of stores on other hand has lead led everyone ponder over the future of malls/stores in the city.

Figure 11

Future of Modern Formats in the City

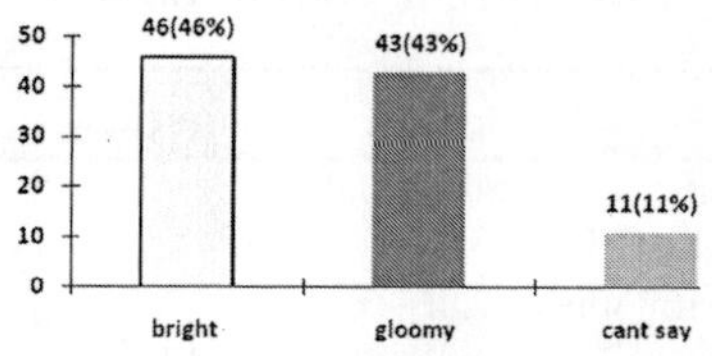

It was seen that nearly 46 per cent of respondents said that future of malls and stores in Amritsar appeared bright whereas, 43 per cent of respondents found it to be gloomy. Remaining respondents held a mixed opinion (Figure 11).

Bright Future

Those who were of the opinion that malls and stores have a bright future gave reasons to support their arguments. Of these, nearly one fifth of respondents were of the opinion that these modern retail formats provide customers with a better quality of goods, services and schemes than local shops (Table, 7.10). Nearly, nineteen per cent of respondents said that malls/stores cater to needs of all classes and provide facility of entertainment along with shopping, and ample space for parking to customers which is a gross problem faced by shoppers in this overcrowded city. Also, modern stores deal in wide variety of goods that are displayed on stacks and rows.

So that they can choose and buy as per their need and pocket. Nearly, sixteen per cent of respondents said that malls and stores will keep on doing because of increasing affluence and shopping habits of people of Amritsar.

Another factor that highlighted a prosperous future of modern formats in the city was tourism. The development activities in the city are on hike hence the respondents anticipated that in future there will be more demand for luxuriant places of consumption as tourist activity takes leap.

Table 7.11

Future of Malls/ Stores/Marts

Bright	**Response**	**Percentage**
Quality, services and schemes will make Malls and Stores to flourish	19	20.00
Caters to the needs, entertainment with shopping, parking facility, no need to carry shopping list, shopping as per need and pocket, ample variety	18	18.94
Malls and Stores will flourish because of affluence of classes and improving shopping habits of people and tourism, development graph is going up in the city	15	15.79
Youngsters and old prefer Malls and Stores for easy shopping, there is a craze for Malls among	15	15.79
people Brands/Malls have become a status symbol	12	12.63
Will work well but Innovation and improvement is needed, rates must be low	6	6.31
People are adjusting themselves with times	5	5.26
Location specific Malls and Stores will work,ie., those near residential area or posh areas	5	5.26
Total	**95***	**100.00**

Gloomy		
Low grade brands, poor schemes/quality/rates	27	22.88
People are not much brand conscious,purchasing power is less and so is the population to absorb abrupt change and overburden of Malls and Store in the city	19	16.10
Class centric, people prefer to keep acquaintance with local retailers	19	16.10
Shops will do better, wont vanish away Mall mania will soon fade away	14	11.86
No exclusive thing at Malls and Stores,	13	11.02
All will not work well, development pace is quite slow, not many malls are performing well and there are more stores than malls	11	9.32
Coexist, different clientele and competitors	9	7.63
Malls are shutting down because they are unaffordable, not catering to the needs of masses/low maintenance/poor quality	6	5.08
Total	**118***	**100.00**

**Multiple Responses*

Nearly, sixteen per cent of respondents said that malls cater to needs of certain sections like youngster, old, upper and middle class. For youngsters, shopping at modern formats is a mere fashion but, for the old, it is time saving, hassle free, provides comfortable environment, variety and quality at moderate prices. Also, 12.63 per cent of respondents said that stores and malls will do well as brands and malls have become a signifier of status.

Shopping habits of people and the place of shopping have become indicators of social class of the customers. Nearly, nineteen per cent of respondents said that stores will work well only if they keep on catering to the needs of the people by lowering their prices and bringing innovation and improvement in their practices. Remaining respondents said that only location specific malls will work well than those located on the outskirts of city or in far flung areas.

People prefer to buy from nearest possible locations therefore, malls and stores located in vicinity of residential areas will definitely have bright future than others.

Gloomy Future

Whereas, others opinioned that malls/stores will die-out due to their malpractices (22.88 per cent), (Table 7.10). Respondents argued that many of stores sell poor quality, low grade brands at higher rates than Maximum Retail Price (MRP). Another 16.10 per cent of the respondents said that stores will not do well as people in city are not so brand conscious and purchasing power of people is not very high and number of retail outlets exceed total population of the city. Excess of mall and stores would just be an overburden to the city. Also number of buyers will remain limited and clientele will be further divided which will bring loss to both malls/stores and shops as people will take some time to change their mindset and break away their habit of buying from local shops to branded stores and malls. Another, 16.19 per cent of people said that malls and stores do not cater to needs of all the classes rather, are class centric and largely cater to the needs of upper and middle classes. While, traditional shops will continue to cater to the needs of all the classes from high to low. Likewise, traditional markets are socially embedded and so social acquaintances play an important role in consumer behaviour. People still prefer to maintain their age old relationship with local retailers.

Similarly, thirteen per cent of respondents said that traditional retailers will not perish as with the increase in competition, traditional retailers will also adopt new ways to lure customers. Moreover, they will do much better as being a part of local culture they know the demands and tastes of customers. Increasing bent of people towards modern formats is just a mania as people want to experience modern retail for a change. Soon these modern stores will become a regular place of shopping and the craze will fade away. Also, 9.32 per cent of respondents said that development activities in the city are on rise but, the pace of development is slow. Number of projects are lying half done and many are still in pipeline. Sue to higher overhead expenses which lead to higher costs not many people are able to be a part of modern consumption. Therefore, respondents were of opinion that only those malls and stores selling goods at low price will work out well and others will get transformed into leisure places.

On the other hand, 7.63 per cent of respondents said that malls stores and shops will co-exist in the future as their clientele is different. In future, there will be polarisation of key players and competitors, i.e., malls will compete with other malls, stores will compete with each other while traditional retailers will have their own competitors. This way, traditional retail will get adequate time to flourish, survive, adjust and embibe techniques of modern retailers. The remaining respondents said many of stores have already suffered losses and have been eliminated from market as they were not catering to the needs of localites as they were unaffordable, sold goods of poor quality, were poorly maintained and were not selling anything exclusive.

General Views on Modern Retail Formats

A few additional questions were asked from the respondents to know their overall response over modern formats in the city. Questions pertaining to quality, variety, services, environment, display, online payment system were asked (Table 7.11). While replying this question, respondents on some issues purposefully differentiated between malls, marts and stores in terms of quality, size, services, variety and display helped in comparing and contrasting between modern formats. Malls and marts are more spacious with multi assortments whereas stores are smaller in size with limited assortments (Appendix IV).

Quality- As shops are owned and run by individual owners, every effort is made to ensure better quality of stock and meet the needs of different sections. In contrast, stores and malls follow policy of stock-grading by categorising and grading products and items as per the city graded, i.e., goods and brands are categorized and distributed quality wise to respective stores/showrooms located at different places or cities by the headquarter as per ranking of area/city. The best products or brands are sent to tier I cities/posh localities whereas, goods are dispersed to tier II and III cities or other areas. Hence, quality of products vary from one store or one city to another city. More than half of the respondents found quality of goods sold at malls and stores was good whereas, nearly 12 per cent of the respondents found quality of goods sold at malls better than stores.

Services- It was also found that a vast majority of respondents were highly satisfied with the services provided by modern retailers. It was seen that 6.60 per cent of the respondents said that malls provide better services than the stores as they maintain good standards, have more formal setting and staff.

While, 3.77 per cent of respondents held an opposite view i.e., stores provide good services to customers than the malls as they are smaller in size and hence more easy to manage and pay more attention to customers.

Variety- Both malls and stores provide ample variety to shoppers. A very significant number of respondents showed liking for availability of variety of goods, brands and rates under one roof. The remaining said that malls have huge diversity, while stores do not provide ample variety to customers.

Price- Price is a relative concept that helps customers establish their priorities and levels of acceptable need satisfaction. It was seen that 39.04 per cent of respondents bemoaned that prices of goods sold at malls and stores were high, schemes and discounts were forged.

Similarly, 34.29 per cent of respondents said that prices at malls and stores were reasonable and there was lot of transparency in prices as all stores have uniform prices. While, 11.42 per cent of respondents were of opinion that prices at malls were higher than stores.

Environment/ Display- The physical environment of modern formats was liked by almost all the respondents and stated it as cool, spacious, hassle free, comfortable. Majority i.e., 89.42 per cent of the respondents liked the display.

While, 2.88 per cent of the respondents said that stores have better display as they are smaller in size and manageable. Only one per cent of the respondents said that the display at malls and stores is poor.

Table 7.10

Views on Malls/Stores

Category	Response	Responses*	Percentage
Quality	**Good**	**64**	**62.75**
	Average	12	11.76
	Malls are better than Stores	12	11.76
	Poor	10	9.80
	Fruit and Vegetable Poor	4	3.92
Services	**Good**	**68**	**64.15**
	Poor	27	25.47
	Malls provide better than Stores	7	6.60
	Stores provide better than Malls	4	3.77
Variety	**Plenty**	**88**	**85.44**
	Limited/ bulk	5	4.85
	Poor stuff	4	3.88
	Mixed	4	3.88
	Malls have plenty while Store have limited	2	1.94
Prices	**High/Fake Discounts**	**41**	**39.04**
	Reasonable	36	34.29
	High at Malls than Stores	12	11.42
	No difference	16	15.23
Online Payment	**Good**	**66**	**66.00**
	Poor	34	34.00
Display	**Good**	**93**	**89.42**
	Malls have good display	4	3.84
	Stores have good display	3	2.89
	Mart is Good	3	2.89
	Poor at mall, mart, store	1	0.96
Environment	**Cool/ spacious**	**92**	**92.00**
	Hassle free	6	6.00
	Entertaining	2	2.00

**Multiple Responses*

Online Payment System- More than half of the respondents said that online payment system was good enough. While, thirty four per cent of the respondents said that it was not good as it was more complicated, problematic, slow and delaying process. The staff at malls and stores in the city was not so well equipped with the system which creates hassle and discomfort for both staff as well as customers when making transaction.

To sum up with the discussion, it can be said that the process of shopping is not only an individual but also a social activity. Customers engage themselves in decision making process of choosing a place to shop on the basis of demographic characteristics, lifestyle characteristics, and other buyer characteristics. Shoppers have different orientations for going at malls and stores which also means that everyone is not going solely for spending money at these formats but also, for recreational purposes. Nearly half of the respondents said that their shopping activity and visit to modern formats have become too frequent as they find it appealing. Likewise, consumer behaviour has been affected in some way or the other by transformation in market, i.e., people have become more quality conscious and prefer to buy branded products. These modern shopping places are playing a major role in integrating families and strengthening relationships as a large majority of respondents stated they prefer to go with their families for recreation at these formats. The findings indicate that traditional as well as modern stores are equally preferred by people for shopping. Transformation in the market has introduced the culture of shopping at fixed prices. For some people, it has made shopping more convenient by saving time and energy whereas, for others it has deprived them of the customer's power to bargain with the seller. Malls and brands have also become signifier of one's social status. Where on one hand, serious shoppers prefer to buy from malls and stores offering facility of one roof shopping. On the other hand, casual or non serious buyers showed preference for malls/stores for recreational purposes. Overall, respondents expressed a mixed response over competition between the modern and traditional retail players.

8

Globalisation and Contentions: Real and Imagined

An overarching trend of our times, Globalisation signifies a transformative force of huge significance. In the globalized world of today, we observe that there are two major trends which are popular and prevailing. Firstly, many of the scholars believe that there is one direction left for the world that is to imitate and incorporate the ideology of the triumphant global free market capitalism and its consequent economic, social, political and cultural paths. Secondly, opponents of the first view see the world of today as a diversified one. In contemporary times, both of these ideologies exist but with their variations (Michael, 2012).

On one hand, Globalisation has resulted in globalized production of homogenization through popularisation of cultural universals whereas, on the other hand, it has also led to globalized production of differences which is evident from certain trends which are indicative of upsurge of cultural distinctions and identities. Contemporary Globalisation represents a major break in the history of capitalism as it now represents an economy that is dominated by services.

The growth in the service industry signifies this. With integration of markets at a global scale, fate of markets has undergone a change. With increasing emphasis on consumption than production, cities and villages are growing in a similar manner. However, cities continue to be a major breeding ground for the proliferation of capitalist culture they are transforming in different ways. The cumulative impact of globalisation can be seen on the patterns of urbanization as well as on transformation of market. Urban spaces, amenities and culture have become a valuable commodity for sale in the global marketplace. Peter Marcuse (2000) claims that cities have become 'quartered', suggesting that although they have always been divided, the origins and forms of contemporary urban division are different and more alarming than before. To him, some divisions arise of economic functionality, some are cultural and some reflect and reinforce relationship of power, some are combination of all three (C.f., Stevenson, 2009). This division has a marked effect on the overall life of the city and its people.

As a result of Globalisation and economic restructuring, cities and regions are being forced to look at consumption and finance activities in order to compete in the growing competition by construction of saleable consumption spaces and a renewed urban image by manipulating for instance, built environment. Power relations informing the city have legitimised the design, and construction of potential symbols of supremacy in the form of monuments, streetscapes, buildings and locations which were earlier confined to metro or cosmopolitan centres.

Particularly to talk of modern retail formats that were truly modern urban spaces designed specifically for the conspicuous consumption of the commodities of capitalist production and aimed to save and promote global culture of consumption so as to achieve cultural uniformity and were subsequently adopted by cities everywhere under the new system of global space. These divisions are apparent in the widespread development of privately owned spaces of leisure and consumption (shopping malls ad store) which are replacing the 'local -main street' as principle shopping places of the middle, upper and lower classes in many cities. Such urban development trends have and are contributing to considerable physical decline and decay of the traditional city centres.

People are consuming similar products and are equally being affected by the changes taking place at national as well as international level. There is no denying the fact that prior to liberalisation policy, sharp difference was seen in socio-economic organization of cities of India. Highly developed cities occupied central position with respect to economic investment, development and policy formation. However, post liberalisation, market has become an important driving force for development of cities as they are now not competing with each other at local level but at global. Cities of today have become cultural expressions of the capitalist mode of production.

Retail Dualism and its Implications

Contemporary society is characterised by modes of life and institutions that are radically different from those in the past. Much of these changes in the Indian society would not have been possible without the 'Policy of Economic Liberalisation'. As a result, India is experiencing almost a similar pattern of change and development as rest of the world. Globalisation is important in the study of Indian cities and urban cultures as process of Globalisation are important element framing the contemporary relationship between capitalist's economic power, the city and accentuating inequalities of all forms, including spatial inequalities.

In this sense, of recent retail Globalisation and its implications have come to dominate academics, political, social and popular discourses with the opening up of retail sector and entry of national and international retailers which are carving newer spaces of consumption in the form of modern retail formats, i.e., malls and stores.

Concerns have been raised that retail Globalisation will have certain implications on local markets and lives of people. This is a problem that has framed recent attempts to explore the ways in which locals have been affected by, responded to Globalisation of capitalism and culture. The case of Amritsar city solves this purpose of analysing the implications of retail Globalisation policy as they city is distinctive in itself on several accounts. Trade and commerce has always been central to the life of the city than religion and politics. Though, the city presents a unique socio-economic history of its own, yet it represents many of the cities of India which have evolved in a similar fashion and so can help us in understanding changes that are bound to take place with retail Globalisation policy at different levels.

The city of Amritsar has always been a commercial hub and embarked on a range of attempts to undertake regeneration and instigate economic development strategies. As a result, today it presents duality (modern and traditional) in terms of its spatial pattern. The traditional marketplace within the walled city of Amritsar since long has been catering to traditional needs of people whereas, the modern market (beyond the wall and expanding) having modern, well structured retail formats is catering to contemporary needs of city dwellers.

The entire investment as well as consumption activity is expanding on the outer area of the city. The walled city market represents and thrive on 'old economy' and caters to the traditional needs of the city dwellers whereas, outer marketplace thrives on 'new economy' and caters to the contemporary needs of people. Both modern as well as traditional retailers are doing businesses in the market but of different levels and different forms. This rapid and uncertain segmental division of market definitely carries implications on local business which this research has focussed upon.

(a) Traditional Retailers

Traditional retail in the city is largely of small and medium size run in traditionally structured retail shops by people largely hailing from business communities. It was seen that nearly half of respondents stated that their business was negatively affected by expansion of modern retail formats and so they were found to be much against the policy move.

Several studies based on the experience of other South Asian countries have been conducted in India since 2006 which include Technopak Limited, Indian Council for Research on International Economic Relations: 2008, India Retail Report: 2007, National Council of Applied Economic Research, NABARD: 2011, Economic Survey: 2013 and NSDC India to assess implications of retail Globalisation policy. Other studies conducted by individual researchers such as, Sridhar: 2007, Chattopadhyay: 2007, Mulky and Nargundkar: 2003, Purohit: 2009 and Neilson: 2010 also bring forth the evidence of loss suffered by local retailers due to expansion of modern retail formats.

Region wise variations on impact of modern retail on traditional retail in India was studied by the 'Indian Council for Research on International Economic Relations in 2008' and brought forward that maximum impact was felt in the western part of the country, followed by both northern and eastern and little in the southern part of India. Sethi's (2007) study of Jalandhar city of Punjab focussed upon the work operation of India's retail giant 'Reliance' (under Reliance-Fresh banner) and reveals how the supply chain of vendors was adversely affected and thrown out to low quality produce. Almost, all of these studies highlighted that traditional businesses has been negatively affected at different rates with the modern retail incursion.

Irrespective of the intense competition, it was also seen that local businessmen are trying their best to maintain themselves in the intense competition by adopting number of strategies such as improving the physical layout of their shops by getting it air-conditioned, improving interior by adding rows and stacks, improving display, adding more variety, selling things on offers and schemes, providing better services to customers, lowering their rates, associating a stylish name to their shop, offering home delivery services and mending their trade practices.

Joseph's (2008) study on impact of modern retailing on traditional retail (at an all India level) also brings forward similar mechanisms adopted by traditional retailers in order to compete with modern retail formats. It means that the new formats of retailing have not only emerged as a model for emulation for the traditional retailers, but also have introduced new ways of doing business by introducing new technologies, new ideas, new values thereby improving the local market. Thus, on one hand expansion of modern retail is being viewed as a threat to traditional business but, on the other hand it has also helped in refinement of traditional retail market.

(b) Employees

Modern retail has not only brought transformation in the market but also has brought about changes in the employment pattern, work and work culture. The profile of people working at modern retail formats is totally different from those working in traditional retail. Youth and women have emerged as a most sought after human resource in modern retail. Katakam's in traditional retail.

Modern retail formats in the city have expanded opportunities of employment (2007) study on 'gender factor' conducted in Mumbai illustrates a similar profile of employees at modern formats. Modern retail provides people with a formal employment which resembles much like corporate organizations in its composition and working. What is drawing people to find employment to the modern formats is not mere the increased options in the market but also, that it provides an attractive work environment and lifestyle alongwith dignity of labour. Modern retail jobs thrive on competency, efficiency and target fulfilling and offer ample scope for career enhancement.

Modern service jobs represents a global economy and so demand people who are adept in particular set of skills. In order to fulfil this requirement of labour in the newly advanced countries market trains individuals to acquire those skills. Gooptu (2009) argues that modern markets are shaping individual subjectivity consonant with needs of market.

This holds true for the modern retail as well. Modern retail is crafting people, training them, making them more skilful in meeting needs of modern market. Employees working at modern formats have to undergo training wherein, they are imparted soft skill training and trained in language proficiency. They are trained in corporate settings, are placed in more formal settings, have to converse in English with customers, have western dress code and are motivated by their employees to work hard and efficiently. The employers in modern organizations value their employees on whom they have invested heavily on training and loosing employees to others (by job switching) is seen as a threat by modern organization. For this, they also try to bind their employees by various means.

Apart from providing comfortable working conditions, employees are provided with ample scope for leisure time activities, easy work shifts, friendly ambience and more egalitarian workplace settings. Employees draw gratification from their job as they see themselves as a part of corporate culture than mere workers. The corporate designations give them some sense of pride and accomplishment than being called and known as a servant or helper. Store management also takes utmost care in presentation of their employees through various mechanisms. Hailing from different classes they try to maintain themselves as presentable as they can. Modern employees are seen as prosperous class which remains passive and satisfied with the work culture and feel more integrated with the system as their material wants gets satisfied by earning through reward systems.

Ford (C.f., Watson, 1980) gave a global vision to consumerism, as a key to peace. He contributed in popularising consumer culture by seeing workers as active consumers. Ford's strategy of paying high to workers in a way has helped in contributing to the growing consumer culture, by making it recognised that with extra pay workers can also actively participate in accumulation of material items which would have been otherwise out of reach. Modern retail players, recognise their employees as important consumers as they have purchasing power and desire to purchase products they sell. Employees at modern formats being surrounded by luxurious goods and in the flamboyant world of consumerism do not feel out of place as their desire to make enough money and buy goods from stores and malls gets fulfilled by earning more through reward system besides the monthly salaries. However, many a times they do feel out of place while behaving as a part of class to which they belong superficially.

Working at malls / stores on the other hand is not always a great experience for employees who have to confront with several problems in their respective malls and stores. Katakam (2007) in her research unveils several problems and constraints of women store employees in Mumbai and their dissatisfaction with the modern retail jobs due to gender discrimination which points out that modern retail is also discriminatory in certain ways. In contrast to Katakam's study, in this study it was seen that employees were by and large found to be satisfied with their management practices. One major reason behind it can be that most of them hailed from lower- middle class background and were adequately and timely paid. Also, it may be due to the fact that concept of malls and stores is new to the city and so employees are not yet fully aware of their rights. Neither any anti-mall/ store response was visible among employees in Amritsar nor was any anti-mall union seen in the city

(c) Consumers

Market affects consumption and consumption pattern of the people. Celebration of culture of consumerism is one of the most prominent consequences of Globalisation which is evident from proliferation of modern retail formats and emerging brand conscious lifestyle. Culture of consumerism is not all about mere consuming of goods and services but entails communication of statuses.

Today, cconsumption has gradually moved into the symbolic realm. This symbolic consumption helps consumer to express his/ her self and achieve a sense of continuity and identity (Chaudhuri, 2010). Bauman (C.f. Singh, 2001) explains this gap between needs and wants as a new function of consumerism i.e., a system of domination. Goods of consumption carry symbolic values and are used for identity formation and class segregation. Such an expression has widened the class disparities by redefining shopping as a means of formation of identities.

The present study brings out that consumers are more likely to use products and patronise shopping locations that are socially visible to others and communicate their identity for which they patronise shopping locations. However, in case of preference for branded goods interestingly, consumers showed consciousness about the looks as well as quality of products along with its functional aspects. Respondents in the present study showed preference of patronising both modern and traditional formats depending on requirement and orientation. For instance, they showed preference for buying monthly ration from traditional kiryana shops but for other goods where they want to exhibit class consciousness they liked to go to modern retail formats. It indicates that there is a likelihood that both modern as well as traditional retail will flourish because of the specific requirements they fulfil of the diverse masses.

To the people who cannot be a part of this flamboyant consumerism, modern retail makes little sense as they cannot afford to pay ready cash for their purchases. The appeal of modern retail formats lie in the fact that they have something to offer for everyone, have better quality of goods, lower prices, are one stop shopping locations, deal in brands and offer provision entertainment alongwith shopping. The plus point of modern formats also is that by engaging everyone under one roof together in the name of family shopping it has been able to latently let people incur more expenses than required. Malls and stores have in a way led to integration of family members as the whole family is now involved in buying decision making and go together to select from wide variety available at these stores which also involves extra spending. Joseph et.,al (2008) study of impact of organised retailing on consumers indicates that shopping activity of consumer's increases with increasing availability of modern locations. This holds true for the present study as well, as most of respondents stated that their shopping activity has increased with incoming of modern formats.

Locating Local in the Global and Challenges Ahead

If we understand the process of Globalisation and the way it is seen as a model for development closely, we can see that development of nations depends much upon the idea of replacement or modification of 'local' values by 'global', which might be delayed or not visible profoundly. A clear case of which is retail liberalisation policy. After seeing the potential which retail sector offers, demand for globalising it was felt by Indian government to give a spurt to the Indian economy. Modern retail formats, which symbolise market homogeneity and modern ways of doing business, modern values and innovation are being seen as a drive to maturity or development of the country. Modern retail has brought number of changes in the market form as well as in relations of market and has redefined market values. For example, credit was a common mode of transaction in local retail and was looked down upon, but in present times, buying through credit card system is looked as a status symbol and as a desirable feature of global market.

Traditional retailers have improved their business practices as well as their businesses by imbibing global business values. Local businesses could not develop in the past, due to certain infrastructural problems as well as restricted policy environemnt. The current pattern of Globalisation provides ample chances to the indigenous businesses to compete with one another through higher level of innovation and rationalization. The notion of reinforcement of global over local can also be seen in spatial patterning of cities. Segregation of space encapsulates segregation of groups so as to help in maintenance of living style and culture. Modern retail with much modern, sophisticated and strategic ways require larger spaces for doing business and so they avoid traditional congested, unplanned market places and choose other untapped locations instead.

It means, over a period of time, new conglomerate are going to stand parallel to the traditional market places thereby creating a dual spatial pattern in the city. Such a pattern of spatial segregation has been well recognised in cities all across. Under global integration, the change in structural and spatial patterns takes place as a result of hierarchical global economic system (Sandhu, 2007). It reinforces the idea that when societies attain certain degrees of modernity, the objects of modernity also decentre traditionality. At the same time, it does not mean that traditional would be totally overtaken by the modern, certain elements of traditionality might remain in the structure as both, traditional and modern are two components of the social structure. Societies are composites of heterogeneity that would always produce and sustain duality in the social system.

From the findings, it may be drawn that due to intensive competition in the market and availability of numerous options to the customers both modern as well as traditional retailers are facing shortage of buyers at their retail formats (i.e., sales of both have declined). With increasing competition consumers have become more informed and conscious of their choices. It is not that the customers are simply going for air conditioned and well decorated stores. They now engage themselves in a rigorous activity and think, compare and then opt for patronizing a shopping place or a product. Over competition has been detrimental to the retail market itself. Chattopadhyay's (2007) study of Kolkata also points that oversupply of malls have proved to be detrimental to business itself. He argues that in Kolkata, all malls/stores are not earning well due to over expansion of modern formats, but at the same time, modern retail has definitely affected business of traditional retail business. Further, he cites example of Chandigarh and Gurgaon where only 50 per cent of malls are functional and rest have perished or still waiting for retailers. Khanna's (2010), study on performance of malls and stores in Chandigarh also points that many shops in malls have actually closed down after running into huge losses and failed to find buyers. With retail dualism, there has been division of clientele as well due to which both modern as well as traditional retailers are facing a market crunch.

Mr Sanjiv Goenka, Vice-Chairman of RPG Enterprises in his statement on future of malls in India said, "Though retail boom is here to stay, yet is a short-term phenomenon as malls which are not successful will eventually be closed down and only few will survive in the long-run," (www.businessline.com). Modern formats all over are emerging as places for entertainment than just shopping. According to KSA Technopak, the 'Conversion Rate', i.e., the percentage of visitors who turn into shoppers is as low as 10 to 15% in Indian malls. Even in the present study, most of store employees said that they got only ten to fifteen per cent genuine shoppers at their stores and more of window shoppers. Seeing the trend, it can be inferred that modern format are fast emerging as entertainment destinations with food courts, eating joints and kids play zones hogging all the business (www.Tribuneindia.com). Hence, dispute that modern retail formats will completely eliminate traditional retail appears less significant.

Numerous evidences of closure of under-performing stores and malls such as Reliance, Subhiksha, 6-Ten, Spencer's, Celebration Mall, More, More 4U and Ebony in Amritsar. Despite, massive propaganda, beautiful interior, attractive schemes and offers they failed to gain ground in the market, as they were providing poor services, outdated stock, rotten variety of fruits and vegetables, negligence in online payments and poor quality products. Such modern stores came in with promising statements that their stock comes from their own farms and is of high grade-quality, perhaps, after a short term their commitments were unveiled. Their overconfidence and mismanagement led them make an exit from the silent doors. No doubt, modern retailers have been able to copycat the material cultural forms and style of retail formats from the west, but have failed to inculcate global values and retail acumen. The failure of these stores point out that, enormity and luxuriousness will not alone fetch retailers any riches for long. In addition only a few bigger projects like 'Tata Trilliam' (the largest in Punjab), 'Omaxe' 'Alpha one' have successfully been able to draw people to their formats.

There are number of examples which also suggest that entry of market players from outside have brought significant positive change to the local market. Some of the big retailers have co-opted convenience stores and are helping them in upgrading under their franchise models, as a result of which there would be no danger to the traditional retailers of elimination from the market. 'Metro' which is a German wholesale chain has started pilot project 'Kiryana Programme' in Kolkata to educate and assist traditional retailers on how to stock, how to manage their stock, how to fix prices and market their wares so as to help them in competition (www.business.outlookindia.com). In a similar manner, government can also come up with certain kinds of reform programmes for the traditional retailers, so as to help them in maintaining their businesses.

Broad based organizations have always been talked of as an essence of modern global societies, which also in a way provide rational means for achievement of the specific goals. These rational organizations consist of several interlocking and interlinking networks of persons with required qualification, experience, age, skills and classes by virtue of which they are demarcated from the traditional organizational system. Under the policy changes, MNCs and Corporates have emerged as modern rational organizations that are involved in the development. It does not mean that traditional organizations lacked rationality, but they have not been able to exercise their rationality to the fullest because of inhibitions imposed by traditional structure. Under the aegis of modern organizations, which are working in a freer economic environment, traditional organizations are equally getting an opportunity to exercise their rational power.

The argument can be supported with findings of the present study, that not only in Amritsar, but also in other Asian countries which had opted for retail globalisation, the traditional sector has also grown along with the modern. The study shows a mixed response over future of traditional retail as traditional retailers and consumers believed in co-existence of both, but employees of modern retail saw future of traditional retail gloomy as the competition is getting intense. As society will continue to transform as a result of Globalisation and so will the emerging needs of people that would create a demand for these modern formats and products. But, at the same time the demands for the traditional goods will also be there which would help in maintaining the existence of these traditional formats that specialise in the indigenous variety of goods. In the contemporary times, both modern as well as traditional businesses are required as modern retailing would promote quality employment, improve business practices, encourage investments in support industries and modernize traditional retailing. On the other hand, traditional retailing will continue to cater to the needs of the masses and fulfil the local and indigenous demands of the consumers. Indian retail sector offers immense scope for the modern as well as traditional retailers to co-exist.

Of recent, the Indian Government has permitted 51 per cent FDI in the multi-brand retail sector and 100 per cent in single brand after a severe opposition which has opened up new dimensions in the debate on Indian retail sector. The immediate effect of further liberalisation in retail was visible in the form of sixty three applications received by government in 2013 for starting single brand retail operations (http://www.retailangle.com). It was equally expected that big players such as Wallmart, Tesco and Carrefour would move quickly for multibranding but not a single application was received till late because of onerous conditions and lack of clarity in the policy. The stringent conditions for retail environment have caused a great hurdle in receiving modern retail investments. Key conditions in the initial policy guidelines include a minimum investment of US$100 million, of which 50% needs to be in back-end infrastructure; 30% of products must be sourced from small enterprises; and retail outlets can be set up only in cities with a population of over one million.

As a result, India slipped to the 14th position from fifth position in 2012 on the Global Retail Development Index for 2013, paving way to three Latin American economies: Brazil, Chile and Uruguay (Business Standard, 2013). The slip of India has been attributed to the 'bumpy' policy scenario in India where two-thirds of the Indian states are still opposed to Foreign Direct Investment (in multi-brand retail) and there is quite an uncertainty over some key issues. Even the six year old Wallmart-Bharti Venture saw a split in 2013 which stated uncertain policy, negative political environment and high corruption risk in India as major reasons behind (http://profit.ndtv.com). It can be anticipated that such an ambiguity on the part of policy makers as well as general people can be consequential for retail sector as well as for Indian economic growth. We may argue on the basis of conclusions drawn from this study that Globalisation is a rational process with powerful social- economic and cultural dimensions. Developing nations are not just what they were fifty or more years ago, and they're not following the same path of development that they did. Sweeping changes in competitive landscape, including the presence of foreign competitors in domestic markets, are driving businesses to rethink their strategies and structures to reach beyond traditional boundaries. To avoid a clash between global economic interests and local political interests, businesses must know how to be responsive to the needs of communities in which they operate, as they globalize.

One of the key conelusions of this study has been that the impact of retail Globalisation is heterogeneous. Since the implementation of policy is recent, it can be envisaged with a degree of ambiguity, the kind of impact it is going to have on different sections of society. The situation may differ, as the competition gets intense. What emerges from the study is that retail Globalisation policy is going to radically alter social relations, spatial expression, traditional markets, lifestyles and consumption patterns of people and employment trend. The gains to be made in the process are so substantial for the powerful parties who drive Globalisation that it is difficult to see the limits of this push to deeper integration (Kaplinsky, 2005). Whatever the normative conclusions, the current policy environment might prove to be a relief for some, providing the opportunity to develop new paths of socal and economic development. For others, it might bring a setback. Hence, a balanced regulatory framework and competition policy is a must for traditional formats and the modern formats to co-exist.

Appendix I

Trade and Commerce (Punjab, Urban) Census 1991

**Main workers other than agricultural labourers and cultivators classified by

industrial category, educational qualification and sex.

Male	Female	Qualifications	Total
75801	3203	Illiterate	79004
12556	131	Below primary	12687
53568	509	Primary	54077
70551	483	Middle	71034
139860	1144	Matric	141004
28269	334	Higher secondary	28603
587	7	Diploma/certificate (non technical)	595
2127	55	Diploma/certificate(technical)	2182
60957	1958	Graduation(non technical)	62915
9735	721	Post Graduation (non technical)	10456
		Graduation/post graduation (technical)	
653	16	....................Medicine.................	669
824	33	........Agriculture/Dairy Farming......	857
144	3	......................Vetenary....................	147
30	0	....................Teaching.....................	30
2389	385	......................Others...............	2774
			467088

census 1991, Pp 177

** Main workers include those who had worked for major part of the year, i.e., who are engaged in any economically productive activity for 183 days or more during the year

Appendix II

Industrial Classification of Main workers by Retail Trade, in Amritsar (1991)

Retail Trade in Food, Beverage etc.	Total – 36787 Urban- 24383
Retail Trade in Textile (readymade, hosiery/knitted etc)	Total – 16464 Urban- 15403
Retail Trade in fuels, other household utilities and durables	Total – 6005 Urban-5186
Retail trade in n.e.c (stationary, books, agriculture inputs, industrial and transport equipment	Total – 8957 Urban-7632
Non specialized retail trade including non store retail trade	Total – 1537 Urban-1281
Retail trade elsewhere classified	Total – 2807 Urban-3122

* *Census 1991, Pp 907-908*

Appendix III

Trade and Commerce (Amritsar District, Urban) Census 1991

Main workers other than agricultural labourers and cultivators classified by Industrial category, educational qualification and sex

Male	Female	Qualifications	Total
11628	482	Illiterate	12110
2077	29	Below primary	2106
8301	76	Primary	8377
10951	72	Middle	11023
21706	175	Matric	21881
5885	66	Higher secondary	5951
89	1	Diploma/certificate (non technical)	90
299	5	Diploma/certificate(technical)	304
10205	304	Graduation(non technical)	10509
1420	77	Post Graduation (non technical)	1497
		Graduation/Post Graduation (technical)	
132	3	..............Engineering..............	135
125	3	................Medicine..................	128
23	0	...........Agriculture/Dairy Farming........	23
3	0	.................Vetenary.................	3

231	37	..............Teaching...............	268
6	0	.............Others............	6
73081	**1380**		**74411**

Appendix IV

Significant Employee Positions (www.nsdcindia.org) :

- **Store Manager/ Department Manager-** Responsible for the day-to-day management of a department/ store. Proficient with spreadsheet and word processor tools to analyze sales and generate sales reports. Ability to devise, suggest, as well as execute sales promotion programmes depending on the sales analysis. Understanding of various aspects of customer behaviour. For e.g., the profile of customer as user/buyer will have impact on selection of merchandise. The person should be able to communicate these insights Transaction processing.
- **Associate/ Billing associate Functional Skills-** The ease of transaction is a key factor in ensuring customer convenience. Key responsibilities involve accurate and quick transaction processing. Requisite computer skills. Understanding of transaction software/hardware such as bar code reading machines, etc. Knowledge of handling credit/debit card payments. Total cash &credit-card transactions and compare with cash register receipts and enter the results in financial records, reporting cash surpluses.
- **Customer service representative/ Sales Associate/Sales person-** Knowledge of current sales promotion schemes of the company and ability to communicate the same to the customers. Ability to sell - i.e., selling skills, knowledge of policies regarding exchanges. In depth knowledge of store offerings. The person should be aware of the offerings of competing stores/brands. For e.g., in case of sales person engaged in apparel retail, knowledge of type of fabrics, styles, etc. of competing brands would be important. Knowledge of product features such as : brand options - warranties - features and benefits, use/application- shelf life/use by dates, care and handling, storage requirements.
- **Merchandising Manager/Sr. Merchandising Manager-** Understanding and knowledge of current market trends - ability

to ensure that items in high demand get more share of the shelf space. For e.g. , an apparel retail merchandiser should know the colours, designs which are doing well at the sale counters and give more focus to the same. Knowledge of products and customer behaviour.

- **Purchase Manager/Category Manager**- Good understanding of the products purchased. Ability to track inventory levels. Knowledge of various sourcing alternatives and ability to search/ select various vendors.
- **Purchase Executive**- Identifying and screening of new vendors. Understand the characteristics of merchandise from probable vendors and communicate the promising vendors to the senior management.
- **Senior Manager**- Key responsibility is to ensure proper availability of merchandise in the retail outlets. Responsible for maintaining the warehouse operations. Should able to come up with continual improvements to drive down the logistics cost.
- **Marketing Manager**- Ability to coordinate with media agencies. Knowledge of CRM/sales promotion activities of competing retail outlets. Should be able to develop schemes which can break through the clutter.

Definations

- **Mall**- Is one or more buildings forming a complex of shops enclosed within a large structure, two-three stories high, may have entertainment facilities, theatre, fast food outlet, restaurant and parking area.
- **Speciality Store**- Narrow product line with deep assortment, viz apparel stores, book stores etc.
- **Departmental Store**- Several product lines- typically clothing, household goods and furnishings- with each line operated as a separate department managed by specialist buyers or merchandisers.
- **Supermarket**- Relatively large, low cost, low margin, high volume, self service operation designed to serve total needs for food, laundry and household maintenance products. It is usually situated near residential areas in order to be convenient to

consumers.The basic appeal at mart is availability if broad range of goods under single roof.

- **Convenience Stores-** Relatively small store located near residential area, open long hours, seven days a week and carrying a limited line of high turnover convenience products at slightly higher prices.
- **Discount Store-** Standard merchandise sold at lower prices with lower margin and higher volumes
- **Work Shift-** it is the time period during which a person is at work. It includes both long term night shifts and work schedules in which employees change or rotate shifts (www.wikipedia.com)

Appendix IV

Maps of Amritsar

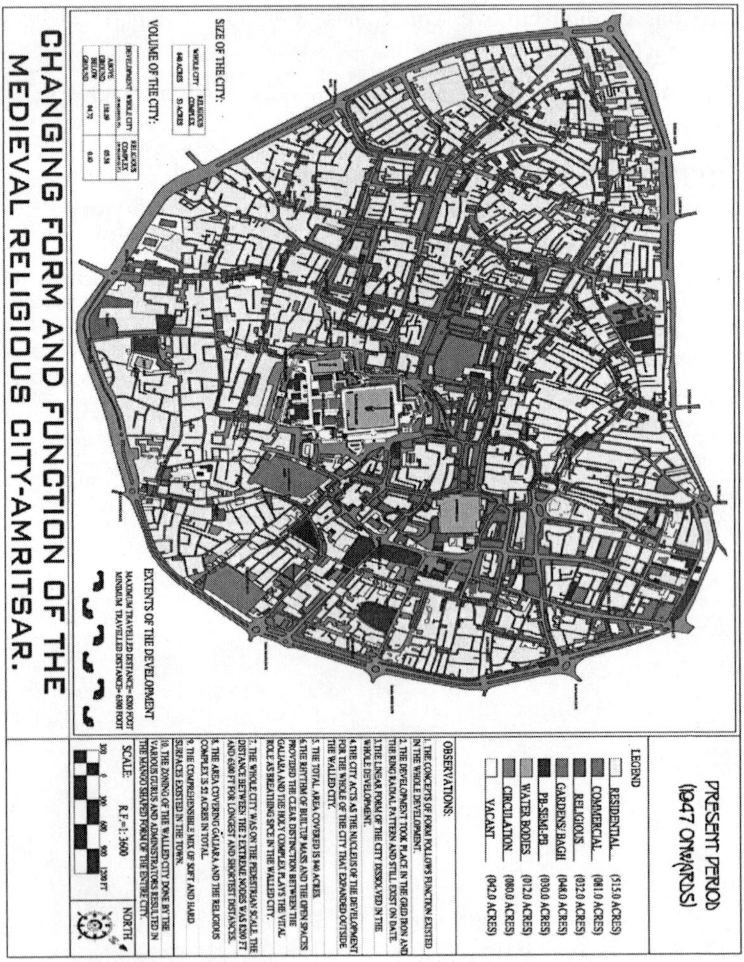

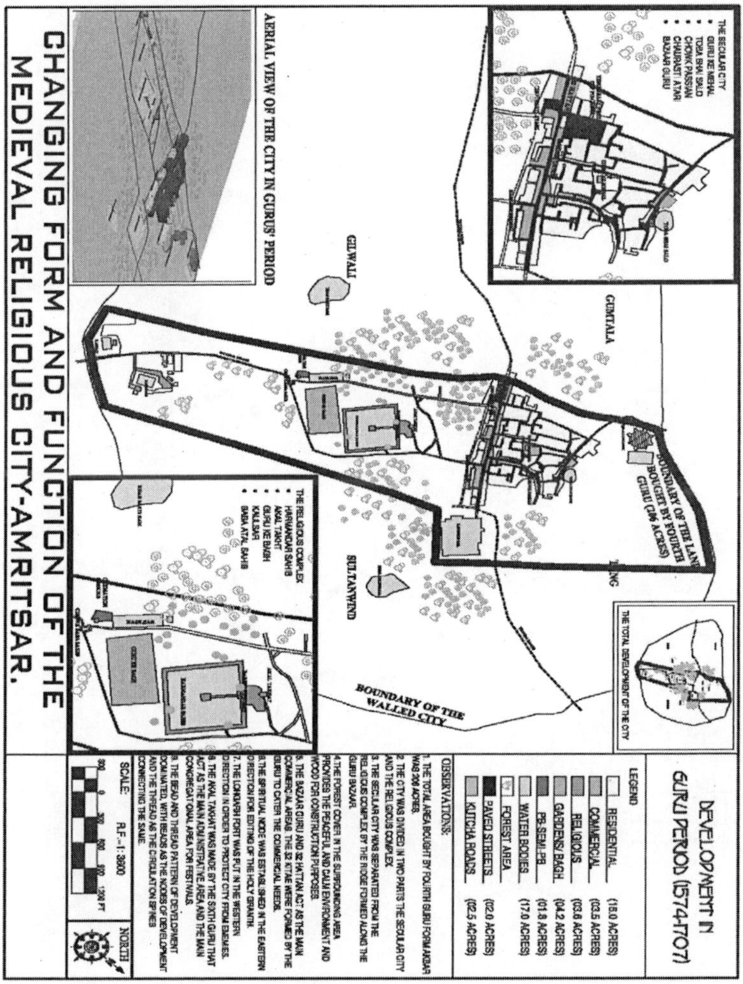
THE SECULAR CITY
GURU KE MEHAL
TOBA BHAI SALO
CHOWK PASSIAN
CHAURASTI ATARI
BAZAAR GURU
GUMTALA
BOUNDARY OF THE LAND BOUGHT BY FOURTH GURU (206 ACRES)
THE TOTAL DEVELOPMENT OF THE CITY
DEVELOPMENT IN GURU PERIOD (1574-1707)
LEGEND
RESIDENTIAL (16.0 ACRES)
COMMERCIAL (03.5 ACRES)
RELIGIOUS (03.6 ACRES)
GARDENS/ BAGH (04.2 ACRES)
PB-SEMI-PB (01.8 ACRES)
WATER BODIES (17.0 ACRES)
FOREST AREA
PAVED STREETS (02.0 ACRES)
KUTCHA ROADS (02.5 ACRES)
OBSERVATIONS:
1. THE TOTAL AREA BOUGHT BY FOURTH GURU FORM AKBAR WAS 206 ACRES.
2. THE CITY WAS DIVIDED IN TWO PARTS THE SECULAR CITY AND THE RELIGIOUS COMPLEX.
3. THE SECULAR CITY WAS SEPARATED FROM THE RELIGIOUS COMPLEX BY THE RIDGE FORMED ALONG THE GURU BAZAAR.
4. THE FOREST COVER IN THE SURROUNDING AREA PROVIDES THE PEACEFUL AND CALM ENVIRONMENT AND WOOD FOR CONSTRUCTION PURPOSES.
5. THE BAZAAR GURU AND 32 HATTAN ACT AS THE MAIN COMMERCIAL AREAS. THE 32 KITAE WERE FORMED BY THE GURU TO CATER THE COMMERCIAL NEEDS.
6. THE SPIRITUAL NODE WAS ESTABLISHED IN THE EASTERN DIRECTION FOR EDITING OF THE HOLY GRANTH.
7. THE LOHGARH FORT WAS PUT IN THE WESTERN DIRECTION IN ORDER TO PROTECT CITY FROM EMEMIES.
8. THE AKAL TAKHAT WAS MADE BY THE SIXTH GURU THAT ACT AS THE MAIN ADMINISTRATIVE AREA AND THE MAIN CONGREGATIONAL AREA FOR FESTIVALS.
9. THE BEAD AND THREAD PATTERN OF DEVELOPMENT DOMINATED, WITH BEADS AS THE NODES OF DEVELOPMENT AND THE THREAD AS THE CIRCULATION SPINES CONNECTING THE SAME.
SCALE: R.F.-1: 3600
300 0 300 600 900 1200 FT
NORTH
BOUNDARY OF THE WALLED CITY
SULTANWIND
GILWALI
AERIAL VIEW OF THE CITY IN GURUS' PERIOD
THE RELIGIOUS COMPLEX
HARMANDAR SAHIB
AKAL TAKHT
GURU KE BAGH
KAULSAR
BABA ATAL SAHIB
CHANGING FORM AND FUNCTION OF THE MEDIEVAL RELIGIOUS CITY-AMRITSAR.

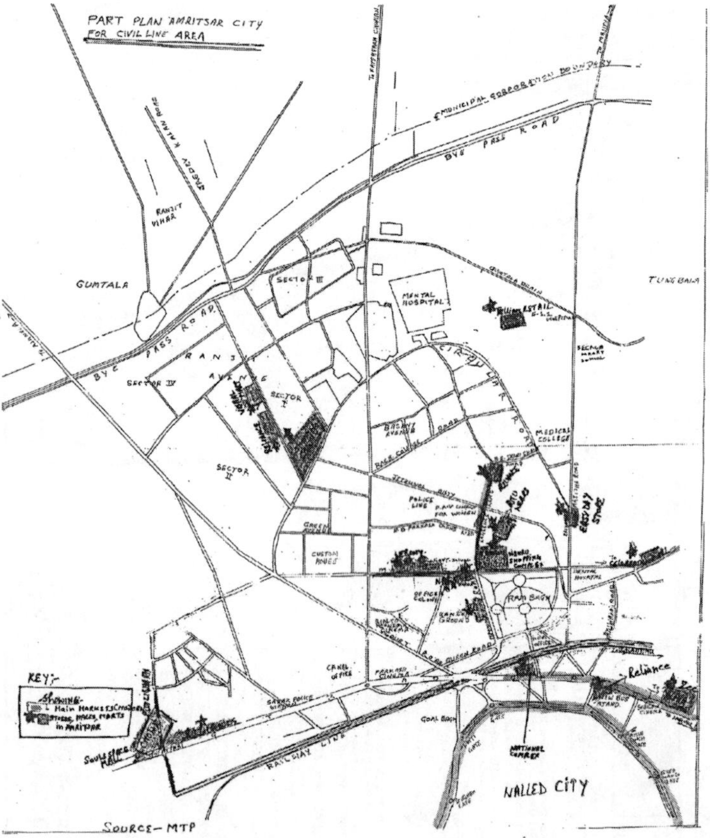
PART PLAN AMRITSAR CITY
FOR CIVIL LINE AREA
MUNICIPAL CORPORATION BOUNDARY
BYE PASS ROAD
RANJIT VIHAR
GUMTALA
SECTOR III
MENTAL HOSPITAL
TUNGBALA
SECTOR IV
RANJIT AVENUE
SECTOR I
SECTOR II
MEDICAL COLLEGE
POLICE LINE
CUSTOM HOUSE
RAM BAGH
DENTAL HOSPITAL
QUEEN ROAD
CANAL OFFICE
RAILWAY LINE
GOAL BAGH
NEW BUS STAND
Reliance
NATIONAL COMPLEX
WALLED CITY
KEY:-
Main Markets, Stores, Malls, Marts in Amritsar
SOURCE- MTP

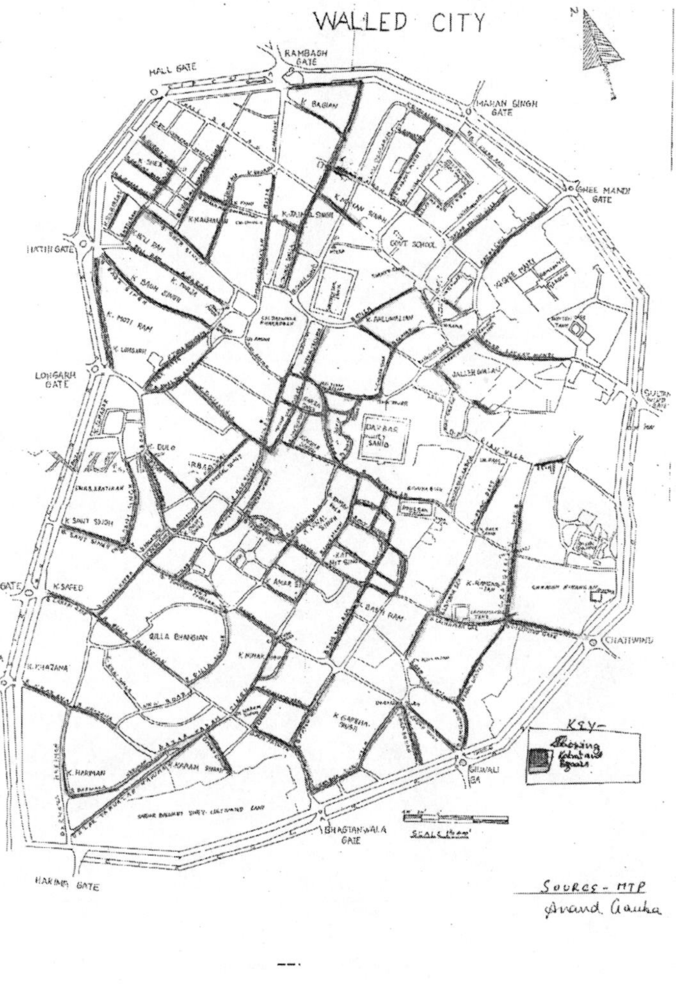
WALLED CITY
N
RAMBAGH GATE
HALL GATE
MAHAN SINGH GATE
GHEE MANDI GATE
HATHI GATE
LOHGARH GATE
LAHORI GATE
KHAZANA GATE
HAKIMA GATE
BHAGTANWALA GATE
CHATIWIND
GILWALI GATE
GOVT SCHOOL
DARBAR SAHIB
QILLA BHANGIAN
K. BABIAN
K. MOTI RAM
K. BAGH SINGH
K. SAFED
K. KHAZANA
K. HAKIMAN
K. SANT SINGH
K. DULO
K. AMAR SINGH
K. GARBHA SINGH
JALLIANWALA BAGH
KEY-
SCALE
SOURCE - MTP
Anand Gauba

References

Ahlawat, S.R. (ed.) 2008. *Economic Reforms and Social Transformation.* Jaipur: Rawat.

Amin, Mohammad. 2008. *Labour Regulation and Employment in India's Retail Stores.* World Bank: Washington DC.

Appadurai, A.1990. "Disjunctive and Differences in the Global Cultural Economy" in M. Featherstone (ed): Global Culture. London: Sage.

Appelrouth, Scott. A. et.al. 2008. *Classical and Contemporary Sociological Theory: Text and Readings.* Los Angeles: Pine Forge Press.

Athique, Andrain and Douglas Hill. 2010. *The Multiplex in India: A Cultural Economy Of Urban Leisure.* London: Routledge.

Baijal, Pardeep. 2002. "Privatisation: Compulsion and Option for Economic Reforms", *Economic and Political Weekly,* Vol. XXXVII, No. 41, Pp. 4189-4195.

Bal, Gurpreet. 1995. *Development and Change in Punjab.* New Delhi: National Book Organization.

----- 2006. "Entrepreneurship among Diasporic Communities: A Comparative Examination of Patidars of Gujarat and Jats of Punjab", *The Journal of Entrepreneurship.* Vol. 15, No. 2, Pp. 181- 203.

Balakrishanan, Pulapre.2003. "Globalisation, Growth and Justice", *Economic and Political Weekly,* Vol. XXXVIII, No 30, Pp. 3166-3172.

Balakrishnan, A. 2007. *Impact of Globalisation and Retaining Strategies for Labour and Employment.* Delhi: Kalpaz Publications.

Banerjee, Arindam and Suresh Divakar. 2001. "Thresholds in a Promotion Intensive Retail Environment: Implication on Consumer Purchase Behaviour and Managerial Insight", Vikalpa, Vol. 26, No. 2, Pp. 15-39.

Basant, Rakesh and Sabastien Moris. 2000. "Competition Policy in India: Issues for Globalizing Policy", Economic and Political Weekly, Vol. XXXV, No. 31, Pp. 2735-2747.

Bawa, R.S and P.S. Raikhey.2007. *Globalisation and Punjab Economy: Issues in Agriculture and Small Scale Industry.* Amritsar: Guru Nanak Dev University Press.

Bert, N. Adama. 2002. *Contemporary Sociological Thought.* London: Pine Forge Press.

Bhati, Usha. 2006. *Foreign Direct Investments: Contemporary Issues.* New Delhi: Deep and Deep Publications.

Black, Jan. Knippers. 2007. *Development in Theory and Practice* (2nd ed.). Jaipur: Rawat.

Boddy, Martin and Michael Parkinson. 2004. *City Matters: Competitiveness, Cohesion and Urban Performace.* UK: Polity.

Bruno, Dorin. 2003. The Indian Entrepreneur: *A Sociological Profile of Businessmen and their Practices*. Delhi: Manohar.

Buck, Nick and Lan, Gordon (ed.). 2005. *Changing Cities: Rethinking Urban Competitiveness, Cohesion and Governance.* New York: Palgrave.

Bucholtz, Mary. 2007. "Shoptalk: Branding, Consumption and Gender in American Middle Class Youth Interaction" in Bonnie S Mcelhinny (ed): *Words, Worlds and Material Girls:Language, Gender, Globalisation.* New York: Mouton De Gruyter

Business Standard India. 2008. Delhi: B.S.Books

Business Line. 2005. "FDI in Retail- Is More a Question of Jobs, Not Ownership" Sept 29.

Caplow, Theodore. 1970. *Sociology of Work.* Allahabad: Central Book Depot.

Chacko, Priyaram. M. 1991. *Caste Business and Entrepreneurship in South India.* New Delhi: Kanishka Publishing House.

Chanda, Rupa. 2003. "General Agreement on Trade in Services: Implications for Social Policy Making", *Economic and Political Weekly,* Vol. XXXVIII, No.16, Pp. 1567-1578.

Chakarborty, S.K. 1991. *Managerial Effectiveness and Quality of Worklife: Indian Insights.* New Delhi: Tata Mc Graw Hill.

Chaudhari, Sudeep. 2003. "Trade in Services: Policy Issues", *Economic and Political Weekly,* Vol. XXXVIII, No. 34, Pp. 3554.

Chattopadhyay, Suhrid. Sankar. 2007. "Unique Co- existence", *Frontline,* Vol. 24, No. 13, June- July 13, Pp. 14-16.

Chinnammai, S. 2008. Globalisation and Consumption Pattern: The Indian Perspective in Gyanan Chandrakar (ed): '*Globalisation and Decentralised Development*'. New Delhi: Deep and Deep Publications. Pp 307-321.

Dasgupta, Biplab. 2005. Globalisation: India's Adjustment Experience. London: Sage.

Dasgupta, Samir. 2006. "Globalisation and its Future Shock" in Samir Dasgupta and Ray Kiely (ed): *Globalisation and After.* New Delhi: Sage publishers. Pp. 143-181.

Datta, V.N. 1967. Amritsar: Past and Present. Amritsar: The Municipal Committee

Davis, Louis.E and Bert. B. Cherns. 1975. *The Quality of Working life: Cases and Commentary,* Vol.2 . London: The Free Press

Delamontte, Yves. 1984. *Quality of Life in International Perspective.* Geneva: International Labour Office.

Dhangare, D.N. 2012. "Globalisation: Towards an Alternative View" in N Jayaram and D Rajsekhar (ed): *Vulnerability and Globalisation: Perspectives and Analysis from India.* Jaipur: Rawat.

Dhingra, O.P and Pathak, U.K 1972. "Professional Background of Indian Professional Managers PACT 11-17", *Indian Psychological Abstracts.* Pp.254

Dholakia, Archana. R. 2003. "Feminization of Poverty and Trade Liberalisation", *Economic and Political Weekly,* Vol. XXXVIII, No. 18, Pp.1810-1812.

Dholakia, Ravindra H. 2001. "Economic Reforms and Trade Performance Private Sector in India", Economic and Political Weekly, Vol. XXXVI, No. 49, Pp. 4566.

Drene, Steve. 2008. *Globalisation on the Ground: Media and the Transformation of Culture, Class and Gender in India.* Los Angeles: Sage.

Economic Survey (2001-02). New Delhi: Government of India Publication.

Edgel, Stephen. 2006. *The Sociology of Work: Community and Change in Paid and Unpaid Work.* London: Sage.

Elliot, Anthony (ed.) *1999. Contemporary Social Theory.* Massachusetts: Blackwell.

Frank, A.G. 1971. *Capitalism and Underdevelopment in Latin America* (revised, ed.,) Harmondsworth: Penguin

Gauba, Anand. 1988. *Amritsar: A Study in Urban History (1840-1984. Jallandhar: ABS Publishers.*

Gadgil, D.R. 1959. *Origins of Modern Indian Business Class.* New York: Institute of Pacific Relations.

Gopptu, Nandini. 2009. "Neoliberal Subjectivity, Enterprise Culture and New Workplaces:

Organized Retail and Shopping Malls in India", *Economic and Political Weekly,* Vol. 44, No. 2, Pp 45-52.

Ghosh, D.N. 2000. "Wall Street *Entrepreneurs: Warts and All", Economic and Political Weekly,* Vol. XXXV, No. 38. Pp.3371-3374.

----- 2005. "Machiavellian Virtue and Economic Globalism", *Economic and Political Weekly,* Vol. XL, No. 31, Pp. 3360-3361.

Ghurye, 1969. Caste and Race in India. Bombay: Popular.

Giddens, A. 1990. *The Consequences of Modernity.* Cambridge: Polity Press.

---- 2006. Sociology (5th ed). Cambridge: Polity Press.

Goel, Anshu. 2010. *"Retailing Opportunities in a Changing Global Business Environment: An Indian Business Prespective"*. Paper Presented in National Seminar on Managerial Challenges in 21st century at Birla School of Management and Techonology (Proceedings)

Goffman, Erving. 1956. *Presentation of Self in Everyday Life.* Edinburgh: University of Edinburgh.

Grewal, J.S. 2008. *The City of Golden Temple. Amritsar: Guru Nanak Dev University*

Gupta, Ashish. 1994. *Indian Entrepreneurial Culture.* UK: Wishwa Parkashan.

Gupta, S.P. 2004. *The Punjab: An Overview.* Chandigarh: Ess Pee Publication. Pp.264

Guruswamy, Mohan and Kamal Sharma. et. al. 2005. "FDI in India's Retail Sector: More Bad than Good?", *Economic and Political Weekly,* Vol. XL, No. 7, Pp. 619-623.

Guruswamy, Mohan. 2005. "Economic Growth and Development in West Bengal", *Economic and Political Weekly,* Vol. 40, No. 24.

Harshe, Rajan. 2002. "Marxism, Capitalism and Globalisation", *Economic and Political Weekly,* Vol. XXXVII, No. 15, Pp. 1407-1412.

---- 2005. "Changing Profile of Imperialism in Global Political Order/Disorder", *Economic and Political Weekly,* Vol. XL, No. 20, Pp. 2073-2076.

Harvey, D. 1989. *The Conditions of Post Modernity.* U.K: Oxford

Hazlehurst, Leighton. W. 1966. *Entrepreneurship and the Merchant Caste in a Punjabi City.* Duke: University Press.

Hoselitz, Bert. F. 1960. *Sociological Aspects of Economic Growth.* New York: Free Press.

Hutton. 1969. *Caste in India: Its Nature, Function and Origin.* Bombay: Oxford University Press.

ICRIER. *2008. FDI in Retail Sector, INDIA (2005-2007)*. New Delhi: Govt. of India Publication (Dept of Consumer Affairs, Ministry of Consumer Affairs, Food and Public Distribution).

ILO. 1984. *Quality of Working Life in international Perspective*. Geneva: International labour Organization.

India Luxury Report. 2006. Gurgaon: KSA Technopak

India Retail Report, 2007. New Delhi: Images Research.

India Retail Report, 2009. New Delhi: Images Research.

ISSER, G.P. 2002. *Changing Face of Poverty and Globalisation*. New Delhi: Gyan Publishers

IT Retailing, 2006. *"Are You in the Loop"*, July 26

Jain, S.C. 1971. *The Indian Manager. Bombay:* Somaiya

Jayaram, N and D Rajsekhar. 2012. *Vulnerability and Globalisation: Perspectives and Analysis from India.* Japiur: Rawat

Jha, Madhu. 2005. *Woman in Decision Making Positions*. Delhi: Kanishka.

Jhaweri, Narendera. 2003. "India's Growth Chase: High Aspiration, Low Inspiration", *Economic and Political Weekly,* Vol. XXXVIII, No. 41, Pp. 4338-4350.

Johnson, J and P.T. Raveendran. 2009. "Retail Patronage Behaviour and Shoppers Segmentation: A Study among Shoppers of Organized Retailers", *Journal of Management*.

Jolly, U.S. 2010. *Challenges for Mega Cities*. New Delhi: Concept Publishers.

Joseph, Mathew and Nirupama Soundararajan et.al., 2008. *Impact of Organized Retailing on Unorganized Sector.* India: Indian Council for Research on International Economic Relations.

---- 2009. *Retail in India: A Critical Assessment.* New Delhi: Academic Foundation.

Judge, Paramjit and Bal, Gurpreet. 1996. *Strategies of Social Change.* New Delhi: MD Publications.

Judge, Paramjit and S.L. Sharma, et.al. 2003. *Development, Gender and Diaspora: Context of Globalisation.* Jaipur: Rawat.

Judge, Paramjit.S. 2008. "Impact of Liberalisation, Privatisation and Globalisation on Agrarian Structure", in S.R.Ahlawat (ed): *Economic Reforms and Social Transformation.* Jaipur: Rawat.

Kahlon, Anuradha. 2007. "Impact of Malls and Small Shops and Hawkers', *Economic and Political Weekly*, Vol. 42, No. 22, Pp. 2063- 2066.

Kambhampati, Uma. S. 2004. *Development and the Developing World*. Cambridge: Polity.

Kannan, K.P. 2004. "For a Fair Globalisation", *Economic and Political Weekly,* Vol. XXXIX, No. 38, Pp. 4217-4219.

Kaplinsky, Raphel. 2005. *Globalisation, Poverty and Inequality*. UK: Polity

Kaul, Subhashini. 2007. "Hedonism and Culture: Impact on Shopping Behaviour- A Research Agenda", *Vikalpa*, Vol.32, No. 3.

Kaushik, Kshma, V and Kaushik Dutta. 2012. India Means Business: How the Elephant Earned *Its Stripes*. New Delhi:Oxford

Kasarda, John. D and Allan, M. Parnell. (ed.). 1993. Third World *Cities: Problems, Policies and Prospects.* London: Sage.

Kapoor, A.N and V.P. Gupta, et.al., 2007. *Dictionary of Sociology.* New Delhi: Radha Publishers.

Katakam, Anupama. 2007. "Gender Factor". *Frontline,* Vol. 24, No.13, July 13, Pp. 17-19.

Kaur, Madanjit. 1977. "The Founding of Amritsar in a Historical Perspective", *The Journal of Sikh Studies,* Vol. 42, No. 2.

---- 1978. "Amritsar under Guru Arjun Dev and Guru Har Gobind (1581-1632)", *Journal of Sikh Studies,* Vol. 5, No.2.

Kelegana, Saman. 2009. *Trade in Services in South Asia: Opportunities and Risks of Liberalisation.* Los Angeles: Sage.

Kumar, Nagesh. 2000. "Economic Reforms and Their Macro-Economic Impact", *Economic Political Weekly,* Vol. XXXV, No. 10, Pp. 807.

Kumar, Ashutosh. 2002. "Globalisation and After", *Economic and Political Weekly,* Vol. XXXVII, No. 4, Pp. 308-312.

Kumar, Ramesh. S. et.al., 2007. " The Role of Point of Purchse in Shopping Behaviour in an Emerging Market- The Indian Context", *Indian Retailing Review,* June- Dec

Lal, Vinay. 2005. "Wall Mart Story", *Economic and Political Weekly, Vol. XL, No. 25, Pp. 2477-78.*

Lencher, Frank,J. and John Boli. 2005. *World Culture: Origins and Consequences*. UK: Blackwell Publishing.

Loudan, Wrenn. Bruce, et.al., 2002. *Marketing Research: Text and Cases.* New York: Haworth Press.

Saiyadain, M.s and Monappa, A. 1977. *Profile of Indian Managers.* New Delhi: Vidya Vahini

Macarov, David. 1980. *Work and Welfare: The Unholy Alliance.* London: Sage.

Macionis, John.J. 2005. *Sociology (4th ed.).* New Delhi: Pearson.

Mahadevia, Darshini. 2003. *Globalisation, Urban Reforms and Metropolitan Response in*

Marcuse, Herbert. 1968. *One Dimensional Man: Studies in the Ideology of Advanced Industrial Society.* London: Routledge and Keagan Paul.

Marquardt, Raymond.A. et.al. 1979. *Retail Management, Satisfaction of Consumer Needs (ed.II).* Hinsdale: The Dryden Press.

Mathur, Manish and Om Prakash.2010. " *Retail Consumer Behaviour".* Paper presented in National Seminar on Managerial Challanges in 21st century at Birla School of Management and Techonology, (Proceedings).

Mehta, Pratap. Bhanu. 2003. "A New Foreign Policy", *Economic and Political Weekly*, Vol. XXXVIII, No. 30, Pp. 2173-3175.

Mein, Benard and Thai Khuin. 1999. "FDI and pattern of trade-Malaysian experience"

Economic and Political Weekly, Vol. XXXIV, No. 22, Pp. M-72-77

Merton, R.K. 1968. *Social Theory and Social Structure.* New Delhi: Amerind.

Michael, S.M. 2012. "Globalisation and Culture: Solidarity with Social Movements for a Humane Society" in Ishwar Modi (ed); *Modernization, Globalisation and Social Transformation.* Jaipur: Rawat.

Mishra, B.B. 1961. *The Indian Middle Classes: Their Growth in Modern Times. Delhi:* Oxford University Press.

Mishra, Sangeeta. 1993. *Status of Woman in Changing Urban Hindu Family.* Delhi: Radha Publishers.

Mitra, Anup. 2009. *"Impact of Trade on Service Sector Employment in India",* Working Paper Series No.E/289/2009.)

Mitra, Jyoti. 1997. *Woman and Society: Equality and Empowerment.* New Delhi: Kanishka

Mohammad, Anu. 2006. "Globalisation and Economic Transformation in a Peripheral Economy: The Bangladesh Experience", *Economic and Political Weekly,* Vol. XLI, No.15.

Mukherjee, Arpita and Nitisha Patel. 2005. *FDI in Retail Sector: India.* New Delhi: Academic foundation, Indian Council for Research in International Economic Relations.

Mulhern, Charlotte. 1998. "Word on the Street: Effect of Retail Store Chains on Small Stores", *Entrepreneur, Feb.*

Mulky, Avinash and Rajendra Nargundkar. 2003. "Modernization in Indian Retailing: Managerial and Policy Perspective", *Udyog Pragati,* Vol. 27, No. 2, April- June, Pp. 1-8.

Myers, C.A. 1960. Industrial Relations in India. Bombay: Asia Publishing House.

Nadarajah, M and Ann. T.Y. (ed.). 2007. *Urban Crises: Culture and Sustainability of Cities.* Jaipur:Rawat.

Nagraj, R. 2003. "Industiral Policy and Policy Since 1980", Economic and Political Weekly, Vol. XXXVIII, No.35. Pp. 3707.

---- 2003. " Foreign Direct Investment in India in the 1990s: Trends and Issues", *Economic and Political Weekly*, Vol.XXXVIII, No.36, Pp. 1701-1711.

Nayyar, Baldev. Raj. 2003. "Economic Globalisation and its Advance: From Shallow to Deep Integration", *Economic and Political Weekly,* Vol. XXXVIII, No.45, Pp. 4776-4782.

Nayyar, Deepak. 2006. "Economic Growth in Independent India: Lumbering Elephant or Running Tiger?", *Economic and Political Weekly,* Vol. XLI, No. 15, Pp. 1451-1457.

---- 2008. Trade and Globalisation. Delhi: Oxford University Press

Nijman, Jan. 2000. "Mumbai's Real Estate Market in 1990s- Deregulation, Global Money and Casino Capitalism", *Economic and Political Weekly,* Vol. XXXV, NO. 7, Pp. 575-582.

Omvedt, Gail. 2005. "Capitalism and Globalisation Dalits and Adivasis", *Economic and Political Weekly,* Vol. XL, No. 47, Pp. 4881-4885.

Pandey, Vinita.2009. *Crises of Middle Class*. Jaipur: Rawat.

Pandit, D.P. 1957. "Creative Response in Indian Economy", *Economic Weekly,* Vol.9, No. 8, Feb 23.

Panigrahi, Nilkantha and Premananda.P. 2000. *Trading Community of India:* An Anthropological Study of Ethinicity. Jaipur: Rawat

Prasad, H. Prdhan. 1997. "Liberalisation in Theory and Practice", *Economic and Political Weekly,* Vol. XXXII, No. 13, Pp. 645-646.

Purohit, H.C. and Kavita. 2009. "Survival Strategy for Traditional Retailers in the Era of Modern Retailing", *Asia- Pacific Journal of Social Sciences,* Vol. 1, No.2, June- Dec, Pp 198-213.

Raheja, Anu and Singh, Nivedita 2010. *"Changing Face of Retailing in India"*. Paper presented in National Seminar on Managerial

Challanges in 21st century at Birla School of Management and Techonology, (Proceedings).

Rahman, Zinab. 2005. *Woman and Society.* Delhi: Kalpaz Publishers.

Rajan, Ramkishan, S. 2004. "Measures to Attract FDI: Investment Promotion, Incentives and Policy Intervention", *Economic and Political Weekly,* Vol. XXXIX, No.1.

Rajagopal, Arvind. 2001. "Thinking Through Emerging Market: Brand Logics and Cultured Forms of Political Society in India", *Economic and Political Weekly*, Vol. XXXVI, No. 9, Pp. 773-781.

Ramaswamy, Ramana. 2003. "Globalisation Capital Flows and Emerging Markets", *Economic and Political Weekly,* Vol. XXXVIII, No. 5, Pp. 449-451.

Rao, Lakshman. V. 1986. *Industrial Entrepreneurship in India.* Allahabad: Chug Publishers.

Rao, P.N. 2008. "Globalisation and Indian Economy: Impact and Evaluation" in Gyanan Chandrakar (ed): *Globalisation and Decentralised Development* New Delhi: Deep and Deep Publications, Pp 102- 114.

Rao, R.R. Mohan and S. Simhadri (ed.) 1999. *Indian Cities: Towards Next Millennium.* Jaipur:Rawat.

Rao, S.L. 1998. "Brand Building in Indian Industry", *Economic and Political Weekly,* Vol. XXXIII, No. 40, Pp. 2566-2568.

---- 2000. "India's Rapidly Changing Consumer Markets", *Economic and Political Weekly,* Vol. XXXV, No. 40, Pp. 3570-3572.

---- 2001. "Foreign Investment in Retail Trade", *Economic and Political Weekly,* Vol. XXXVI, No. 41, Pp. 3891-3892.

Ray, C.N. 2003. *Liberalisation and Urban Social Services.* Jaipur: Rawat.

Ray, Rajat,.K. (ed.) 1994. *Entrepreneurship and Industry in India: 1800- 1947.* Bombay: Oxford University Press.

Ray, Ranjan. 2003. "Understanding Globalisation", *Economic and Political Weekly*, Vol. XXX VIII, No. 2, Pp.121-122.

Ray, Saon. 2004. "MNE's Strategic Alliance and Efficiency of Firms", *Economic and Political Weekly,* Vol. XXXIX, No. 5, Pp. 434-439.

Reddy, Narsimha. D. 2008. Globalisation and Decentralised Development: Bringing Back the Nation State in Gyana Chandrakar (ed): *Globalisation and Decentralised Development,* New Delhi: Deep and Deep Publication.

Robertson, Ronald. 1992. *"Globalisation: Social Theory and Global Culture"*. London: Sage Publications.

Robins, Nick. 2006. *The Corporation that Changed the World: How the East India Company Shaped the Modern MN*. Orient Longman: New Delhi.

Rondinelli, Dennis. A and John M Heffron. 2008. *Globalisation and Change in Asia.* New Delhi: Viva.

Samir, Amin. 1976. Unequal Development: An Essay on the Social Formations of Peripheral Capitalism. New York: Monthly Review Press.

Sandhu, Ranvinder. Singh and Jasmeet Sandhu. 2007. *Globalizaing Cities: Inequality and Segregation in Developing Countries.* Jaipur: Rawat.

Sarma, EAS. 2005. "Need for Caution in Retail FDI", *Economic and Political Weekly,* Vol. XL, No. 46.

Saiyadain, Lash. S. and J Urry. 1994. *Economics of Signs and Space*. London: Sage

Scott, Allen.J. 2000. *The Cultural Economy of the Cities.* London: Sage Publications

Sethi, 2007. "Curious Practices", *Frontline,* Vol. 24, No.13, June- July.

Shah, Amita. 2011. "Retail Chains for Agro/Food Products: Inclusive or Exclusive", *Economic and Political Weekly,* Vol. XLVI, No. 33. Pp. 25-28

Sharma, Kamal and Jeevan Prakash Mohanty. 2005. "FDI in Retail: A Question of Jobs, Not Ownership", *Business Line, Sept* 29.

Sharma, K.L. 2003. "The Social Organization of Urban Space: A Case Study of Chanderi-A Small Town in Central India", Contributions *to Indian Sociology,* Vol. 37, No 3, Sept- Dec.

---- 2007. *Indian Social Structure and Changes.* Jaipur: Rawat.

Sharma, Rachana. 2010. "Contouring Exclusion in an Urban Social Milieu", Guru Nanak Journal of Sociology, Vol. 31, No1, 2.

Sharma, S.K. 1986. *Development: Socio- Cultural Dimensions.* Jaipur: Rawat.

Sharma, S.L. 2003. "Globalisation and Socio-Cultural Discontents", in Paramjit Singh Judge (ed): *Development, Gender and Diaspora- Context of Globalisation. Jaipur: Rawat.*

Shaw, Annapurna. (ed.,) 2007. *Indian Cities in Transition.* Chennai: Orient Longman.

Siddharth, Mallavaarapu. 2005. "Globalisation and an Indian View", *Economic and Political Weekly,* Vol. XL, No.8, Pp. 737-739.

Siddharthan, N.S. 1999. "WTO and the Globalisation of the Enterprise", *Economic and Political Weekly,* Vol. XXXV, No. 10, Pp. 1287-1291.

---- 2004. "Globalisation: Productivity, Efficiency and Growth", *Economic and Political Weekly,* Vol. XXXIX, No.5, Pp. 420-422.

Singh, Daljit. 2004. *Punjab: Socio- Economic Conditions (1501-1700 AD).* Delhi: Commonwealth.

Singh, Jaspal. 2003. *Rationalization of Social life.* New Delhi: Kanishka Publishers.

Singh, Fauja. 1977. *The City of Amritsar: An Introduction.* Patiala: Punjabi University Press.

Singh, Gopal. 1987. *Punjab Today.* New Delhi: Intellectual Publishers.

---- 1994. *Past, Present and Future.* New Delhi: Ajanta.

Grewal, J.S. 2006. *Religious Movements and Institutions in Medieval India. India:* Oxford University.

Singh, Kamla. 1992. *Woman Entrepreneurs.* New Delhi: Ashish Publishers.

Singh, Narinder. 1988. "Amritsar: A Blend of Sacred and Secular", *The Sikh Review.* Vol. 36, No. 4, Pp. 11.

Singh, Rajendra. 2001. *Social Movements: Old and New.* India: Sage.

Sinha, B.P. 1990. *Work Culture in the Indian Context. New* Delhi: Sage.

---- 2004. *Multinationals in India: Managing the Interference of Culture.* New Delhi: Sage.

Sinha, Piyush. Kumar. 2003. "Shopping Orientation in the Evolving Indian Market", *Vikalpa.* Vol. 28, No. 2, Pp. 13-22.

Smart, B. 1993. *Post Modernity.* London : Routledge

Sklair, Leslie. 1995. *Sociology of the Global System.* London: Prentice Hall.

Smelser, Neil. J. 1965. *Readings on Economic Sociology*. New Jersy: Prentice Hall.

Sridhar, Kala. Seetharam. 2010. *State of Urban Services in Indian Cities: Spending and Financing.* Delhi: Oxford University Press.

Sridhar, Y. 2007. "Retail Invasion", *Frontline*, Vol. 24, No.13, June- July, Pp. 4-13.

Stevenson, Deorah. 2009. *Cities and Urban Culture.* Japiur: Rawat.

Stiglitz, Joseph.A. 2002. *Globalisation and its Discontents*. London : The Penguin Press.

Stiglitz, Joseph E, 2002. "Employment, Social Institute and Societal Well Being", *International Labour Review,* Vol. 141, No. 1-2.

Subramaniam, V.1971. *The Managerial Class in India.* New Delhi: All India Management Association.

Swedberg, Richard. 2004. *Principles of Economic Sociology.* Jaipur: Rawat.

Thakur, Manish. 2012. 'Globalisation, Middle Class Consumerism and the Declining Welfare State: Some Sociological Reflections" in N Jayaran and D Rajsekhar (ed); *Vulnerability and Globalisation: Perspectives and Analysis from India.* Jaipur: Rawat

Timberg, Thomas, A. 1978. *The Marwaris: From Traders to Industrialists.* New Delhi: Vikas

Timberg, Thomas. 2004. " Why is India Shining", *Economic and Political Weekly,* Vol.XXXIX, No. 39 Pp. 4324- 4328.

Tiwari, Sanjay. 2011. Service Sector in India: Performance and Reforms. *Zenith,* Vol 1, Issue 7 (Nov) Pp. 155-170.

Tomlinson , John. 1999. *Globalisation and Culture.* University of Chicago Press: Chicago.

Tripathi, Dwijendra and Jumani Jyoti. 2007. *The Concise Oxford History of Indian Business.* Delhi:Oxford University Press.

Trivedi , Madhusudan. 1991. *Entrepreneurship among Tribals.* Jaipur: Printwell.

Turok, Ivan et.al., 2004. "Sources of city Prosperity and Cohesion: The Case of Glosgow and Edinburg" in Boddy Martin and Michael Parkinson (ed); *City Matters: Competitiveness, Cohesion and Urban Governance. UK: Polity.*

Uberoi, J.P.S. 2008. "Sociology of Commerce and Industry: The Three Lives of Things", *Sociological Bulletin,* Vol 57, No1, Pp. 41-59.

Valaskakis, K. 1999. "Globalisation as Theatre", *International Social Science Journal,* Vol. 51,No. 160, Pp. 153.

Veblen, T. 1953. The Theory of the Leisure Class. New York: Mentor.

Virmani, Arvind. 2003. "India's External Reforms Modest Globalisation Significant Gains". *Economic and Political Weekly,* Vol. XXXVIII, No. 32, Pp. 3373-3390.

Voyce, Malcom. 2007. "Shopping Malls in India", *Economic and Political Weekly*, Vol. XLII, No. 22, Pp. 2055-60.

Volti, Rudi. 2008. *An Introduction to the Sociology of Work and Occupation.* Los Angeles: Pine Forge Press.

Waters, Malcom. 1995, *"Globalisation"*. London: Routledge.

Wattal, Jayshree. 1997. "Implementing the TRIPS Agreement I: Policy Option Open to India", *Economic and Political Weekly,* Vol. XXXII, No. 39, Pp. 2641-2668.

Watson, Tony.J. 1980. *Sociology of Work and Industry*. London: Routledge and Kegan Paul.

Theses/ Dissertation

Bal, Jatinder. B.K. 1994. *"Woman Entrepreneur in Amritsar City"*. M.Phil. Dissertation, Department of Sociology, G.N.D. University, Amritsar.

Bandhu, Vishav. 1989. *"Industrial Development in the Punjab: A Study of Amritsar (1849-1947)"*. M.Phil Dissertation, Department of History, G.N.D.University, Amritsar.

Jaggi, Sangeeta. 1989. *"Business Communities in the City of Amritsar- Late 19th to Early 20th Century"*. M.Phil Dissertation, Department of History, G.N.D.University, Amritsar.

Kalia, Rajesh.2010. *"Displacement* and *Rehabilitation: A Sociological Study of Galiarra Scheme in Amritsar"*. PhD Thesis, Sociology, G.N.D. University, Amritsar.

Kaur, Kanwaljit. 1996. *"Non Punjabi Business Communities in Amritsar City"*. M.A. Dissertation, Department of Sociology, G.N.D. University, Amritsar.

Kaur, Sukhwinder. 1985. *"Business Communities in Punjab"*. M.Phil Dissertation, Department of History, G.N.D.University, Amritsar.

Rampal, Jyoti. 1989. *"Job Satisfaction and Work Values"* M.A. Dissertation, Department of Sociology, G.N.D. University, Amritsar.

Sacher, Rashmi. 2009. *"Consumption Pattern of Youth: A Case Study of Amritsar City"* B.Ssc (Honours School), Guru Nanak Dev University, Amritsar.

Sen, Monica. 1983. *"Wholesale Trade and Traffic and Transportation in the Walled City Amritsar"*. M.A. City and Regional

Planning, Guru Ram Das Post Graduation School of Planning ,G.N.D. University, Amritsar.

Singh, Balwinder. 1979. *"Some Social Aspect of Urbanisation With Respect to The Book Sellers of Bazaar Mai Sewan"*. M.A. Dissertation, Department of Sociology, G.N.D. University, Amritsar.

Singh, Rawal. 2006. "Changing Form and Functions of the Medieval Religious City: Amritsar" M.Tech Dissertation, Guru Ram Das School of Planning, G.N.D. University, Amritsar.

Newspapers

The Tribune (8/8/ 2007) '*Foreign Support Firms Ride on Indian Retail Sage*'. Pp.1.

The Tribune (8/8/ 2007) *'Real Estate Funds Scout For Elusive Right Projects'*. Pp.1.

The Tribune (11,10/2007). '*Big Retail Not Welcome in Punjab*'. Pp.2.

Dainik Bhaskar (24/10/ 2007). '*Punjab Mein 900 Crore Lagaegi Germany ki Company*'. Pp.3.

The Tribune (15/1/ 2008). '*Mumbai Traders Protest against Organized Retail*'

Dainik Jagran (15/1/2008). ' *Aadhunikta Ki Chaka-Chondh Me Doobega Amritsar'*.

The Tribune (21/4/ 2008). '*Glossy Malls, Retail Chains enter Rural areas*'. Pp.1.

The Tribune (1/12/2008). *'Go Exclusive' Real Estate*, Pp.1.

The Tribune (14/1/2011). *'MC Kinseys Report on Urbanising* India'. Pp 1.

Websites

www.globalissues.org (Consumption and Consumerism). Accessed 4/3/2009

www.paggu.com. Accessed 4/3/2009, 8/6/2009 and 31/9/2010

www.wto.org/english/thewto_e/coher_e/mdg_e/development_e.htm#fntext1. Accessed on 19/5/2009

www.mngt.waikato.ac.nz/ejrot/cmsconference/2005/proceedings/criticalmarketing/Varman. (Consumer Culture and Working Class Stream: Rohit Varman). Accessed on 8/11/2009.

www.financialexpress.com (Rising Lifestyle Spend to Boost Retail Sector updated 4/9/ 2003) Accessed on 8/11/2009.

www.Uk.geocities.com/balihar_sanghera (Sociology of Consumption: Outlines of Consumer Culture.) Accessed 8/12/2009.

www.business.mapsofindia.com (Indian Organized Retail Sector's impact on Lifestyles). Acccessed on 20/11/2009

www.news.webindia123.com/news/articles/India/20080526/962374.html.(Organized Retailers affect unorganized retailers- sales, profit study: 26/5/2008) Accessed on 21/11/2009

www.indiaRetailbiz.com/blog/2009 (Bharti Retail decides to close 4 to 5 non-performing stores of 'Easyday' supermarket Retail chain, 12/3/2009) Accessed on 21/11/2009

www.expressindia.com (Malls with the Right Retail Mix Will Survive) Accessed on 23/11/2009

www.tribuneindia.com (Shops in Malls Fail to Attract Business, Ruchika M Khanna: 8/2/ 2010) Accessed on 6/6/2010.

www.ey.com/india (India Retail Report 2005- 07) Accessed on 21/4/2010

www.ey.com/india *(RNCOS: India Retail Sector Analysis Report: 2006-2007)* Accessed on 21/4/2010

www.emergreen.in (Punjab Retailing) Accessed on 21/4/2010

www.voxeu.org/ (Service with a smile: A new growth engine for poor countries.) Accessed on 5/5/2010

www.punjabgovt.nic.in/ECONOMY/ecofinal (Punjab Economy) Accessed on 5/5/2010

www.scribd.com/doc. (Effect of Organized Retailing on Unorganized Sector). Accessed on 5/5/2010.

www.scribbed.com/doc (Effect of organized retail on unorganized sector, Dissertation-Kamlesh Kumar Rathore.) Accessed on 6/6/2010

www.scribbed.com/doc/13082656. (Impact of Organised Retail on Unorganised Retail in India) Accessed on 6/6/2010

www.slideshare.net (ICRIER Study on Impact of organised Retailing on Unorganised Retail in India, Sarvjeet). Accessed on 6/6/2010

www.andhracafe.com Accessed on 1/7/2010, 8/3/2011

www.planetretail.com Accessed on 1/7/2010, 31/7/2010, 4/10/2011

www.amritsar.nic.in (Amritsar) Accessed on 1/7/2010

www.retailrise.com Accessed on 1/7/2010, 22/7/2010, 31/8/2010

www.legalservices.com (Sexual Harassment). Accessed on 1/7/2010

www.technopak.com (An Overview of India's Consumer and Retail Sector. Accessed on 8/8/2010

www.india-reports.com,.(KSA Technopak Consumer Outlook Report 2004). Accessed on 8/8/2010

www.indiafdiwatch.org. (FDI in Retail III: Implications of Wall Marts Backdoor Entry). Accessed on 8/8/2010

www.cmie.com Accessed on 29/8/2010, 6/9/2010

www.tribuneindia.com (City of Nawabs Embraces Mall Culture:10/2/2007) Accessed on 29/8/2010

www.tribuneindia.com (Ansal Set to Change Amritsar Skyline, Estate Talk- 26/2/ 2007). Accessed on 29/8/2010

www.pl.neilson.com/trends/documenets/globalisation.pdf(Consumer Insight into Globalisation, Report: 8/2006) Accessed on 21/ 9/2010.

www.atkearny.com (Selling the World on Modern Retail). Accessed on 21/9/2010 www.cpasind.com . (FDIs in India's Retail Sector). Accessed on 22/9/2010

www.planetretail.net (CPAS Study, "Will India Catch-up with China?", Tamoghna Das Sharma) Accessed on 29//10/2010

www.businessstandard.com (Beyond Grain Security: Agriculture Tomorrow, Ashok Gulati Pp. 1-23). Accessed on 29/10/2010

www.wakeupwallMart.com/facts/amrightatwork. Accessed on 20/10/2010

www.ibef.org (Retail) Accessed on 6/12/2010

www.censusindia.gov.in (India) Accessed on 7/1/2011

www.verdant.net/society_howaffect (Why Overcoming Consumerism). Accessed 12/12/2010

www.punjabgovt.nic.in/budget. Accessed on 18/4/2011

www.socyberty.com (The Four Theories of Globalisation, Alexendra Berany). Accessed 1/5/2011

www.infed.org/Globalisation (Globalisation) Accessed 1/5/2011.

www.nabard.org (Organized Agriculture Food Retailing in India: Report 1/ 2011). Accessed on 1/6/2011.

www.itftindia.com (Pravasai Punjabi Diwas). Accessed on 15/6/ 2011.

www. Palgravejournals.com (Management of Indian Shopping Malls: Impact of the Pattern of Financing', Harwinder Singh, et.al.:2010) Accessed on 15/6/2011.

www.articles.economictimes.indiatimes.com (Modern Retail Outgrowing Kiryana Stores in India: Nielson Study: 15/6/ 2011). Accessed on 15/6/2011.

www.rediff.com/ business/slide-show (India's 2010-2011 GGDP at 8.5 % updated 31/5/2011) Accessed on 5/7/2011

www.fibre2fashion.com (Indian Retail industry- Its Growth, Challenges and Opportunities). Accessed on 5/7/2011

www.unidow.com/ indiahome eng/ statewise_gdp.htm. (Economy of Federal states for year 2010 and population of year 2011). Accessed on 5/7/11

www.indiaretailing.com (Emerging markets- opportunities in cross border retailing) Accessed on 14/8/2011

www.oppaers.com. (Factors Influencing Retail Store Atmospherics). Accessed on 20/8/2011.

www.nsdcindia.org (Human Resource and Skill requirement in Organized Retail Sector 2022: A Report). Accessed on 29/8/2011

www.csi.McKinsey.com (The Great Indian Bazaar). Accessed on 29/8/2011

www.imagesretail.com (India Retail Report 2005) (Punjab 2001 and beyond) Accessed on 29/8/2011

www.Indiaretaiing.com (India Retail Report 2007, 2008) Accessed on 29/8/2011

www.deloitte.com (Indian Retail Market: Changing with the Changing Times, 8/2010). Accessed on 21/10/2011

http://www.ibef.org/industry/retail-india.aspx 'Retail industry in India' Last Updated: sept 2013. Accessed on 27/11/2013.

www.nytimes.com (India's Path Was Paved by Soviet Fall, 19,2009) By Akash Kapur

http://profit.ndtv.com/news/cheat-sheet/article-why-wal-mart-bharti-split-in-india-328426 'Why Wall Mart Bharti split in India'. Updated: 9/10/2013, 16:51. Acessed on 5/12/2013.

E-Books

www.infibeam.com 'Shelf-life-supermarkets and-the changing-cultures' by Kim- Humphery's. Accessed on 22/5/2010

www.google books.com 'Handbook of the Sociology of Gender' by Janet Saltzman Chafetz,2006. Accessed on 22/5/2010.

www.bharatbook.com 'India Retail Sector Analysis, 2006-2007'. Accessed on 30/7/2010.

www. googlebooks.com 'World System Analysis: An Introduction' Immanuel Wallerstein, 2004. Accessed 21/9/2010.

www.books.google.co.in 'Developed India: The Role of Service Sector' by G.N. Brahmanandan in, Talpuru Sreenivas (ed): Service *Sector in Indian Economy.* Accessed 1/1/2011.

www.books.google.co.in 'India's Experience with Globalisation' by Montek Singh Ahluwalia in K R Gupta: Liberalisation and Globalisation of Indian Economy. Accessed 1/1/2011.

www.books.google.co.in 'The Rise of the Network Society' Manuel Castells, 2000, Accessed 14/4/2011

www.books.google.co.in 'Local and Global: The Management of Cities in the Information Age'. Manuel Castells, 1997, Accessed 14/4/2011

www.googlebooks.com ' The Sociology of Work' Keith Grint, 2005. Accessed 25/4/2011.

Statistical Sources

Census of India. 2001.

Municipal Corporation Amritsar and Municipal Town Planning Amritsar- Primary and Secondary Sources

Punjab Handbook of Industrial Policy and Statistics. 2005-2006.

Punjab Statistical Abstracts. 2001 to 2009

Amritsar: Town Directory Schedule, 2011. Amritsar: Munciple Town Planning.

*****